A PADDLE IN HOCKLEY BROOK

Ron Smith

First Edition February 1988
Second Edition August 1988
Third Edition March 1990

Previously published by Weldon Press Limited.

Fourth Edition February 1998

Published by Waveney Publishing, Birmingham, England
Designed and printed in England by Clarkeprint Limited
45-47 Stour Street, Ladywood, Birmingham, B18 7AJ
Waveney Publishing is a division of Clarkeprint Limited

ISBN No. 09523 84915

British Library Cataloguing in Publication Data.
A catalogue record for this book is available
from the British Library

Ron “Smudge” Smith

Ron “Smudge” Smith was born in Hockley, Birmingham, in 1928.

Drawing and painting has been a part of his life since childhood, and in particular, cartooning during his varied working life.

CONTENTS

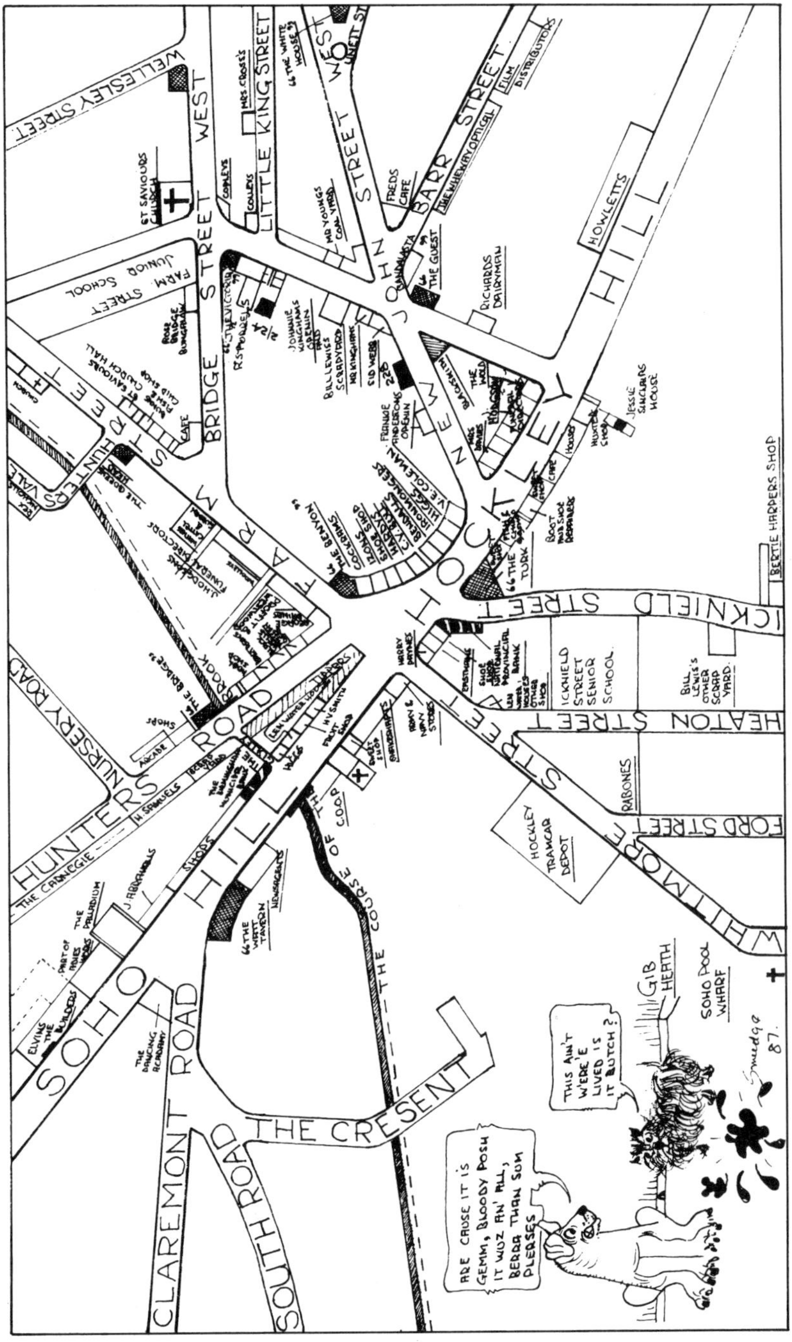
WELLESLEY STREET
ST SAVIOURS CHURCH
BRIDGE STREET WEST
FARM STREET JUNIOR SCHOOL
LITTLE KING STREET
MRS. CROSS'S
STREET WEST
BARR STREET
FILM DISTRIBUTORS
THE WHEWAY OPTICAL
FREDS CAFE
MR YOUNGS COAL YARD
HOWLETTS
HILL
RICHARDS DAIRYMAN
66 THE GUEST 99
JOHN
HOCKLEY
JESSIE SINCLAIRS HOUSE
BERTIE HARPERS SHOP
BOOT AND SHOE REPAIRERS
ICKNIELD STREET
ICKNIELD STREET SENIOR SCHOOL.
BILL LEWIS'S OTHER SCRAP YARD.
HEATON STREET
RABONES
FORD STREET
HOCKLEY TRAMCAR DEPOT
WHITMORE STREET
GIB HEATH
SOHO POOL WHARF
HUNTERS VALE
FARM
BRIDGE
HUNTERS ROAD
NURSERY ROAD
THE CARNEGIE
H. SAMUELS
SHOPS
ARCADE
THE PALLADIUM
SOHO HILL
ELVINS THE BUILDERS
THE DANCING ACADEMY
CLAREMONT ROAD
66 THE WATT TAVERN
NEWSAGENTS
SOUTH ROAD
THE CRESENT
THIS AIN'T W'ERE 'E LIVED IS IT BUTCH?
ARE CAUSE IT IS GEMM, BLOODY POSH IT WUZ AN' ALL, BERRA TURN SUM PLERSES
Smedge 87.

The Brook

A Paddle in Hockley Brook

INTRODUCTION

MEMORIES, memories of Hockley through a child's eyes. This Hockley was my home, my town, my village, it was everything to the innocence of childhood. All the dreams, whether at night or just day dreams, were of my small world. Like the child in the country, they knew nothing other than green fields, streams, leafy lanes, clear blue skies, and a closeness to God's animals either on farms or living free in the woods or forests of their particular location. My world of hustle, bustle, the noise of factories, tramcars, buses, cars, the acrid smoke and grime were, through my eyes, love and comfort. Like the country child I knew nothing other than this way of life and to me it was beautiful. The love and kindness shown by most of the people living in Hockley was another character of that particular era, but I do believe this was created by our sharing one particular common cause - *poverty*. Like everywhere else I imagine this particular situation was prevalent, but we can only think, write, or talk about our own locality. This has been handed down from generation to generation and will continue to be so. The saying to sum it up I would think is, give kindness, respect and truth to all others, hoping to God they will reciprocate.

Memories as soft and gentle as a cooling breeze on a warm summer day sweeping in and out of your mind. The laughter at some particular incident, the enjoyment for that immediate time, and other memories like the crash of thunder or the flash of lightning on a dark rainy night, bringing tears flooding down your cheeks. The harsher vivid side of life, which in those days was nearly an everyday occurence.

I shall attempt to give you, as near as I possibly can, life in Hockley in the 'thirties, which will be of course as I saw it as a child; God willing I will carry on further for as I grew up, naturally the story changed drastically, as my observations on life changed. In other words I shall use myself, with the help of my family and friends, as a vehicle through these times and hopefully bring with it memories, both happy and sometimes sad, to the people who shared these times with me. You will find I shall mention in detail my family, roads, streets, pubs, and business places, referring to them on and off throughout this book. My explanation for this is, I assure you, to make the memories become more vivid, for how often have you said, "Good God, I had forgotten that." Or, "What was the name of that street? I wish I could remember." The names are not fictitious, because the story is not fictitious, I hope no-one will take offence, because I assure you, none is meant.

Ron Smith

CHAPTER ONE

"The Start"

I CAME into this world January 3rd 1928. According to all concerned I was late, apparently due before Christmas Day. I suppose it would be fair to say that "our Mom" wanted things settled before the Christmas celebrations, for I must admit it was the one time of the year in those days when nearly everyone really enjoyed themselves. It was a time when people became close, forgetting for the moment all their problems, which were many. All arguments appeared to have been forgotten and the call of "Merry Christmas" to one another was an absolute sincere gesture.

My birthplace was two, back of twenty-four, Guest Street, a two up and one down house at the top of the yard. I was the fifth child of Lily Snow and Arthur Stanley Smith. The eldest child was Lilian, then Violet, Hilda, Arthur, and me. Did Arthur and Lil stop then? No, after me came our Audrey, Dorothy and the "Babby", our Betty, and at least one that aborted.

The immediate neighbours in the yard were Mr. and Mrs. Twigg on the left of the entry, looking from our house. On the right was our auntie Bertha, Mom's sister, uncle Alf and cousin Bertha. In the house in front of the Twiggs were Mr. and Mrs. Tyne (I was in love with Mrs. Tyne when I was seven) and in the one in front of auntie Bertha's, Mr. and Mrs. Evericks (Mrs. Evericks used to be on the stage, or so the story went.) Naturally, I have no recollection of sleeping arrangements when I finally appeared on the scene, but the earliest ones I do know of were Lil, Vi and Hilda in a double bed in the one bedroom, and in the other was a double bed and a single bed. The single bed was occupied by Audrey and Dorothy at the top, with our kid Arthur and me at the bottom. In the double bed was our Mom and the "Babby" Betty during the week, but on Saturday night Dad used to be in there as well. Dad was on permanent night work at Bradfords Bakery in Norton Street. The only other times he occupied his bed during the night was whilst he was on his week's holiday (which he sometimes did not take in order to obtain a little much-needed extra money) and Bank Holidays.

Our Dad's favourite local in my early days was "The Guest", an Ansell's pub on the corner of Guest Street and New John Street West, opposite the blacksmith's shop. He would frequent, on occasions, other pubs like "The Victoria" on the corner of Guest Street and Bridge Street West, by Farm Street Junior School, near St. Saviours Church in Villa Street. The reason I mention pubs is that most people do not realise how big a part they played during this particular period. They were in fact, on occasions, a necessity. The landlord and his wife were not tied down so much with red tape as they are these days, so consequently if relatives or friends came to see you they would more or less, on the spot provide you with sandwiches, pig's pudding, cheese, pickles etc., charging next to nothing due to the extra ale that would be supped. The Sick and Dividend Clubs met and paid out there, the local money lender would do the round of pubs in his or her area supplying or collecting money, the foreman of some works and shops would pay out for the "Gaffer" in pubs on Saturday night, giving a drink to each employee as a gesture of goodwill, or was it a blind to cover the poor wages he was paying them? There would be a plentiful supply of buskers providing very good musical entertainment. The two I remember vividly were Mr. Moseley out of Guest Street, playing banjo and Mr. Beddoes who lived in New John Street West, playing accordian, who sang a very good duet whilst playing their instruments.

I have hazy recollections of the introduction of balloon tyres to replace the rigid rubber ones on the corporation buses, on route numbers twenty-nine or twenty-nine "A", which would halt fleetingly outside the fish and chip shop in Hockley Hill, just by the Turks Head on the corner of Icknield Street, on its outward journey to the far reaches of the world, Perry Barr; coming from an equally far distance, Baldwins Lane, Hall Green. With an open cab, the only protection being a piece of shiny black tarpaulin fixed to the top of the crude dashboard and hung by two pieces of rope from a small wooden roof over the cab, the winter snow and rain would fall on the drivers; coupled with the harsh wind, even harsher when the vehicle was in motion, and the heat in the summer, it would I imagine have been practically unbearable with the engine alongside the driver.

Now I must admit that trams were my great love. The whine of the motor, the steady rhythmic clacking noise, like that of a train, quickening and slowing with the fast or slow motion. The rocking, swaying and general clatter as it went over cross points, the clang of the driver's bell warning other traffic of its approach, the "ding ding" of the conductor's bell telling the driver that all the passengers had alighted or were on board.

It was on very rare occasions we kids rode on these wonderful vehicles. For me it was always on Sunday when four, or six of the eight "Smith" kids would board the tram at 'Hockley Brook' by "The Watt" pub, opposite "The Palladium" cinema, on a visit to my Father's Father, Grandad Smith. The tram would start laboriously up Soho Hill, into the posh area, past Abrahams, General Plumbers Merchants, Elvins the Builders, Naden Road and Adies until it reached the summit by "The Roebuck" on the corner of Hampstead Road and Wretham Road, running back to Hunters Road, and Richmond Road running likewise to South Road. After a stop for passengers exchange the tram would move off at rather a faster pace along the level section of Soho Hill passing the R.S.P.C.A., Mists Garage, The School Clinic, Handsworth Post Office, "The Beehive" Dennisons Watch Company, Park Avenue and Soho Avenue to the junction of St. Michael's Hill and Villa Road, when we stopped again. On we would go down the hill of Soho Road passing Piers Road and Whitehall Road, Mottershead and Smith's garage and sales, "The Ivy House" on the corner of Ivy Road until we reached Handsworth Railway Station which was part of the London, Midland and Scottish Railway network. On occasions if we were lucky, and if we were on the upper deck, or saloon to give it its correct name, we would with great excitement see a train either pull in or out, steam clouds filling the immediate area. Our tram would move on along the Soho Road passing Thornhill Road, Holliday Road, The Library by Stafford Road, stopping there only if requested, "The Frightened Horse" on the right side, and the next stop was at the junction of Ninevah Road and Grove Lane. This junction was the exit for route number twenty-six tram where it would go down Grove Lane on its journey to Oxhill Road. We continued up the slight long ascent, still on the Soho Road, past "The Pump Tavern" to "The Cross Keys" where we stopped again. Past Linwood Road, Boulton Road, Murdoch Road on to "The Queens Head" by Rookery Road to the stop we kids had to alight at, Booth Street, at the junction of Soho Road and Holyhead Road.

When the eldest of the troop, which would be either Lil, or Vi had assembled us on the pavement prior to our continued journey, giving us a reprimand and sometimes a backhander when we objected, which resulted in a grizzling match, we

"Our Mom and Dad"

would then proceed down Booth Street to the railway bridge at the junction of Crockets Road. The station, just to the right of the bridge looking down Booth Street was the Handsworth and Smethwick junction of the "Great Western Railway" system. I remember that as we went under the bridge bawling and laughing to one another and listening to the echo which would follow - quite a mystery to us kids - with great reluctance and often another backhander, we would eventually emerge to carry on the journey. Many things frightened me as a child, most predominantly "The Bogey Man". Things I still remember vividly were the two gas tanks, one in Booth Street at the corner of Foundry Lane, the other one opposite in Rabone Lane. I always had a fear they would topple over and land on us, so what I used to do was walk as close as I could to the wall surrounding the first tank, usually to the amusement of the others, and crouch low so that the tank could not see me until I reached the end of the wall at Foundry Lane. I would then run across the lane and repeat the procedure on the other side. This wall was much higher so it was not necessary for me to crouch, but I would run for my life up the hill past "Tangyes" to the canal bridge by "George Burns" foundry, usually leaving the others in my wake. On arrival at the bridge I would turn and look back at the tanks and think "Yo ain't got me this time 'ave ye" in my imagined conquest. Sometimes we ventured through the entrance to the canal and stood at the top of the descent leading down to the tow path, looking over the iron rails waiting for a barge to pass, with the woman, man or sometimes children leading the big shire horse pulling it. Of course we were now well and truly into a "Foreign Land", Smethwick, Staffordshire. This you could tell not by the written notice, but by the change in the paving bricks, lamp posts, and "Suff Grates", but most predominantly the dialect, which was different from "Brummijam" but not quite like "Black Country". On from the canal bridge up to *The White Horse* at the junction of Soho and Rabone Lane, sometimes we saw a single deck "Midland Red" bus of the "S.O.S. Class" passing on its way to Warley from the New Inns. Its livery of bright red with gold lines and lettering on the sides, with the Staffordshire Knot motif on the rear door all in gold with a black back-up, shining and immaculate. It was a rare thing for vehicles, whether engine driven pulled by horse, or even pushed by man to be in a dirty or dilapidated condition in those times. It was I imagine pride in what business men sold, or the service they gave that prompted them to keep whatever vehicle they ran in tip top condition; we must also remember the vehicle was one of the main motivations of selling their product or service.

We turned left along Soho, over the bridge which was another part of the London Midland and Scottish Railway system, housing Soho station. This location was also the number thirty-one tram route terminus. This tramcar differed in style to the tramcars on the route we had just taken, the difference being the previous was completely enclosed, whilst the tramcar on the Soho Route was open front and rear in the upper saloon. Past "Walsh Graham" the timber merchant we would go, crossing to the other side of the road to the little huxters shop at the bottom of Market Street. Up the hill we would trudge, by this time tiring a little, but happy we were nearing "Grandad Smith's". Whilst walking up towards twenty-one, which was on the left nearly at the top of this long street, I always looked at the huge wooden cross perched precariously on the top of the high wall running alongside the end houses and was filled with wonderment at this huge symbol standing out toward the heavens. To get to Grandma and Grandad's house we by-passed the front door, admiring their orderly garden on our way. Whoever heard of anyone using a front door when down the entry stood a very adequate rear door. This entry divided eight attached houses, four either side. On reaching the bottom we turned left and went to the last house of that four, with its beautiful rear garden, where we knocked the door and waited for a voice from within bidding us enter. We had arrived!

I can see the kitchen now, the fireplace on the left - with a fire blazing up the chimney whatever the time of year, the flames reflected in the highly polished iron work, so was the abundance of brasswork which surrounded it. Over the fire, suspended on an iron bracket bolted to the chimney breast, hung a huge iron pot in which the vegetables for Sunday dinner bubbled. On the left of the fire was a large oven which housed the joint of beef, with potatoes snuggled around it, giving off the most beautiful smell. The door leading upstairs was to the left of the wall facing, and on the right was a passage leading to the front parlour, which was forbidden territory to us kids. The floor consisted of twelve by twelve red quarries, with an old herden sack at the door, and a bit of carpet in front of the fireplace. Surrounding this was the bow, and fender with dogs (not the canine type) at either end, again all in brass. In his wooden chair to the right of the fireplace, his back to the stairs door, sat Grandad Smith, a big man, with a shock of closely cropped white hair, his large nose set in a big red face, with big blue twinkling, but constantly watering eyes. His red and white spotted handkerchief was much in evidence as he wiped them. Grandad's generous mouth housed a set of good strong teeth, and his gentle but authoritative voice made itself heard. Usually he wore a union shirt, slightly threadbare, but spotlessly clean, and darned well, with his thick woollen vest showing where his top button had been left undone. Over his shirt would be his dark waistcoat, which I should imagine he could not fasten due to his build. Then the thick black belt with its huge brass buckle, attempting to hold his dark coarse trousers up, coupled with a pair of wide braces as well. Thick woollen socks under his canvas slippers, that was "My Grandad". Now our Gran was just the opposite to Grandad, being slight in build, her complexion pale and almost yellow in colour, her hair was black with streaks of grey, brushed tight to the scalp to the rear of her head where it terminated in a huge bun, fastened with pins and hair grips. She had large brown eyes sunk into her small face, with a lovely twinkle to them. The nose was big and hooked, and a mouth which was wide, and again was sunk into the face, but this I fancy was due to her having no teeth, as like so many in those days, they refused to wear dentures, that's if they could afford them. Peeping from her floor length black frock were shiny bootees. A cameo was usually pinned to the neck of the dress completing my child's eye description. On reflection she would have given a good impression of a witch, but of course that would only have been a physical view, for as much as I knew my Gran she was the most kindly and gentle, although abrupt, lady. *The Smethwick Telephone*, a local paper, sadly like my Grandparents long since gone, did a beautiful write up in the fifties showing a picture of them in the kitchen. To this day I still have and treasure this article.

Our stay would be short, for we would begin to get restless as children invariably do, but also we had to get back to "Guest Street" for our dinner before going to Sunday School at St. Saviours Church Hall in Farm Street. Our fervent hope throughout the visit was that Gran would dip into her big black bag and give us a 'a'penny each for the return journey on the tramcar, which I must admit she never failed to do, well not whilst I went anyway. It would certainly have been a long walk home if Gran had failed us! On these visits my Grandad would never fail to tell me "When yo gerra mota car ole mon, you can come 'ere an' put it in that shed at the top of the gardin, until yo gu um again." I would thank him and tell him, "I'll 'urry up an' get one Grandad."

The tramcar route numbers on these visits conveying us to Booth Street were seventy-four terminating at Dudley, going via West Bromwich and Great Bridge, seventy-five terminating at "The White Horse" Wednesbury via West Bromwich, but at "Farleys Tower" at Carters Green she would turn right and move on to her terminus via Black Lake and Hill Top. The other routes available, but not on a Sunday were twenty-three which terminated at "The Hawthorns", West Bromwich Albion's Football Ground (The Baggies), seventy-three terminating at Carters Green, seventy-six terminating at Great Bridge, and seventy-seven terminating at Spon Lane.

These tramcar rides became more frequent later on, because our "Auntie Bertha" moved from one back of twenty-four Guest Street up to the snob area, "Handsworth". She moved into number seventy-three Douglas Road which ran from Grove Lane by the Park to Linwood Road. Auntie Bertha I must admit was my favourite aunt. She was my Mother's younger sister, a big woman like Mom with rosy complexion and dark hair scraped back into a bun, which was a style most women adopted. To me she had a quiet, gentle disposition, caring, with a voice as soft as billowy clouds. These characteristics as far as I knew never altered from my boyhood right through to manhood.

Uncle Alf was as different as chalk from cheese to our Aunt Berth. He worked for a good many years at "The Mint" in Icknield Street and was very popular. After an evening at 'The Pub", on one of their rare visits to our house, he would have the bloody place in an uproar with his continual humour, goodwill, and non-stop laughter. He was indeed the life and soul of any party. Smaller in stature than our Aunt Berth, blue twinkling eyes, laughing through his metal framed glasses, a shock of ginger hair, thick wavy and shining, good teeth with an apperture between the two front ones, and a gruff type of voice, it sounded as if he had a permanent mucus congestion in his throat, which funnily enough added to his comical character.

Cousin Bertha was a quiet studious type of girl. She worked at Lucas's in Great King Street for a good number of years in the offices. I thought she was a pretty girl with a slender figure. She wore glasses like her Dad, but this seemed to enhance her appearance. What I really loved about her, although to this day I don't think I have mentioned it to anyone, was her piano playing. The tune which always reminds me of her is *Smoke gets in your eyes* which she would sometimes be playing in the front room when us lot from 'ockley' descended on them in Douglas Road, via the front door. In all probability shattering what for them was a peaceful, quiet Sunday morning.

The journey to Aunt Bertha's was initially on a number twenty-six tramcar, and later for a short period on the number seventy bus when the tramcar service on these routes finished in March 1939. Less arduous than the journey to Grandad Smith's due to the shorter distance. Circumstances changed as well because our Mom, and don't ask me why, suddenly became more benevolent, giving us lot enough money for the journey there and, wait for it, the return trip too! So when Aunt Bertha and Uncle Alf gave us a 'a' penny, or sometimes a whole penny, we would spend it on sweets at the little shop on the right hand side of Douglas Road when heading for the tramcar (bus) stop situated just outside one of the entrances to Handsworth Park by Holly Road.

Then there was our Aunt Nell who lived opposite All Saints Hospital in Lodge Road, or "The Asylum" as it was known locally. I really enjoyed this particular journey, not so much for the visit itself, although I must add I loved Auntie Nell, and

2 back of 24. Guest Street

cousins Bertha and Violet. The visit would again occur on a Sunday, but with a great difference, because on this trip we rode on the number "Thirty-two" tramcar, which was the older type with the open front and rear upstairs, like the Thirty-one route tramcar I have already mentioned. There would be a rush when we boarded to get to the front open balcony, if not already occupied, and it usually wasn't when the weather was bad. We dived into what we considered the driver's seat and despite all weathers remained there until the last minute, driving the tram in our child's mind until we reached Auntie Nell's, when we reluctantly handed over to the driver downstairs to complete the journey to the terminus at Victoria Street in Smethwick.

If I remember correctly we varied our route to board the "Thirty-two". My favourite way was across the "Brook" and down Whitmore Street, past Heaton Street, to the "Tram Sheds" (Hockley Tramcar Depot) on the right, where I would stop and gaze at the goings on, until a bang up the ear 'ole brought me back to reality. Sometimes we turned left up Ford Street, past "Rabones" and on reaching the junction with Park Road turned right past Piddock Street up Lodge Road. Other times we would carry on up Whitmore Street bearing left at the entrance to Soho Pool Wharf, where the little tank engines of *The Great Western Railway* shunted the big trucks of coal for distribution to the various merchants who dealt there. On up the rest of Whitmore Street we travelled to the junction with Park Road, where we turned right and took the first left into Goode Street, ascending the steep hill of this street to the top, turned right and the tramcar stop would be just on the left.

On other occasions we would cross the "Brook" at New John Street West to the *Turks Head* and turn left into Icknield Street. The "Turk" was our favourite watering hole in later years. Along Icknield Street we stepped up to Nortons at the junction of Key Hill, turned right and went along the "Flat", on past Little Park Road as the locals called it, although it was in fact a continuation of Park Road, past Piddock Street, then straight up the steep incline to our tramcar stop on the right. Scribban's Bakery was a very notable part of the Hockley landscape, with its dome alike to St. Paul's Cathedral, the carved stonework and the pillars, scrolls, and small castle-like windows, descending to an ultra modern building below housing the bakery itself, offices, stables, transport, garages, store rooms for bread, cakes, flour, and sundries. It covered an area from Goode Street down Lodge Road toward "The Flat", terminating at *The Leopard Inn* more than half way down. The other way it dominated nearly all the right side of Goode Street. The one thing above all others about this magnificent building was its absolute immaculate cleanliness. If ever a business deserved its logo, which was "Scribban's Purity Bread" this one did.

We would wait expectantly, one or two of us with our ears against the tall posts that supported the overhead lines, waiting for the first quiet buzzing tone, which I assume was something to do with the electrical system echoing from the lines into the hollow posts, indicating that a tramcar was approaching, but in which direction we could not ascertain. This buzzing would naturally become louder and louder, until we had to remove our ears from the post, for to leave them there would mean experiencing the dull sound in our ears for quite a few minutes after, which was not at all pleasant. If the tramcar we heard at the post was inbound for the City we would see it long before it arrived at the stop on the opposite side to us, by Fred's Cafe, because you could see right up to The British Oxygen Company, and Tinegates the Timber Merchants at the top of the steep incline, where the tramcar would come into view, the roof first and then the rest of its structure little by little, due to the very steep descent on the other side. We watched with excitement as it sped towards

Gran and Grandad Smith

us, stopping only if requested at the stop just past Tinegates. The driver slowed down before reaching Paxton Road on the right, to negotiate the very sharp left, and then right bend by Abbey Street before coming to a halt just past us, with the conductor shouting "Scribbans's, The Hydraulic, and Goode Street." We then knew that the next buzzing sound inside the post, after the inbound tramcar had gone, would be ours. It would grind to almost a halt when it arrived at the corner of All Saints Street and Lodge Road, because not only was it an acute turn, but it was also a quick change from slight descent, to a very steep ascent. The aroma of bread being baked at Scribbans's, mixed with the steam from the many trains passing under the bridge further up from the tramcar stop, these trains on the *Great Western Railway* running from Snow Hill Station to destinations beyond our little minds, created a most wonderful atmosphere.

The big 'uns would push us little 'uns on to the tramcar when it finally arrived and as I stated earlier, there would be a rush for upstairs. Sometimes, however, this was not always convenient due to the upstairs saloon being full, so very disappointed we would have to travel in the inside saloon. The upstairs of this type of tramcar had separate wooden seats facing toward the front. When it reached its terminus at "Vittoria Street and Wellington Street", these seats could be reversed by simply moving the back support which worked on a pivot system, to the opposite side. You would again be facing the front.

The inside saloon was designed differently. The seating arrangement was a long wooden, carved bench, facing in ards either side the whole length of the saloon, which meant the passengers were facing one another. I presume that would have satisfied the grown ups, but you know kids, they always want to look out of windows and not miss anything. Mind you, I'm still the same now I don't think men, as a rule, quite release their hold on childhood fantasies, which is probably why I'm writing this book, in order to record these events. If we did have to go inside, we would climb on to the long bench and either stand, or at least kneel to see what was happening as the tramcar moved off and continued on its journey. The situation remained only if there were no protests from the other passengers, or the conductor. If there were we would be swiftly and roughly swivelled round by "The Big 'Uns" with the usual comments "If yo don' be'ave yo'll gerra tannin a'cross yer bloody backside."

When all the passengers were aboard the tramcar we moved off up the steep hill, taking the double bend slowly, to the top, past Harmer Street, over the canal bridge (we used to swim in the basin there), if not requested to stop by *The British Oxygen* past the new Ford Research Establishment on the right and the Nurses Home on the left, speeding up on the steep slope downwards. We pulled up at the stop by Norton Street; the Outdoor on the corner run by our coalman Mr. Kavanagh. On we travelled downwards, the complete left side of Lodge Road being completely occupied, as it is today by *All Saints Hospital*. On the right we passed Kent Street North - Lees Street on our way to the next stop opposite *The Devonshire* public house, situated at the corner of Devonshire Street and Musgrave Road. Up the steep hill, to a sharp left bend which contained the entrance to the hospital, passing Talbot Street and Don Street in the process, until we reached our stop just past Bacchus Road, where we would get-off and wait for the tram car to move off.

We crossed Lodge Road to the first entry past the garage on the corner. Up the steep entry we would climb, due to the houses being built much higher than the road level. At the top of the entry we turned left along a very wide blue bricked space, separating the houses from their individually beautiful long gardens. Like our

Grandad's we would enter our aunt Nell's via a latched back door. I can only vaguely remember our auntie Nell because she died before the Second World War commenced, but I do remember she was one of the real old brigade, wearing a man's flat peacked cap when she went out for any reason. Recollections of the big glass dome covering a stuffed animal of some kind, resting on a metal plinth in the front room, of "Uncle Fred", who, said the "big uns", was not our proper uncle: 'E's on'y a lodger!'

I have vague recollections of other aunts and uncles but I'm afraid as a child I did not participate in the ins and outs of their lives. I do however recollect the names and approximate locations. Aunt Doris and uncle Jim lived at twenty-one Farm Road, just off Unketts Road, leading off Thimblemill Road, Warley. This address I have cause to remember - I walked there from 'ockley' once when I was about seven. My cousin 'Jim' entered The Birmingham Police Force some years later and rose to quite a high rank. Cousins Bertha and Violet Knowles, auntie Nell's girls, auntie Vi and uncle George with cousin Vic from Doncaster, auntie Lil and uncle Bill Woods with cousin Edna lived in Moilliett Street, Smethwick, auntie Kate and uncle George from Coventry, and then there was an uncle living in Blackpool. Lastly, (or was it?) a mystery aunt Sarah, whom I never met, apparently owning a hotel somewhere in London.

CHAPTER TWO

"The Old Hockley"

THE BROOK" was the centre pin of Hockley. From there it spread to Villa Road and Lozells Road to the North, to Spring Hill and Dudley Road to the South. Eastwards it terminated at Summer Lane at the junction with Snow Hill, and to the West, Wellington Street with a part of the Black Patch Park included, although it came under the jurisdiction of Smethwick Parks Department at one time. Some people living on the perimeter of Hockley would declare they were residents of Smethwick, Handsworth, Birchfields, Edgbaston, or even Townies. Why they chose to do this was entirely their own business, I can only think that they shied clear of being a 'ockley'-ite, but since I was old enough to really understand I've always thought it was "you" other people love, respect, cherish, and understand, not the locality in which you were brought up or lived.

Right in the middle of the "Brook" itself was the traffic Bobbie in his long white mackintosh and white mittens when the weather was bad. On sunny days he wore white armlets over his black uniform sleeve. His helmet had a silver spike on top and a big badge containing the Birmingham Coat of Arms at the front, and the leather chin strap usually held just beneath his mouth instead of running right under his chin. The tunic was fastened with silver buttons right up to a clip on the collar at the top. This collar displayed the police officer's number. Around his waist would be a black belt and silver buckle, his smartly creased trousers and highly polished leather boots completing the picture.

Around the Bobbie in the near vicinity was Hockley Hill leading to the city, Icknield Street leading out to Edgbaston, Whitmore Street leading to Winson Green. The termination of Hockley Hill where it merged into Soho Hill took you out to Handsworth and West Bromwhich, Hunters Road heading towards Handsworth Wood, with Farm Street eventually merging into Aston.

The bobble really had his work cut out directing the flow of traffic from the six entrances and exits leading into and away from the Brook. Of course one must remember the amount of horse traffic those days, far outnumbering the mechanical traffic, which was probably why a lot of the older generation say "Life wus a bloody lot easier in them days." This of course is debatable due to the type of work you followed.

I can see the different liveries of the horse-drawn vans and carts now. Bradfords Bakery, dark blue, gold lettering with a red back-up stating "Bradfords Bread and Cakes". The trade mark on the rear doors, a round red ring with gold dots on it representing the pimples they had on the bottom of certain types of their bread. Wathes, Cattell, and Gurden out of Farm Street with their cream coloured floats, green lettering with a red back-up, and red and green lining, all painted by hand. Scribbans's, cream top and rear, with panel of brown either side, the kick board in front, a red edge to the roof at the rear. There was a mixture of black and gold lettering, with green, orange, and black back-up respectively. R. White the pop people out of Western Road by "The Workhouse" Summerfield Hospital, and Brookfields House, with their green drays and gold lettering and lining, with a black and red back-up. Tommy Shaw's out of Burbury Street, and Jack Holt from Cowper Street, were dairymen with both their colours being red with gold lettering and black back-up. Then there was Harry Marsden on the Handsworth border in Heathfield Road with his brown drays and floats, and gold lettering with a red back-up, George Baines out of Finch Road round the corner from Marsden's with their maroon vehicles and a picture on the side of green hillside and a cottage in the background, the sun's rays spreading outwards, again gold lettering with a black back-up. The drays of Mitchells and Butlers Brewery, with their dark blue livery, gold lettering with a light blue back-up, and their motif of a deer leaping across a ravine. There were a variety of carts that were horse drawn, floats, drays and semi-box vans the dairymen favoured. Boxed vans of all kinds and sizes, both four wheeled or two wheeled. Flat carts of a heavier build were used by The Great Western Railway, out of All Saints Road, Hockley Goods and Passenger Depot, Leonard Leigh, and the Co-Operative Society Coal Department located in Wharf Lane, at the junction with Wharf Street. It was wonderful to see these big shire-horses pulling the heavy flat carts with their loads of iron, wood, or machinery - God, what strength they had.

The immediate areas which us 'ockley kids' considered our territory, because all kids had their own particular territories, was all Guest Street, the last part of New John Street West, from Guest Street to Hockley Hill, all "The Brook" was ours, the first part of Farm Street down as far as Bridge Street West, and along there back to Guest Street by the "Vic". We looked after it like a fort! Naturally, on occasions we ventured outside our territory, "we 'ad ta gurra skule din we?" Or perhaps a visit to Burbury Park, or Recreation Ground to give it its full title. Or 'ans'worth Park in the nobs area, perhaps once a year, with the inevitable milk bottle of cold tea, with a piece of paper screwed up and put in the top to stop it slopping over into the Blackwell's carrier bag. A fruit cake or caraway seed cake which our Mom made on a few occasions, coupled with a call from Mom to one of the "wenches" - "Don't yo gu an' spill it, mek sure yo keep it stood up, or yo'll wet the bloody cake." When you did venture away from your area, and then only at the invitation of a school mate, you were still very wary once outside your patch and kept your "eyes skinned" for any trouble from the kids on the particular territory you had ventured into.

The names, people and places in this small area, return, bringing long lost memories flooding back. On the "Brook" itself at the junction with New John Street West was Elsie and Violet Coleman, Newsagents, for whom I worked for a short time. They also sold toys, cigarettes etc. Moving down in the Handsworth direction was Higgs the tobacconist, Bendall's bread and cake shop; an alley divided them from C.V. Bull the butcher, Hardy's the Off-Licence, The Ideal shoe shop, Izons the Chemist, Cockram's Butchers leading us to the junction of Farm Street which housed *The Benyon* Public House, a Mitchells and Butlers establishment. From *The Benyon*, looking diagonally across to the left at the junction of the "Brook" and Hunters Road, was Tippers the Outfitters. Taking the left side of Tippers the next shop was H.V. Smith, bakers and confectioners, then a fruit shop, bringing us to Len Waterhouse's. " 'e charged our 'cumulators for us when Our Dad bought a wireliss set at last, one o' the ol' Cossors." I vaguely remember lisening to the Tommy Farr - Joe Louis fight on that. The next shop was the second of the Higgs' shops situated on the corner of the passage leading to Hunters Road, or "The Gulley" to give it its local name. On the other side of "The Gulley" was the Birmingham Municipal Bank who allowed Mr. Phelps to sell his papers from their doorway in an evening. You could hear the call "Patchy, Mail, Patchy, Mail" from Arthur Phelps' gruff, bronchial voice. He was of course selling *The Birmingham Mail* and *The Evening Despatch*.

Hockley Brook

I worked for Mr. Phelps for some considerable time after I left the Colemans and he was without doubt one of the kindest, caring men I have ever met.

There was a row of shops after the bank whose names I'm afraid I cannot remember, but among them were a toy shop, a womans fashion shop, cooked meat shop, and just before Abrahams the plumbers' supply merchants was a high class sweet shop, bringing us to "The Palladium" or again, to give it its 'ockley name, "The Palladidalum". Looking back I can see me queuing for the Tupp'nny crush on a Sat'day arternoon arter a look at ole mon Blackwell's, an' scroungin' some specks (fruit turning bad) ta stuff while we wus watchin "Buck Jones, Johnnie Mack Brown, or the Whisperin' Shadder". Looking across from the cinema to the corner of Claremont Road, set in a beautiful forecourt of rockery, conifers and an abundance of rock flowers and plants, was a Dance Studio and Hairdressing Salon. The Dance Studio provided tuition for the posh kids ("bloody lot of cissies") in acrobatic, or tap dancing. In the evening there would normally be held a dance.

Returning down the "Brook" toward the "Fanny Brown" Town, and immediately behind the main tramcar stop - it was amazing how many pubs were situated just outside a tramcar or bus stop - was *The Watt Tavern*. Next door was a Newsagent's shop, bringing us to the bridge that spanned "The Brook" itself, running some thirty feet below. Over the bridge to a very ornate structure which housed one of the hundreds of "Co-Operative" grocers, then lying back off the road quite a way, with a wonderful frontage of tall aspens and conifers amidst a floral show set in lawns either side of the path leading to the impressive building of the Methodist Church, its wrought iron gates and railings on blue brick walls artistically laid surrounding it. Following on we had a sweet shop, and then the next three shops were occupied by W. Shakeshafts, a real old fashioned grocer, who packed loose tea into their own printed packets, weighed the sugar up as you the customer required it into blue packets, roasted and packed their own coffee, served butter and cheese (with the rind round it) off big blocks, the butter being patted into the square shape with two wooden spatulas. The aroma of smoked bacon, roasting coffee, mixed fruits in their large sacks, and a hundred other smells emitting from the shop, God it certainly played havoc on a little fella's nostrils. On the corner of Whitmore Street next to Shakeshafts was an Army and Navy surplus store, where "The Sally Ann Band" usta play on a Sunday arternoon, an' trying ta gerrus to join em. The shop on the corner opposite belonged to Harry Payne, boot and shoe repairers, and the next shop was Eastmans another butcher, this is where "Our Dot" lived - over the top - many years later; going on past Eastmans was a shoe shop. The near corner of the next junction with Icknield Street was the National Provincial Bank, a big official looking building running from "The Brook" well into Icknield Street itself. At this bank we watched the money from the tram depot being deposited, unloaded by several tram drivers and conductors from a converted old "A.E.C." bus. Over the way was *The Turks Head* another of Ansell's Churches, occupying part of Icknield Street, pushing upwards into Hockley Hill. In later years our Mom called *The Turks Head* Dad's second home. The reason I use the term "churches" is because one of my Dad's favourite sayings was "Come on, gerra move on, I don' wanna be late for the service" this being applicable naturally on a Sunday. "The Turk" was managed for several years by a Mr. & Mrs. Atkins. Next to "The Turk" was a sweet shop, further up was the Fish and Chip Saloon, past the entry alongside was another boot and shoe repairers, a huxter's shop, a couple or three houses, the dairy shop, a few more houses, at the rear of these houses Jessie Sinclair used to live. Then we came to a business place lying back from the main road opposite Guest Street, with its cream painted walls and grained and varnished doors and windows, showing an abundant amount of brass, including the plate indicating the name of the business, which try as I may I cannot remember. Situated on the corner of Guest Street and Hockley Hill opposite was "The Wold" cycle repair shop. The owner was a kindly man, whom we called Mr. Wold simply because we never did find out what his correct surname was, but this wasn't really important to us. When I finally got a bike of my own (I brought it for "Two Bob" off one of my paper round customers in Prescott Street) years later, Mr. Wold would give me and other kids advice about the repair and maintenance of our cycles, and sometimes do a minor repair for nothing. Returning back down Hockley Hill would be T. Hodgson and Sons Funeral Directors, which us kids kept well away from. God knows what we thought they kept in there. Next door was yet another newsagents bringing us to Mrs. Davies's, the Herbalist.

Many a night during the early part of the war we finished up there with a hot fruit drink, "chewin the rag" until Mrs. Davies kindly reminded us that it was getting a little late, and we would disperse. Next door to the herbalist was an old pub, now a second hand place selling almost everything under the sun. This building was situated on the corner of New John Street West, bringing us back in a complete circle to Elsie and Violet Coleman's. We return to "Tippers" at the junction of Hockley Hill and Hunters Road, but this time we take the right side of this shop and venture up the left side of Hunters Road. The first shop before we reach the other end of "The Gulley" was not so much a shop, but more of a window and door, put in by the builders of "Tippers" as an afterthought, for it was indeed a one storey continuation of the outfitters' majestic building. In this window and door another electrician had his business. Past "The Gulley" was a long line of high advertising hoardings, erected by Sheffield Advertisements, and behind this facade was a thriving scrap iron business. Next to this was Charles Kirby, Wholesale Grocer, his red Ford vans outside being loaded by a number of brown cowgowned men; on past "Charlies" was the original building housing "H. Samuels" the Jewellers, who extended their premises and also built a new block opposite with an overhead bridge running between, in the post war period. The Corps of Commissionaires man looked resplendent in his black uniform with red piping and gold badges and buttons, white shirt and gloves, and a black tie. His boots were highly polished, his cap set squarely on his head. A black patent "Sam Brown" with a pouch attached, presumably for carrying documents, lay across his shoulders. Next door to Samuels, extending nearly to Naden Road was *The Carnegie* with its statue of the Virgin Mary holding Jesus in her arms set into a beautiful designed arch. "All the Moms usta tek their kids inter there if they wus feelin' poorly." Opposite Samuels on the corner of Nursery Road returning down to the "Brook" was first, a wall, what was behind there I had no idea, that was one of many mysteries I didn't solve. Following this wall and lying well back off the road was a row of shops. I remember the first shop was a toy shop, for every time we passed we would linger for a while wishing we had some of the toys ourselves - wishful thinking! I remember also there being a big shoe shop as well, but alas I do not remember the others.

In front of these few shops, extending to the pavement, was the most ornate arcade of metal pillars, wonderfully designed and continuing overhead in an arch up to the wall of the shops just below the upstairs windows. In between the arching stays was thick glass, and this whole structure gave protection to the shoppers. Well, I say shoppers, it was used more as a temporary refuge from a sudden downpour, or for kids to play in, until the shopkeepers shouted for us to "bugger off". At night time I imagine it would have its fair share of courting couples. At the end of this arcade, the buildings jutted out again to the pavement. The first business was a wool shop, which lead us to an alley, which not only provided an entrance to the rear of the shops I have just described, but I think there was a building yard down there as well.

Over the other side of this alley was *The Bridge* public house, frequented by a faction of the Irish community after Sunday morning service at Saint Francis of Assisi situated on the corner of Hunters Road and Wretham Road. Probably searching for "The Poteen", to help raise their spirits after the Priest's admonishments for their sins committed during the week. The pub's name was naturally obtained due to the bridge being a continuation of its facade, with the "Brook" running merrily thirty feet below, in the direction of Aston.

This "Brook" you will recollect ran from alongside the "Co-op", when it went through the tunnel there, and went under Hockley Hill itself, continuing beneath the Bank, "The Gulley", then Hunters Road and finally emerging by the pub.

First shop past the bridge was for babies clothing, wool, knitting implements etc., and after that was Bartram's the butcher (our Mom's butcher).

On occasions when our Mom didn't go to Bartram's herself to fetch the meat (which was usually on a Saturday, it was very rare to go in the week, as most of us could not afford it) I would be told to fetch it "An' don't ferget ta tell 'im I want a lump of fat thrown in fer the cookin" she would bawl after me as I ran down the yard. On Mr. Bartram's counter was usually a big packed mound of home made scratchings. No packets in those days. He would always break some off and giving them to me would say " 'e' yar nip, get that lot down ya, it'll stop the mice nibblin'."

Next door was Blackwell's the greengrocer, Mrs. Messenger's Off Licence, bringing us to George Baines shop, Bakers and Confectioners, on the corner of Farm Street. Turning left and going down Farm Street in the direction of Aston, was Proffitt and Westwood the corn and seed merchant, (I usta get the corn fer me Dad's cocks an' 'ens from there, cus that's when we all flitted to Two Twenty-Eight New John Street West into Mrs. 'all's posh 'ouse).

She went into the dairy further up the street, opposite Mrs. Dutton's grocer's shop, selling all farm produce. At the end of the building housing Proffitt and Westwood's was a wide passageway leading to the rear of the shops in Hunters Road. Continuing down past this passageway there were a number of small factories, one occupied by "Woolleys", where later my sister 'ilda worked for years.

Next to these factories was another very wide passage. It had a big wooden sign high up running between the two side walls, held by iron brackets bolted to these walls, stating "T. HODGSONS and SONS, FUNERAL DIRECTORS" in gold letters with a black back-up, set on a light blue background. This appeared very mysterious to us kids, more so than the shop in Hockley Hill, and under no circumstances would we venture down that openin'! The bigger kids used to scare us by telling us they kept all the dead bodies down there, but of course in reality, as we realised in later years, this was where they stabled the beautiful black horses and highly polished hearse and coaches.

Past the opening was Wathes, Cattell and Gurden's Dairy Shop, where you could buy all your dairy products if you did not require them to be delivered, or if you ran short of anything. The shop, like the dairy itself was open seven days a week. Inside it was always cool and spotless. Standing on the counter were three or four big

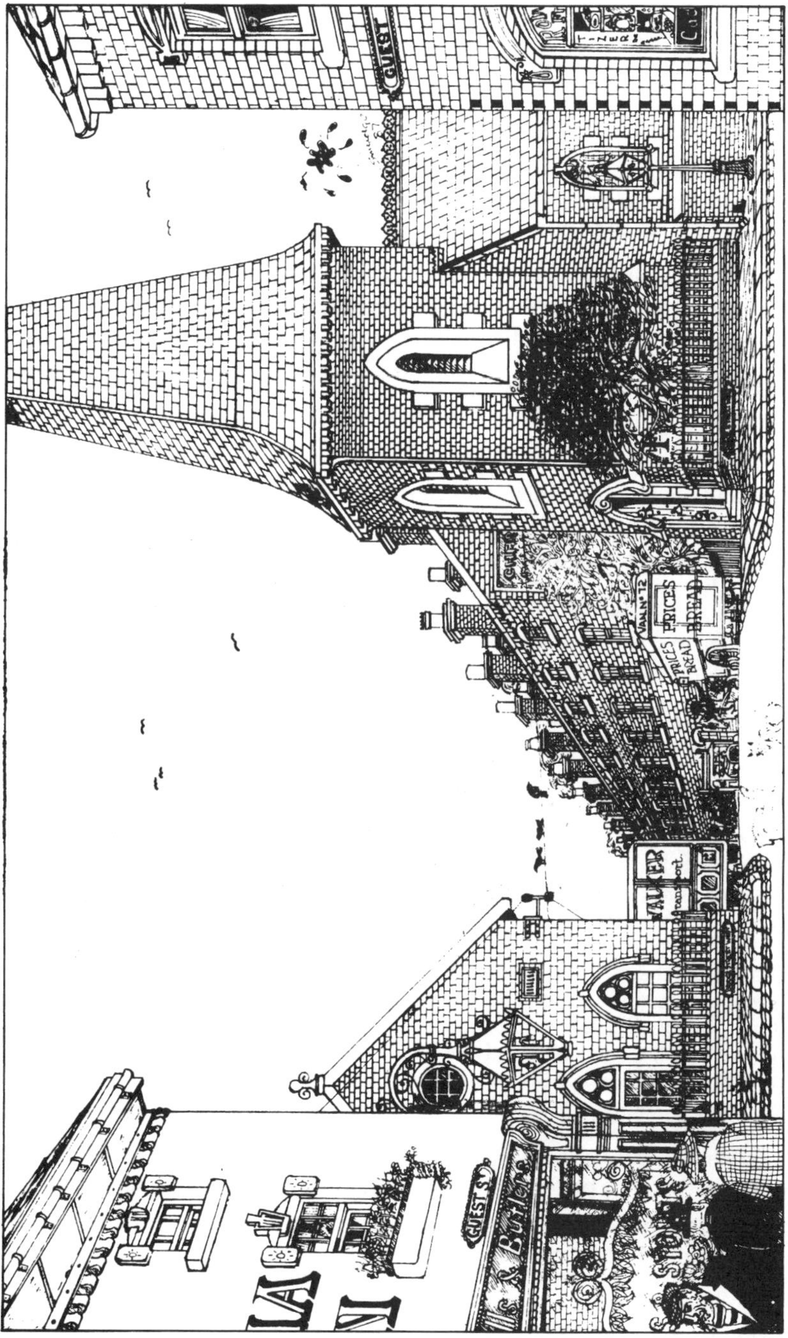

The Victoria Inn, Farm Street junior School, St. Saviours Church

earthenware pots containing fresh milk, with muslin covering the top, and the steel half and one pint measures ledged on a further pot filled with clean water covering them. Bottled milk was available, but like most new ideas people were suspicious and loathe to change. Consequently, in most small huxter's shops you would find, in all probability, one of these earthen pots serving you pure fresh milk.

At the side of the shop were two big wooden gates leading to the milk depot itself. (The head Office of Wacaden was in Nova Scotia Street off Doe Street, at the junction of Grosvenor Street in town). Here was a Hive of Industry, with roundsmen and their supervisors coming and going. Stable staff were always busy, for the stables had to be cleaned, food and water and fresh bedding provided for the horses. Harnesses to be cleaned and small repairs made, while the big lorry brought its load from Head Office and returned with the empties. The drivers for the dairy, as I remember, were Mr. Hunt and Bill Tyne. Sometimes when we had finished school at half past four in the summer, we would go to the depot and ask the stablemen if we could take any horses to the Blacksmith's in Abbey Street off Park Road. One of my mates, Stan Yates, lived there. Occasionally they would let us and seemed pleased to be relieved of this time consuming business, for if one or two of them had to make this trip, they had to wait until the horses were shod and then bring them back. With us kids doing this they could get on and finish their normal duties a little earlier.

They put a canvas halter over the horse's head, then tied some rope or string to the two down pieces, running the length around the neck, which served for reigns. Then they threw a herden sack over its back, picked us up, or gave us a leg up to settle us on the horse's back. God we used to be out of our mind with pride and happiness, as we rode our horse out of the gates, turning right up Farm Street towards the "Brook", especially if we saw some of our mates. The Bobbie on point duty would see us approaching to go straight across into Whitmore Street and hold all the traffic up and call us across. As we passed, thanking him, he would give us a big smile and sometimes pass a remark like "Ride 'em cowboy" or "They went thataway pardner" pointing down to the Tramcar Depot, and that would see us safely on our way.

On past the Dairy towards Aston there were a few terraced houses with a small greengrocer's in the centre of them, bringing us to *The Queens Head*, an Ansell's pub on the corner of Hunters Vale. In the Vale lived a couple of my old school mates, Dickie Sheppherd and Tommy York. The Vale itself consisted of terraced houses on either side for the first part, up to the right hand bend, leading down to Villa Street. On the left, right in the bend, was a Grove consisting of ten or twelve houses. Facing Farm Street was the modern factory of Rex Nicholls, continuing down to Villa Street, with Middlemore's the Builder and "Moons" the Newsagents. Just to the right of Rex Nicholls were some old cottages, lying well back off the Vale itself, with a frontage of long narrow gardens; Dick lived in one of those cottages. On the other side was a complete row of modern type maisonettes running from "The Dispensary" in Villa Street, turning into the Vale and continuing back up to the bend. "The Brook" gurgled on its way at the rear of these maisonettes where Tommy York lived, and protecting the residents from the thirty foot drop was a wall with steel railing on top.

Returning to Farm Street once again, on the opposite corner to the *Queens Head* were a few smaller type houses, and Iying back off the road with an impressive frontage consisting of a small brick wall, with an iron fence emerging from it, two wrought iron gates and a slabbed area and path leading to some concrete steps, was a majestic church. Next door to this was a well known builders merchants T.W.

Brough, whose yellow and red lorries were always seen to be busy. Following Brough's was "The Pawnshop", one of the two our Mom used. If she didn't use this one, she would use Pawsons in Icknield Street. I think it was the 'a'penny she had to find for the fare on the number eight Inner Circle bus, or maybe she didn't have the money to redeem the items that deterred her sometimes. It was always early on a Monday morning that one of us kids would be sent off to the "Pop Shop" before our Dad arrived home from his night's work at Bradfords. On to the "Dispensary" at the corner of Villa Street, and on the other three corners, rotating from left to right was *The White Swan*, a Mitchells & Butlers house, Doctor Targets surgery and Farm Street Junior School with Mr. Margerisson the Headmaster. Mr. Warrener I remember well, a thin man with dark hair, brylcreamed and brushed well back to his scalp, brown eyes, in a very thin face, a moustache under a long narrow nose. His mouth was generous, and when he was happy it lit up, but when he was angry - watch out, that was when his Welsh streak would be at its best. I can see him now, smoking one cigarette after the other when giving us instructions for the football match to be played the following day, Saturday. He was the Sportsmaster as well as the normal duties he carried out as a teacher. The mere mention of Farm Street School stirs memories of old school friends. Where are they now? Ray Izons who played in goal, Vic. Hughes from Burbery Street, a brilliant forward, Roy Hayling who lived in the next yard to Vic, Gordon Mann, brother of Johnnie Mann the boxer, Dennis Mann, a relation of their's out of Wheeler Street, Kenny Hughes who lived by *The Rosebridge Bungalow* in Bridge Street West, Ray Whittle from Lennox Street, Arthur Allbut, Frankie Deeley and his girl friend Gwennie Munn, whose parents had a shop in Barr Street (bloody posh they were), Tommy Smith from Bridge Street West, Bertie Harper and Les Yeomans from Farm Street (I have met up with Les again, he now lives by me in Lichfield), Ronnie Dolphin from Villa Street, Tommy Tandy, Alfie Mobbs from Little King Street, Nunky Collins from Bridge Street West, Jimmy McDonald and Gordon Hipkiss out of Farm Street, by the "Brook", Harry Webster who lived over Bull's the butchers on the "Brook", Freddie Nicholls, he met with a tragic end just after leaving school, and Bruce Spinks whom I met in Tripoli briefly, both from Little King Street, and not forgetting Fat Wagstaffe. Johnnie Kingham, Chubbie and David Moseley, Jimmy Perry, Ray Rickards, Dennis Clark, Lennie Hunt and Harold Bearsmore, the local tough guy, all out of Guest Street the Best Street. Frank, George, and Dennis Anderton, Jackie Walford all lived down the openin' in New John Street West, Jackie Thornton and Bernard Osbourne from Guest Street, Kenny Bates from Wheeler Street, and the other Ronnie Smith out of Whitmore Street, and the Girls, Olive Shellis who lived in Villa Street, Barbara Wilson, Bridge Street West, Florrie Pinchbeck from Wheeler Street, Gwennie Brueton, New John Street West, Pat and Joan (I cannot remember their surnames) living in Ventnor Road, Joan Hardy, whose Mom and Dad had the Off Licence on Hockley Brook, Doreen Cattell from Unett Street, Nancy Cotton, Connie Wadhams, Hilda, Mary, and Connie Clark, (they moved out into the country, at Glebe Farm) out of Guest Street, Jessie Sinclair, from Hockley Hill, Lena Palmer, from Cowper Street, and Elsie Guest out of Tower Street.

Of course there were many more of these friends, I can see them now, but cannot put a name to them. I know they will forgive me. Like a mist by water on a cold morning, dispersing quickly when the sun appears, so their names have gone, but the memories of a brief moment spent with them, remain forever.

On then past the school, back toward "The Brook" was a row of houses, with a wide passage in between leading to a builders yard. At the end of this block of houses was St. Saviours Church Hall - what happiness us kids had there, Captain Davies of The Church Army, The Boy Scouts whom I shall never forget, the kindness and understanding these people had for kids like us, all in the same circumstances, was wonderful. I remember the Christmas Breakfast on Our Lord's Birthday down at the Hall. After opening our few presents at home, our Mom put us into our Sunday Best clothes, and off we trooped. The Scouts greeted us with paper hats, crackers etc., and wished each one of us "A Merry Christmas". When we had all sat down we said our prayers and the Senior Scout gave a condensed version of The Christmas Story which we listened to in awe. On completion of this, several Scouts entered the hall from behind the stage with great platefuls of steaming food - bacon, sausages, eggs, tomatoes, which they served on the plates in front of us, and God did we tuck in, for we knew we could ask for more, and we certainly did. After the breakfast was cleared away we played games and sang carols, but the highlight of the morning was the arrival of Father Christmas with our presents. He had to be real, despite the older kids' doubts, "Cus 'ow would 'e know our names w'en 'e gid us our present a', ans'a that then?" In the summer the Scouts took us from the hall on a double deck Midland Red Bus up to Snow Hill Station on a Saturday lunch time, to catch the train to transport us a million miles away to Barnt Green. What a thrill as the train entered the station, steam blowing about all over the place, and finally stopping for us to scurry aboard; waiting anxiously in the carriage for the first pull and jerk as we left the platform, watching it recede into the distance behind us. On arrival the Scouts would form us into some sort of order. We then walked to our destination which was a large field, with a big wooden building in it. We played games in this field, supervised by the Scouts, and possibly enjoying themselves as much as we were. Then we would have our tea outside (that was a thrill) on long wooden tables. Cakes, bread and butter, jelly, blanc-mange, trifle and custard, and as much Pop as us little uns could drink. Eventually after what seemed years, and with our presents in our hands we returned home, tired but very happy children. Later I joined the Life Boys at "The Hall" and though I tried really hard I never managed to save the nine-pence needed to buy the "Sailors Hat" which formed part of the unihrm. I did, however, get the badge which cost three pence.

Next to "The Hall' was a shop that had been converted into a house, then on to Dudley's Fish and Chip Shop, beautiful and clean, a sweet shop and a couple of more houses brought us to the café on the corner of Farm Street and Bridge Street West. On across the street for the last part of what we considered "The Real Brook".

A wide entry gave access to houses and a large yard at the rear of another huxter's shop on the right, in Farm Street, and a house on the left in Bridge Street West. A row of houses brought us back in a complete circle to the *Benyon.*

I have taken great care in describing the general layout of Hockley Brook in the thirties, but of course what I have written is seen through my eyes. Naturally there are certain things I have probably not included, being unaware of them or, maybe, they will appear in later chapters.

To write a complete history of anything or anywhere is an almost impossible task, but if one gives pleasure to those reading whatever you choose to write, and satisfaction for yourself in writing it, then you have certainly won through.

CHAPTER THREE

"Early Memories"

IT WAS a general practice in those days for working class women and men to attempt to hide the harshness of life, to relieve themselves if only momentarily of the continual struggle to survive, let alone live the life God had given them.

Saturday Night was the best night to carry out this deception with a visit to *The Guest*, *The Turk*, *The White Horse*, in Unett Street, *The Vic* or sometimes *The White Swan* in Farm Street, or if "Yo felt like it, start early, an' gu a pub crawl, tekkin in the lot." Pubs in 'ockley' (like everywhere else) were dotted about like fleas on a mangy dog.

People succeeded in putting all their worries behind them with a "Good Booze up" (but the worries still returned afterwards.) They had their fill wherever they went and sometimes returned to one another's houses for a continuation of the merrymaking, purchasing several bottles of beer from the last pub visited, well before "Time Gentlemen Please" was called.

The end though was as predictable as the sunrise after sunset. Everything would be alright for a while, and then, in all probability there would be a "scrap" between one or other of the sexes, or both together, or two families, or with people from another area. One thing was pretty certain, there would be a "scrap" of some sort, to get rid of the frustrations of life I suppose. Predictable people didn't bear malice, and there would be the making up in "The Pub" on Sunday dinner time.

Now with "kids" it was vastly different, for although we had "Our arses out, holes in our boots and socks, and silver sleeves, through constantly wiping our noses on them" we were happy, due to that wonderful protection God gives to all children - INNOCENCE.

Kids can be happy in the most distressing situations, by the God given fact that he does not equip them to understand, as adults do the stark fears and trauma of life. Also one should remember another predominant fact, that most children in Hockley shared the same standard of life anyway, as poverty was not a problem for them. Of course there were a few exceptions to this poverty rule. These "posh kids" with their nice manners, nice clothes, and general cleanliness were the butt for our rather cruel attitude towards them which I suppose was mainly due to our ignorance, not knowing that we should ail be living like those fe , not those few living like us.

One thing most people of "good ol' Ockley Brook" had in common, was a strength of feeling and a real helping hand in trouble. This would prevail through any type of trouble, financial, sickness, law, death, you name it and there would be help from some quarter. This common bond has been revealed in all walks of life, but it was very pronounced in "Hockley Brook" with the working classes of the thirties and during the Second World War, and for a while in the aftermath.

As kids we had our pastimes and our drama. I used to dream of far off places I'd heard people talk about, or had seen (when I had been taught to read) on tramcars, buses, or other vehicles. Places like Dudley on seventy-four tramcars. Or Wednesbury on the seventy-five, or the terminus of the twenty-six tramcar at "The Uplands", a journey I did travel later, taking you through "The Nobs" area, past

Handsworth Grammar School in Grove Lane and into real countryside by Wassons Farm and Wassons Pool. Johnnie Kingham's father had an allotment there, "an' grew Flars an' evrythin' ". The number eight, Inner Circle bus crossed "The Brook" from Icknield Street into Farm Street, then they changed the route and buses went up Hunters Road. On its route the bus went through such districts as Aston, Nechells, Saltley (they used to call it Saltley Docks) Bordesley, with the Morris Commercial Works there, Small Heath, Sparkhill, Edgbaston - another "nobs area" - then back through Monument Lane, into Icknield Street to good ol' 'ockley.

I have good reason to remember the Inner Circle. When I was about nine, I took my two younger sisters, Audrey (our Ginge) and Dorothy (Dot), for a 'walk', which if I remember correctly was a journey covering some fourteen miles. Dot was in the pushchair and Ginge walked *part* of the way, but most times climbed in the pram with our Dot, and I pushed both of them. The navigational system I used during the trip was I would wait for a "Number Eight" to come into sight. Then noting the direction it took I would follow, or I would see a "Number Eight" coming towards me, and take the direction it had come from, which proved completely successful. What did I get for my trouble? "A bloody good whalin' off our Mom for worryin' 'er ta death, wanderin w'ere we wus."

One of our many self-made pastimes was to remember tramcar and bus numbers and destinations, then compete with one another to see who could attain the highest amount. We also went on "The Brook" by Tippers to collect used tram and bus tickets. Having collected them we separated them into their monetary denominations of halfpenny units and stored them for future games of tram or bus conductors. To be a conductor you required a ticket rack, so first you either scrounged or knackered a piece of wood, approximately nine or ten inches long, by an inch and a half to two inches wide. But the size wasn't the real problem, it was the elastic you needed to stretch over the length of the wood. The usual answer was to have a look in the "Fillery's" toffee tin, which served as a sewing container for our Mom - when she wasn't there of course. If that didn't prove fruitful, then you resorted to knackering some other kid's garters, for to use your own led to the inevitable whaling from you-know-who. Once the elastic was put over the wood you placed your collected tickets underneath it in value order, starting on the left with the 'a'penny ticket, then the penny, three 'a'pence, and so on right up the side of the wood, then turned it over to fill the other side, providing you had enough of the right denominations.

After the "old uns" had let their hair down on Saturday night, and if they still had any money left, a Sunday dinner time session would be in order, then it was back to the grindstone for them on Monday. Monday dawned, and with it the reality of life, and the same old process would start all over again.

Our Mom, bawling up the stairs, "Lily, Vi, 'ilda" woke us - "come on its time ta gerrup, an' don' pretend yo' ain't 'eard me, cos I've 'eard yo three talkin' an' this is the larst bloody time I'll call ya, so bloody gerrup." I snuggled closer to "our kid" Arthur in the single bed that we shared with my sisters Audrey and Dorothy. Me an' our kid at the bottom an' our two wenches at the top, their feet sometimes guin up ya shirt, instead of up the bed, or sometimes fetchin' yo' a wallop in the face.

My wick day shirt, damp, and stiff from the nights sweating, and sometimes urine, which turned to ice cold when yo' finally goorup the nerve ta gerroura bed. We darsena tell our Mom we'd piddled the bed, 'cus she'd just ge us another soddin' whalin.'

Me by Johnnie Kinghams "op'nin"

I lay quietly for a change, for to use our Mom's most expressive term for me, "Yorra noisy bleeder forra little un' ", and listened to the whistle, banging and general clatter of the trains at 'ockley station, in All Saints Road, as they shunted the big wagons about ready for distribution, or as the express trains sped through, thinking of all the wonderful places that they might be guin' to, hoping that someday I could gu' with 'em, when I had lotsa money, say five shillin', or maybe more.

Our Lil an' Vi gorrup an' got themselves ready ta gu ta work. Lil at "Wheway Optical" in Barr Street, an' Vi at 'owlets in 'ockley 'ill. But our 'ild would wait 'til the larst minnit afore she med a move, with our Mom's screeching voice warning 'er of all the fates that awaited 'er for not doin' as she wus tol'.

A little longer an' I would 'ear "Terra Mom, see ya dinner time", from me three big sisters as they went off ta werk. Then sometimes I'd 'ear Uncle Alf, 'oo lived in our yard, 'e'd say "Tarra luv" to Aunti Bertha, as 'e went orf ta "The Mint" in Icknield Street. Mr. Twigg 'oo lived the other side o' the entry dain't gurra werk, cus 'e wus a 'undred years old, an' 'is missus wus a witch an' med us kids drown lickle kittens, cus she dain't wannem, in a bucket o' water in the brew 'ouse in the yard, an' she'd promise us 'a'penny, an' never paid us, the rotton sod.

Then I'd 'ear our cousin Bertha gu ta werk at a posh time, not like our wenches, 'cus she werked in an orffice, bloody lah-de-dah, at Lucas's in Great King Street, an' she wus 'igh class enyway 'cus she wus alis clean an' smelt nice, even in the wick.

The "Bulls" for the workers had already put forth their wail, 'owletts, Wheways, The Bandalasta, Swallow Raincoats, Lucas's an' God knows 'ow many more wus guin' at it, no rest for the wicked?

Then it wus our turn, with "Mom's warning of tanned arses if we weren't down quick", an' believe me that wus enough warning, 'cus she really mea'nt wot she sed, 'specially if she 'adn't got the rent in the Chirms Book fo' the rent mon w'en 'e called. She usta gerrus up an' bugger us orf, an' then gu an' 'ide in one ov the neighbours, until she thought 'e 'ad gone, pretendin' next wick that she dain't 'ear 'im, or that she'd gone out.

Out on to the bare, cold, wooden boards, an' get me trousis from under the bed by a pot full of piddle, matchsticks, an' nub ends, (Gold Flake) in it, forra "Dad" usta use it in the day, for ya see 'e werked perminent nights, six day's a wick (as I've already told ya). On wi' me socks if I 'adn't already gorram on cus o' the cold, mind you I'd sometimes sleep in 'em even if it worn't cold. They'd be as stiff as bloody boards, (you know 'oo washed once a wick, on a Monday) with the muck an' wet comin' through the 'oles in the bottom of me boots, an' the cardboard "our old mon" usta purrin dain't last long. Arter tuckin' the 'oles in the 'eels of me socks underneath I shoved me boots on, an' if it wus cold, an' I 'appened ta 'ave one, I'd stick me ganzi on as well. Our kid an' me sisters, Ginge an' Dot (the youngest "Our Bet, the Babby" 'oo dain't 'ater gurra skool 'cus she was too young yet - lucky sod - she stopped in bed 'til our Mom fetched 'er down) went down the dancers to the one room which served for ev'rythin' an' ge our Mom credit (you've gorra be jokin', nobody would) she nearly al'is 'ad a nice fire guin up the grate, but then ag'en I suppose it wus natural, for she did most of 'er cookin' on the fire, presumably to save on gas, for arter Sunday there worn't much bloody money ta throw around, so you know 'oo didn't wanna put any pennies in the box down the "bogey 'ole."

Into the "bogey 'ore" entrance, a little four by five place with a concrete sink, an' a choice of cold water, or none (I preferred the latter), a quick splash in the tin bowl,

Guest Street

"Don't yo' ferget to wash yer bloody neck ya dirty little bugger" from 'er, an' back inta the "dining room", well it wus wornt it, it wus the on'y room we'd got, for breakfast. Breakfast - a quick cuppa tea in a cracked cup, unless yo' wornt quick enuff, an' ad ta wait for somebody ta finish theirs afowa yo' could 'ave a drink. A piece of scrape, usually lard or drippin', or if yo' wus lucky yo'd 'ave ya bread toasted.

A bit of bread an' somthin' wrapped in larst night's "Mail", if we'd 'ad it, cus sometimes the paper bloke wouldn't leave it cus we 'adn't paid 'im 'is tanner for the wick's lot. If not, it would be somebody else's or "The Despatch" that it wus wrapped in, an' that would serve as our mid mornin' snack, an' sometimes if yo' wus feeling' like it yowed ge yower mate a bit on it, but not bloody often.

One thing we had nearly always got plenty of, of course, was bread. The reason we had this ample supply of bread was naturally "cus me Dad wus the Foreman at Bradfords Bakery in Norton Street, just off Park Road, an' e' allis brought us sum 'um when 'e could manage it, which wus offen. I loved me "Dad" 'an I usta snuggle up ta 'im when I could (luv 'ad gorra be shared with eight of us) 'specially when 'e cum 'um from werk, cus 'e usta smell luv'ly of bread, an' flour, an' terbaccer, an' also 'e could draw enythin', 'e could, enythin' in the world, smashin'. "Our Dad" showed me 'is 'oss 'e 'ad in the war, which 'e drawed while 'e wus fightin' the Germans, in France, 'an it wus the most luv'ly thing yo've ever sin; it wus more than smashin', a million times more.

"Our Dad" also wus gassed by the Germans, the rotton sods, an' I tol' me mates this, orl on 'em, an' sed 'e'd got sum medals forrit, an' they sed I wus a bloody liar, an' I offered them a fight, but they wouldn't tek me on, so I sed "Bum then".

Guin along the witches side of the yard was a place called "Spurrells" I donno wot they med, but the noise they kicked up, bangin' an' thumpin' all the time deafened ya, but wus as precise 'as the tickin' of a clock. This was accepted, not only in 'ockley, but nearly everywhere in the area, and the people got used to this particular type of noise in their local vicinity, this then was the price we paid for industry.

What we all found rather strange though in our little area, when work finished on a Saturday dinner time, was the deathly silence everywhere due to the machinery coming to a halt, it was heaven. "We dain't 'ave ta shout at one another ta mek ourselves 'eard".

"Our Mom" gid us a quick look over, and with a "I suppose yo'll bloody do" she shooed use orf ta school. My school at the time was Burbury Street Infants, by Lucas's in Bridge Street West, an' it covered the area right through to Farm Street the other end.

Down the entry I'd run an' inta Guest Street. I'd turn left toward "The Vic" an' start lookin' for sum ov me mates, an' when I found sum, I'd shout for them ta wait for me, an' then when yo all got tagether yowed start ta do wot ya Mothers 'ad tol' ya not ta do, "play it up."

Sometimes we'd stop an' look inta the small, low, an' dirty windas, at Spurrells. These windows were at pavement level, due to the construction of this building, and the slope of Guest Street. We'd watch the wenches, they wus all wenches in this particular workshop, cus it wus wenches werk I suppose. They'd wallop the 'and presses over with force, to do whatever they were doin', an' it looked real hard werk ta me. If one o' these wenches wus ta look up, we'd stick our tongues out at 'em, or pull funny faces, an' they'd shout 'orrible thins' at us, but we couldn't 'ear 'em enyway cus of the bloody noise they med. Then off we'd run, across the road past

Copley's sweet shop, where Mr. Copley 'ad got summit a marra with 'im cus 'e couldn't keep still, an' 'e kep' pullin' funny faces, an' kep' fallin' all over the place, like sum blokes did when they cum outer th' pub. If yo' wanid eny sweets it ud tek 'im 'alf an' 'our ta purrem in th' bag, but one good thin' though 'e nearly allis gid ya overweight, cus I suppose it wus too much trouble to tek 'em outa th' bag agen. (Parkinsons Disease). We'd turn right into Bridge Street West past Saint Saviours Church, where "Mr. Joseph" wus the vica, 'e wus a nice man 'e wus, an' 'e gid us some tea once in 'is back gardin, which wus at 'is big 'ouse in Wretham Road. Sometimes 'e wus stern an med us be'ave oursols, but this dain't mek any diff'rance ta the twinkle in 'is blue eyes though, just like the stars at night they wus.

When we arrived at school, which wus further along Bridge Street, past Wellesley Street, an' just arter Ventnor Road, where Pat an' Jean lived (they wus some o' the posh kids that smelt nice they wuz), we 'ad ta gu in the second gate, cus the fust one wus for the big kids (Seniors), down past the woodwerk shop where they cut wood up an' everythin', which we wornt allowed in, cus we wus too small ta cut wood, an' finally into our playground.

Our playground was separated from the big kids playground by iron railin's, an' an iron gate, but yo couldn't get through the gate cus the caretaker 'ad alis got the key.

At nine o'clock one of our teachers would ring a big brass 'and bell, 'an w'en this wus rung yo all 'as ta stand still. Then the teacher would shout "Clarses" in a posh voice, an' we'd ave ta gu into little mobs, which wus our own classes. When we wus all ready, the teacher would tell us to march inta school one class at a time, an' ta be quiet abaht it, or we would know wot we would get if we didn't.

No children were allowed into school prior to the above precedure, with the exception of the monitors (I never attained that regal position) who would help their particular teacher prepare the milk and biscuit money list, for collection when the class was seated, after the register was called.

On our entrance into the school the first thing you did was put your top clothes into the cloakroom, usually this happened in the cold period of the year. It never bothered most of us though "cus we dain't 'ave eny underwear ta purron, lerralone coats, macs, or overcoats" an' we dain arf tek it ourra them that 'ad gorr overcoats an' all, cus it's them that wore bloody cissie underwear as well.

From the cloakroom you went into the big 'all, where one of the teachers (cus the 'eadmaster old Locker was tekkin the big kids, seniors, in the other 'all wus up on the stage, an' another one o' the teachers wus sat at the pianner. The teacher on the stage u'd say a prayer, and we'd all say "Amen" like bloody sheep, an 'God 'elp ya if yo' sed "Amen" afore the teacher 'ad finished sayin 'is bit, for yowed be forrit then. We'd all sing summat like "All thin's bright an' beautiful" or "Praise morsole the Kin's of 'eaven". The teacher would tell us if they wanted ta see anyone (usually for a wallopin') or tell us some news, an' then we'd be dismissed to our separate classes.

Miss Butterfield wns our teacher, an' she 'ad black straight 'air, which wus cut square all the way round. An' she worn't too bad, well not all the time any road up, but she wus a little bit fat, an' wus sometimes red in the face an' neck, like she'd bin boozin'. She'd read out our names, an' we'd answer "ear Miss" an' she then gid us a red tick, but if you worn't 'ere yowed gerra black cross. If yo got too many black crosses, the School Board bloke 'u'd be roun' to yower 'ouse, an' yowed be forrit. Unless yower ol' lady 'ad kep' yarra way cus yo wus poorly, or cus ya bloody boots 'ad dropped ta bits, or the ole in yar arse wus to big ta mend, or most likely she 'ad kep; yarrat 'ome cus she wonnid ya to do summat forra. But "Our Mom" wus allis glad ta "gerrus out the bloody way, from under 'er feet", or did she just mean me w'en she sed this?

With the register complete, the monitors would come round for the milk an' biscuit money, so that they could check the total against the amount they 'ad ta order. Again this dain't bother us lot, cus our Mom's couldn't afford 'a'pennies for these luxuries, burrit dain't stop us scroungin' a drop o' milk from them 'as 'ad gorrit, 'an if they wouldn't geus any, we'd sometimes knacker it off 'em.

I dain't like school, except for some things, like when we went ta Wood Lane Playin' Fiel's in 'answorth Wood. That wus nice, 'specially the buz ride there an' back. It wus a special buz, cus it 'ad no conducta'ta tek eny money orf us, 'e'd 'ave a bloody job tryin' ta tek eny orf some on us eny road up, cus we never 'ad none anyway.

I like drawin, an' paintin', me an' Ray Izons wus good at it, so the teachers sed, but wot I liked best of all wus gerrin' ta the next book, for learnin' ta read.

The system the teachers used at that time for advancement in a pupil's ability was different coloured books. Hence you would move to say, a blue book, when you had completed reading, to the satisfaction of the teacher, the yellow book, and so on.

It certainly worked, for you can imagine the competition it created within the children, without them realising how it taught them quickly. "Look at Smiffy" you would hear. " 'e's on'y on the blue book, an' I'm on the red 'un, 'e's a dunce 'e is". So it came automatically that you would try even harder in order to escape this ridicule, for there was only one way to stop it, and that was for you to get the yellow book finished as soon as possible, to get on reading the blue one.

School, the endless writing with scratchy pens and the ink that was always getting onto your fingers, shirt, and face, and when you finally did manage to put some of it into the exercise book, with its one inch regulation margin down the left side of the page, you would always manage to put a blot or two down as well, much too late for your blotting paper to absorb. This misdemeanour rewarded you with a smack on the hand with a ruler from "Miss" and a big red circle put round it to indicate the mess you had made. I used to think "Bloody 'ell Miss, I can mek inuff mess without yo' startin' as well."

I remember looking out of the tall church-like windows up to the sky and dreaming all things small boys dream about, wondering if it were possible to dance from one fluffy cloud to another, like some children did in the books we read, or the teacher sometimes read to us. "We 'adn' gorreny books at 'um', an' even if we 'ad "our Mom" wus allis to busy fo' readin' ta us lot."

Dreaming, about aeroplanes, airships, and autogiros, wondering if they could fly for ever, and ever, "Cus the sky 'ad no end 'ad it?". Then I would switch my dream, and I would be a tramcar driver, bus driver, train driver, and then wanting to go home and fulfill these different roles in a child's wonderful world where everything was a reality. Clang, clang, the tram bell would sound when some silly bugger ran in front of me. I would use the lower cupboard doors as the handles for starting and stopping my tram, and the sofa for my passengers, which normally consisted, under protest, of "Our wenches", the young un's that is, Audrey, Dorothy, an' the Babby, our Bet. One minute I'd be the driver and the next a conductor, with me piece of wood an' elastic an' tickets, an' God 'elp 'em if they dain't gimme me tickets back arter we'd finished playin'. "Fares please" I'd shout, an' then "Yo should 'ave gorroff at the Roebuck missis, but gu on I'll let yarorf with it this time, but don't yo ferget next time, its three 'a'pence to 'ockley Brook' from the Uplan's."

Then I'd be drivin' a van for 'An'sworth Dairies, deliverin' milk, an' 'urryin' back to the warmth of the Morris ten 'undred weight, arter puttin' me milk on the doorstep of the customer on a cold mornin'.

"Ouch" the bang on my head from Miss Butterfield's ruler would bring me back to reality, and to much laughter from my classmates. "Smith, save your daydreaming for when you go home, or you will stay behind, alright?" "Yes Miss, sorry Miss" I'd say, but under my breath "You rotton ol' sod."

The handbell would sound at ten in the moming for "Playtime" and then again at twelve noon for "Dinner". At the latter bell there would be a rush to "gerrout" the playground fuss, with a lingering smell of boiled fished, an' boiled puddin's, for those unfortunate enough to have to stop at school for dinner. God, it smelt bloody terrible. I know we'adn't got much to gu 'um for, but it wus berra than that lot, anytime o' the day.

Back 'um I would run then, where "Our Mom" would 'ave a stew or somethin', with lots of taters an' carrots, an' onions, but yo allis 'ad a job ta find the meat, most times it was because there warn't any. But agen yowed 'ave thick lumps of bread ta fill "yer'oles" up with.

We 'ad ta be quiet w'en we cum 'um forra dinner, cus the "Ole Mon" wus upstairs sleepin', an' Christ 'elp ya if yo woke 'im up, it ud be a whalin' for sure. Not off me Dad, off me Mom. Bloody 'ell she could lay it inta ya, when she belted yower arse yo felt it forra wick arter.

After dinner we would play in the street for a bit, an' then back ta school for two o'clock, where the arternoon would be spent alternately dreamin' an' 'alf lis'nin to or workin' for a particular lesson, broken only by a mid-afternoon break at three o'clock, when all the teachers would guzzle tea, an' 'ave biscuits whilst us lot were stuck out in the playground. Greedy sods.

Then the final bell at four thiry, an' we wus free to gu 'um an' play with no old uns ta gu on at us, tellin' us not ta do this, an' not ta do that.

Home fust though to assure "Our Mom" that we were okay, for although we were poor, the love was strong, in a funny way, and defended with fierce pride. A quick cuppa tea, an' a piece o'lard, then rush out, with "our Moms' words ringin' in me ears "now don't cho gu gerrin' inta eny mischief ya little bugger, or I'll whale ya bloody arse for ya". Off I would go to meet one of the many friends I had.

The most popular place for us to meet was an area alongside Bill Lewis's scrap yard, which was situated at the rear of some houses at the top of Guest Street, before you came to New John Street West. This spot was known to all as "Johnnie Kingham's opening".

I would first go to Johnnies 'ouse, but yo 'ad ta gu roun' the back up 'is openin', cus'is ol' mon wus a boot an' shoe repairer, an' in the 'all at the front of the 'ouse, leadin' past The Front Parlour (bloody posh), wus a counter which lifted up an' down on 'inges'. This is where Mr. Kingham took the boots an' shoes orf the customers, or gid 'em their boots an' shoes back, arter 'e 'ad mended 'em, an' 'ad the money orf em. The prices for the repairs were marked up over the front door in large sign-writing,

"Two and Sixpence sole and heel, with real leather, and One and Sixpence for sole only", it dain't say nuthin' abaht heelin' on'y, burr I don' think 'e dunnit for nuthin.

When Johnnie an' me cum away from 'is 'ouse, we would either call for, or meet the rest of the mob. Chubby Moseley, 'ose Dad played the banjo, Donnie'Arbridge, 'is Dad wus ever so clever at mekin's thin's, with wood an' ev'rythin', Dennis Clark, 'oo 'ad a lorra sisters, but 'e dain't 'ave a brother like I did, although we usta scrap at times, burr I alis beat 'im. Ray Rickards, 'oo wus a bit posh, they lived in an 'ouse on its own at the top of a yard, burrit 'ad its own gardin' an ev'rythin', burr 'e worn't as posh as sum on 'em. These meetings were pretty well a regular thing, unless we 'ad a bost up with one another, but by and large the same faces gathered, and when we had we would then decide what game we would play. "Cowboys and Injuns" - "Coppers and Crooks" - "Tramcars or Buses?" it wus a difficult decision ta mek at times. But one thing was certain, we always found something to do, even if it was only climbing over Bill Lewis's scrap yard lookin' for treasure, with one on us keepin' dog furr enyone comin', 'specially Mr. Gilbert, cus 'e wus a "Coppa". But we nearly allis 'noo w'en 'e wus comin' cus yowed 'ear 'is little three wheeled "Morgan" cum down the openin', kickin' up a bloody row.

Mr. Gilbert wus eva sa good gerrin' 'is little car inta 'is back gardin', an' we usta watch 'im sometimes, 'opin' 'e'd mek a mistake, burr 'e never did. 'e wus a nice bloke forra coppa 'e wus, 'e 'ardly usta say enytin' to us kids at all 'e probably wouldn't trust 'imself, or 'e would 'ave thumped the bloody lorron us.

Whatever we decided to play, one of us would be despatched by "Johnnie", for he was the recognised gang leader, to fetch 'is sweetheart Jessie Sinclair. Jessie lived just over the 'Brook' opposide "The Wold", in a back 'ouse, an' she 'ad a brother called Bob, 'oo wus as 'ansome as Jessie wus pretty.

It was generally agreed, no, it was naturally accepted, that "Johnnie" would be the particular hero of the day (although l disputed this right with "Johnnie" at one time, but that was another story which l will relate further on). "Johnnie Mack Brown" - "Tom Mix" - "Buck Jones" - "Buck Ryan" - "Robin Hood" - "Flash Gordon", or if we were playing tramcars or buses, you could put your money on there being a crash or some misdemeanour on the road, and "Johnnie" would sort it out, or save the victim from death, but you could put further money on, that if a crash occurred with his bus, tram, or whatever vehicle he was driving, it would never, never, be his fault, he always came out of it smelling of roses.

I would like to point out at this stage, that we did not have any equipment or toys to use during these games, because our Moms and Dads could not afford such luxuries. Imagination was our equipment and toys, we used to run around and go through the motions of the different actions, with hands, feet and our clothes sometimes. If we decided to play tramcars for instance, we would get a piece of wood or steel from Lewis's, and the tram lines - passenger stops - and islands, and anything else that was required for a game was marked out in the dirt of "The Openin'" to indicate their whereabouts.

"Johnnie" told us what character we were to play in the game he had decided upon, and probably, with the exception of one of us, who would be selected to be the limping, drunken idiot portraying his sidekick, we would all finish up either outlaws, rustlers, gangsters, indians or some other guys from the wrong side of the fence.

Without exception, one thing on the chief's orders taken for granted, and no arguments, was Jessie Sinclair, for she was always "Johnnie's Girl", never a bad girl, and they always without doubt went off into the sunset together. Oh, we would on occasions capture her during the progress of the game, but always Johnnie would be there eventually, and *without* the cavalry I might add to rescue her, defeating us single handed.

We played for hours enjoying ourselves, completely oblivious of time, or anything. I suppose the only time we were concerned about time was either going to school, or waiting for the bell to indicate school was over.

The call from one of "Our Wenches", the old uns, or even on occasions "Our Mom" 'erself, would bring the night's playing to an abrupt halt. "Ronnie, come on it's time fer yo ta gurra bed, I know yower there, (I always went to ground on hearing them call, unless they sneaked up on me of course) an' if yo don't cum out, an 'urry yerself up, yow'll be gerrin a tannin' from our Mom."

I knew why our wenches wanid ta get me in quick, I worn't bloody barmy ya know. The sooner they gathered the flock in for bedtime, the sooner they could gu out with their workmates, or a chap if they wus seein' one.

"Our Mom" allis liked us up the "wooden hill to Bedfordshire" by seven o'clock ev'ry night, but the three big uns were allowed up until ten.

So inta the 'ouse, an' sometimes yowed gerra cuppa cocoa, if the Ole Lady 'ad eny money forrit, which worn't offen, but normally it would be straight up the dancers, throw all ya clo'es under the bed by the piddle pot, "ceptin' ya shert o' course, an' inta kip yowed jump.

When we wus all up the dancers, up ud cum "Our Mom' an' say Gu Night, an' then she'd turn the gas out, an' we'd snuggle up in the dark, an' wait 'til "Our Mom" went down, an' then listen for the stairs door ta close. Then we'd av a talk, or we'd push, an' fight, but not too loud, cus if "Our Mom" 'eard us, she'd cum stormin' up an' we'd gerrour arses tanned.

"Our Mom" wus 'ard, but allis fair, for it dain't marrer 'oo started it, or what we wus doin', we all bloody well copped it.

Gradually we'd all gu quiet an' withdraw into our own particular fantasies, knowin' that all wus safe 'an sound, even from the bogey man, so we all snuggled up together, an' with "Our Mom" downstairs adding the extra security to our little minds, we'd eventually drift off into the trail of "The Sandman", our fantasies becoming real once again in our dreams.

CHAPTER FOUR

"The Truant, and Love all at Perry Hall"

I SUPPOSE it would be fair to say that "playing the wag" (being truant from school) was an occasional accepted thing, amongst us kids anyway in my schooldays. On reflection I think that if you worked it right you would get away with it. Well, you thought you would get away with it, for the teachers generally were compassionate towards us, due to the times we were living in, vast unemployment, poverty, standard of living, and the constant threat of a Second World War overshadowing us. I can imagine one of us being away, and the teacher smiling, and thinking, "Well, the poor little bugger deserves a break". When the offender returned she (yes the girls did it as well) or he would receive a slight reprimand and a caution, and that would be the finish of the matter.

There was, however, always the clever sods weren't there, and Kenny Bates who lived in Wheeler Street ('is sister wus a clippie on the buzzis w'en the war wus on, an' she wus beautiful like a film star) and Frankie Anderton from down "The Openin'" in New John Street West" 'e wus one o' me bestist mates 'e wus, and two or three others including "Smiffy", planned what we thought was the perfect scheme.

The schedule on Monday afternnoons at Burbury Street Senior School was we assembled in the playground until two o'clock, when the duty teachers would ring the bell and we would all stand still, until the second bell, and then we would group into our own particular classes. On completion of this we would then be marched into the school, but unlike the morning procedure, we would not attend assembly, but go straight into our classrooms. Once settled in the classroom our teacher called the register, and you would give the appropriate answer "Here Miss, or Sir" as was applicable. The register call completed, we normally commenced with the lesson allocated for that afternoon. But on Mondays all the lads would stand at the teachers order and file out of the classroom again, for on Mondays the lads of our class were scheduled for "The Metal Work School" in Vittoria Street, off Warstone Lane, for our "Art lesson in Metalwork". What a giggle, the old man that took us for this lesson was a very kind gentleman, who did not worry about the administration side of education, but was genuinely interested in trying to pass on his great skills to his pupils. I really did (as I do to this very day) appreciate art in any form, and further, I loved to put it into practice. According to all concerned amongst my many teachers, this talent should have been pursued, but due to the poverty stricken times etc., this was never realised.

All us lads would leave the school for our walk to Vittoria Street, with no teacher in charge, for they knew approximately how long it would take us to arrive at our destination. Nevertheless we would dawdle along Bridge Street West to Great King Street by Lucas's, there we would turn right, taking our time, and have some "Donnuck" (fun) on the way up to Hockley Hill, with Key Hill opposite. Across there we would run, and then head towards "The Fanny Brown" until we came to the junction of Great Hampton Street, where we turned right into Vyse Street opposite Well Street, with "The Swallow Raincoat" (Fine in the Rain) factory on its corner. We would then trek up to the "Clock" at Warstone Lane and Frederick Street, turn left down the lane, first right into Vittoria Street and the Metal School was down there on the right.

I must admit that I honestly liked the work we did whilst there, but I'm afraid this vast interest was soon overwhelmed by that short period of freedom between Burbury Street and Vittoria Street. In a very short time we fell to trying to elongate this short lived freedom by a foolproof scheme. We must have spent hours figuring this problem out, but in the end we had to rely on "The Old Man's" reluctance towards administration.

We decided on a trial run, and it was "Batesy" and I who were the trialists. The decision was that we would 'play the wag' and if we were found out, we would say we had "Stummickpains 'an went 'um", hoping this would suffice, but if the "old man" said nothing, we considered this would be the answer to our problem. Well, we reasoned with oursleves, what could go wrong, if the 'ole mon dain't miss us we could all "play the wag" in turns.

On Monday afternoon we had decided to carry out our plan, I was nearly 'doin' it in me trousers, cus I 'new warrour old lady ud do ta me if she copped me", and believe me I was a "bloody pest" nearly all the time to her, although I saw it in a somewhat different light, but you can't argue a point of fact with your Mother when you're only ten going on eleven can you?

The time came, however, and we all left the school, but instead of turning up Great King Street with the rest of the lads, "Batesey" and me carried on along Bridge Street West, after arranging to meet Frankie Anderton and the rest at the "Clock" in Warstone Lane at half past four to see what had transpired in "Metal Work". Off we went like a couple of scouts exploring in front of the main party, with best wishes from all our mates, who had given their oath that come what may, they would not utter a word. Well, I say they gave their oath, they knew they had better keep quiet or "We'd do 'em". Where Ken and I went on that particular afternoon I cannot remember, other stories I can, and will relate to you further on.

We were early at the "Clock" though, after our afternoon of wandering, because we were apprehensive as to what had happened. After what seemed an eternity, "The Lads" came out of Vittoria Street into Warstone Lane, and when they saw us they ran, shouting and laughing, until they reached us. "It's okay dokey, 'e dain't even arsk where yo' wus, 'e dain even check us, 'e dain even say enythin', it's bloody werked, we've dunnit" they shouted. "Are yo' shure" we queried, thinking they might be pulling our legs, "Cause we'em shure, 'e dain even know if *we* wus there lerra lone yo', 'e wus that busy messin' about with 'is bits o' metal ta know 'oo wus there or not, so don' worry". After a while Ken and I accepted that it was so far so good, but we had still got to attend school the next day, so we were both still concerned, although we put on a brave face for the others and joined in the "donnuck" back down Vyse Street to the "Hockleychem" by Hockley Hill, where Kenny and I parted. He went towards town along Great Hampton Street with his friends, and Frankie Anderton, the other kids and me went in the opposite direction towards the "Brook" down Hockley Hill.

The next morning I was up and ready for school in a shot, I couldn't get there quick enough. "Wot's up wi' yo' " our Mom quipped, "It's bloody strange fer yo'ta gu rushin' orf ta school like this, what's a marra, yo bin playin' up agin? Cus if yo' 'ave I shall soon bloody find out, 'an then yow'll gerra bloody good whalin' " I paid no heed to the threats or answered the question, I dain' even ge 'er no lip which was unusual. I ran down the entry into Guest Street, across there and down to St. Saviours, with me birra bread an' jam wrapped in *The Birmingham Mail*, along Bridge Street and into the playground. I met my mates, and naturally we all put on a brave face, averting the immediate problem we thought we might have.

Eventually the bell rang and we formed into our classes, then marched into "Assembly". How we managed to get through it I'll never know, but the time arrived, after what seemed an eternity, for Mr. Locker to give his end of assembly talk, and after that to read the names of the pupils he wished to see in his office. We thought, "any second now 'e's gunna call out Bates an' Smith", but thank God, there were many others, but *not* us.

How we managed to get through the first morning session, bringing us up to playtime at ten fifteen I do not know. There were knowing winks, and nods, with secret thumbs up to one another, but it was when the bell went, and we emerged into the playground that we really congratulated one another, on our successful mission. Needless to say Ken and I had praise from the others for sticking our necks out to gain this success, but in the end the attitude we adopted foolishly led us to complacency, and ultimate ruin.

Every Monday from then on, there would be three or four of us "Playing the wag" until we just didn't care anymore. We didn't bother to see who was going to "Metal Work" or who was "Playing the Wag". Ken, Frank, a couple or three others and myself just didn't attend "Metal Work" at all, and this situation prevailed for some considerable time, until one day I came home from school for my dinner and there was "you know who" waiting with her arms folded across her huge chest and I thought, "wot's a marra now".

"A right" she started "now wo't the bleedin' 'ell 'ave yo bin up to, an' don't tell me any on ya bloody lies, cus I know all abaht it, cum out with it ya little bugger?" "Nuthin' Mom, 'onest, I dain't dun nothin' " which immediately brought about my first wallop across the head, which started me grizzlin'. 'Yo cun gu on grizzlin', cus it ain't gunna 'elp ya, now bloody tell me what yo've bin up to, cum on out with it ya little bleeder", and in between sobs, " 'onest Mom I don' know watcha mean", - bang! - another wallop which brought on a fresh bout of "grizzlin". "I've 'ad the bleedin' School Board bloke 'ere this mornin', and 'e sez yo' ain't bin guin ta school for wicks now, so worr'ave ya gorra say abaht that then, ya little sod?"

All my world crumbled about me, how could they have found out? The "Ole Mon" didn't tell them, or did he, the rotton old sod. What could I do? Well, I didn't want any more thumping around the earhole did I? I came to a decision rather quickly, under "Our Mom's" threatening look. I would relate what I had been doing and depend on "you know who" showing a little mercy. Mercy? You've really got to be joking. I told the whole story, only interrupted by a wallop here and a wallop there, but did not reveal that my mates had been "playing the wag" as well. It wasn't because of loyalty I didn't mention them, it was fear of "being dun" if I did. Anyway the School Board Inspector would have this information, so it didn't make a lot of difference.

I had my dinner, for nothing would affect my appetite, and went to school feeling right miserable, and quite sorry for myself into the bargain, wondering what was going to happen next. I didn't have to wait long for the answer.

We had just sat down in class for the afternoon session, when the teacher informed me that I was to go to Mr Locker's office straight away. I went amongst hushed whisperings from my classmates, wondering I've no doubt what I had done.

When I arrived at the corridor behind the back wall of the main hall, I received a shock, our Mom was there. She didn't speak to me, she just glared, until we were summoned to enter by the Headmaster. Once inside he asked Mom some questions and then he turned to me and requested me to tell him the whole story, from beginning to end, and reminded me not to tell any further lies about the affair. I did as he requested, but I still did not involve my mates. He listened without interruption, and when I had finished, he informed me that they knew about all the other culprits involved, so there was no need to pretend any longer. Mr Locker then gave me a severe reprimand and told me to return to my classroom, leaving our Mom in there with him, persumably to confer with her on what they intended to do.

I was soon made aware of what they intended to do, for within a very short time of me returning to my classroom one of the Senior Monitors knocked on the door, and on entering went to our teacher and said something very quietly to him, and then left. My teacher then said "Smith the Headmaster would like to see you again, off you go quickly boy." More whisperings, but this time louder. "Shut up, all of you" from the teacher, and I left the room in quietness. On arrival at the office in the corridor, no Mom in sight this time, which was a bit of a relief, but I was naturally still apprehensive. I knocked the door, and the deep voice of Mr Locker bade me to "Come in."

Once inside I stood to attention in front of his desk. "Yo sen' fa' me Sir?", I said. He stared at me for a while, and then commenced to repremand me further in the wickedness of my ways, and the results of what would happen if I did not alter drastically. Then he went on, with me snivelling, and telling him how sorry I was, and how it would never happen again. I thought it would never end, but eventually it did, but *not* the way I expected it to. On completion of his reprimand, I thought he would tell me to return to my classroom again, but no, he took his cane from the cupboard and said "Smith, I am going to attempt to put some sense into you, and believe me when I say it will hurt me as much as it will hurt you, but I assure you it is only to prevent you from reverting to these ways again. Do you understand me?" I didn't understand, but to say I didn't would have been insubordinate, I had a pretty good idea what was coming, so l didn't want an extra helping, so naturally my reply was "Yus Sir", but I don't think he believed me anyway. He then proceeded to give me six of the best, three on each hand, and I thought to myself, "It's a bloody funny way to put sense into me, through my hands." Although I didn't grizzle in front of him, I certainly did when he dismissed me back to my classroom. After grizzling for a few minutes in the hall, I wiped my face on my shirt front (Handkerchief?, you must be joking) and resumed my journey back to the classroom.

When school finished that day and we poured out into the playground to go home, all my mates came round to enquire what had happened, and so I retold the story, but in a slightly different version. Well, by this time I was feeling a bit heroic wasn't I? I could hardly tell them that I had "blarted", or that I had been sorry either, so I gave the impression that we (Mr Locker and myself) had negotiated amicably.

I went home after a short time, and "Our Mom" gave me another belting, saying, "I've tol' ya Fertha the bloody antics yo've bin gerrin up ta, an' yo' wert' till 'e gets 'olt on ya', 'e'll belt ya bloody arse till it's raw, now bugger orf ourov 'ere fower I ge' ya some mower." I went back out without having any bread and lard, or a cuppa tea, not daring to ask for any, for I knew what the answer would have been, and I'd have probably got another bang up the earhole "Ta gu on with."

That night I stayed out until one of "The Big 'uns" came bawling for me to go to bed. I hid for a while to give my Dad time to go to work, and hopefully avoid the threatened belting. "The Big 'uns" must have had a date that night, for the hands when they found me were't too gentle, and so my guided tour back home that night was a rough one, and I thought to myself, "It just ain't bin my bloody day ta day."

The tanning that was promised from my Dad never materialised, probably because he thought I'd had enough already, for nobody knew "Our Mom" like our Dad. I could visualise him smiling, with that wonderful twinkling in his blue eyes, behind "Our Mom's" back of course, and thinking to himself, "The crafty little bugger."

After a short time the whole issue was presumably forgotten, or at least it seemed to have died down, so it was a further shock to me when I was suddenly transferred from Burbury Street School to Icknield Street. Whether or not it was anything to do with me "playing the wag" I shall never know, but I rather suspect it was. I never did hear what fate the other kids suffered. I expect it was something similar to my punishment though, for it was the usual treatment given all round in those days, and us kids just learned to accept it. I did meet all of them in turn, at one time or another but we managed not to bring the subject up. It's easy to forget when you want to, isn't it?

It was during one of these Monday afternoons off that Ken, Frank, two other lads and myself decided to go to Perry Hall Playing Fields, at Perry Barr, right by the Dog Track. We had heard they had positioned some anti-aircraft guns there in preparation for a possible war with Germany. Naturally we were curious, and thought what a lot of fun it would be to go and have a look.

It was a beautiful sunny afternoon as we set off along Bridge Street West. As usual, we were quite carefree, all the initial worries and apprehension of "playing the wag " now clearly forgotten. We said "Tarra" to the rest of the lads, not knowing, or caring for that matter, what they were going to do, which was of course our ultimate downfall, we should have kept a check on the number who were "playing the wag." I mean, we could all have decided not to go to "Metal Work", then even "The Ol' Mon" would have been suspicious wouldn't he? Probably that's what dropped us all in the S... at the end!

It would have been a giggle though wouldn't it? Can you imagine *one kid* turning up at Vittoria Street, and the "Ol' Mon" peering over his glasses and saying, "Good heavens boy, the class is small today, whatever has happened to your friends, eh? And the kid replying, if 'e'd gorreny eighteen pence, "Well Sir, yo' ain't gunna believe this, but some bloody Germans landed in Great King Street an' knackered all the rest on 'em, but I wus a bit quika than 'em, cus I nipped down a "Suff 'ole" (Drain) an' escaped through the sewers ta gerr'ere an' tell yo'." Any road up, we never found out how we were rumbled, but we were, so that was that.

We went along Bridge Street, past Tommy Smith's house opposite Lucas's, until we arrived at Well Street. We turned left towards Wheeler Street, skirting well around the school in case anyone saw us. Originally we would have gone straight up Wheeler Street to Lozells, but when we arrived at "The bottom of Well Street" (good joke which we used often, *well* we thought it was any road up) we decided to nip along to Withers bread and cake shop, to see if they had any cakes, stale ones of course, "Ta ge us", which was normally the usual thing.

So off we trooped, anxious to fill our ever-hungry stomachs, past Cowdrills the bike shop, and then over Great King Street to Withers on the right. Surrounded by Joseph Lucas' works, they covered a vast area of 'ockley. Into the shop we went and asked "Gorreny stale cakes yo' don' wan' Mista, please?" The bloke must have been in a bad mood that day, an' 'ad got one on 'im, or something had disagreed with 'im, because his reply was quick, to the point, and even us kids got the message abundantly clear "Sod orf ya little buggers, afoa I call a bloody coppa to ya, now gu on an' bugger orf'. Now this reply deflated our feelings of '*Goodwill to Man*' somewhat, so we ran out of the shop and back up toward Great King Street (we couldn't go any other way, because that's where our school lay, we shouted to the bloke, "Stick ya' cakes up yarr arse then." He couldn't get around the counter quick enough to catch us, and he was too fat anyway, eatin' all them cream buns I shouldn't wonder, the greedy sod. Up Farm Street we went like the clappers out of hell, turning left at Great King Street, and immediately left again into Berners Street. Just along there on the left we ducked into Burbury Street Rec.

Through the "Rec" we went quickly, for we "dain't wan' the Parky ta see us" in case he wanted to know why we were not at school. We would have to explain, "Cus 'e wus a birrof a Coppa worn 'e? an' 'e'd 'ave marched us back ta the school, an' that's the last thing we wanted to happen wornit?"

We climbed over the railings into Gordon Street. There was no point in going to the gate by Lozells Street, it was too far up, and anyway we intended to go up Berners Street, past Berners Press Works opposite Gordon Street, and Chuka Baileys house just on the left inside Berners Street itself.

Up Berners Street we went heading towards Lozells Road at the top, crossing Clifford Street on the way. When we arrived at the junction of Gerrard Street we spotted a Purus's bakery van, one of the 1934 Fords, parked over the other side on the left. Still feeling hungry after our unsuccessful "request" at Withers, we decided to knacker a cake or two off this van.

We looked into the shop on the corner, thinking that the roundsman might be serving in there, but the shop was empty. So we had a quick scout round, and not finding any sight of him we assumed he must be in the pub on the opposite corner having a drink. So whilst the rest of us kept "dog", one of the lads opened the rear doors of the van (they only had the latch type of doors on the vehicles at that time). We thought he would just knacker a *few* cakes for us to share out, but "The silly sod", instead of taking a few, he started to pull the whole bloody tray of cakes out. As soon as we saw what he intended to do, being the heroes we all were, we were off like a bat out of hell up Berners Street toward Gower Street. I was still the last in the queue, the other buggers were quicker off the mark than me, leaving the kid that was doing the actual knicking to fend for himself. Well, we could always deny being with him if he was caught, couldn't we?

But I will give him his due. Whether he was determined to show us how good he was, in the face of us weak kneed berks, or he was so frightened seeing us leave him in the lurch that he forgot he had the tray, I don't know, but he hung on to it anyway, and it was more than half full of cakes. I mean, he could have dropped them and chased after us bloody heroes. On the other hand he must have thought that if he left the cakes behind, he'd have "'ad a taterin'" from us. However, he *did* hang onto the wooden tray of cakes, and round into Gower Street he came, with us heroes already hiding up an entry.

We made sure no-one was chasing him, then called him, seeing that he had indeed still got the cakes. When he came to us we commenced to slap him on the back and tell him how good he was, just like we would have done it (what a bloody lot of liars and hypocrits we were, but hopefully, convincing.)

After eating what cakes we could manage and putting some into our pockets for later (well, we couldn't take the wooden tray to Perry Hall with us, could we?) we threw the rest of the cakes and the tray up another entry, then proceeded down Gower Street, past The Manor Vinegar Company. Phew! What a pen and ink (stink) from the brewing of the vinegar. This firm also made toffees there as well, but we thought we wouldn't like a bag of them even if they "Gid us sum", or even if "We could a 'nicked sum". They most likely put vinegar in them for a laugh sometimes. Some bloody joke, I don't think. On we went right down to Guilford Street, where we turned left up to Lozells Road. Once across there, we ran down Chain Walk to Birchfield Road, where we started the long trek to our final destination.

On we went, gaming about, talking, pushing and shoving one another, past the *Odeon* at the junction of Canterbury Road and Thornbury Road, keeping an eye open for coppa's from "the nick" just up Canterbury Road on the left, then onto *The Birchfield Cinema* passing The Broadway and Bragg Road on the right, and Livingstone Road and Willmore Road on the left. The Corporation Bus Garage was opposite the cinema. On we strode to the junction of Wellington Road and Aston Lane, with *The Crown and Cushion* on the left corner, and an old pub opposite which was referred to as *The Old Crown.* If you were giving directions to anyone around that location, you would refer to the *Old Crown and Cushion* or *The New Crown and Cushion* so that people would not get confused.

Over the bridge, with Perry Barr Station beneath on The London, Midland and Scottish Railway network. Just beyond the bridge was the tramcar terminus for route number 6. The line of the L.M.S., running to the left, skirted Perry Hall Playing Fields, before going on its way to Great Barr Station, situated alongside Rocky Lane, then on through Hampstead, right through the colliery to Walsall via Bescott Station. There was a junction on the line before Great Barr Station which veered to the left on another route which passed by Wood Lane. Under Wellington Road it went and then onto Hamstead Road by *The Endwood*, emerging from the tunnel into Handsworth Wood Station, situated more or less in Handworth Park itself. This line would travel onwards to Handsworth Station in Soho Road, passing right through the park, going under Holly Road, and then after Handsworth puffing its way in the direction of Winson Green, past "The Soap Hole" signal box by Averys Weighing Machine and Scale Works, through Soho, by me Grandad's, Smethwick, on its way to the "Black Country" and beyond.

We moved on past Perry Barr Station which bought us to some pretty little cottages on the left. Beyond these, lying a good distance back off the Walsall Road was The Perry Barr Stadium (The Dog Track).

By this time we were, according to us 'ockleyites' out in the country. We crossed a huge expanse of grassland, with large trees and bushes situated directly in front of the track, to gain access to Regina Drive, just before Teddington Avenue. This drive was more of a path, leading to the entrance of Perry Hall Playing Fields. On the right of the drive were garages and a door alongside them, locked of course, which led into the very large gardens at the rear of the "Posh Houses" in Teddington Avenue. On the left side were corrugated iron sheets, bolted together, standing about five sheets high, and running practically the whole length of Regina Drive, painted dark green, containing the track on the other side.

At intervals, and at various heights, you found some of these iron panels prised slightly apart, to provide a peep show for those unfortunates who could not afford the admission fee, presumably. Where this iron wall terminated, and then turned left following the contour of the track, was a path. On the other side was a Tea Shop, catering for people visiting the park in the Spring and Summer months, and just beyond that, the entrance to the park itself, with its huge gates of iron open to welcome us.

Into the park we rushed with whoops of joy and delight, scaring the birds momentarily out of the trees, which were in abundance. A woodland path ran to both left and right, following the course of the river which ran through the park. Onto the bridge which crossed the river we clattered, stopping half way to lean over and look into the dark water below, hoping to catch sight of a fish or two, unsuccessfully, then listening to the birds whistling and chirping. A distant train whistle, and the huffing and puffing as it steamed past the park on the far left of us. God, this was heaven. We forgot all about school, playing the wag, our dirty little houses in Hockley, with their small cramped yards, brewhouses, communal lavatories, gas lights, and the never ending smell of the factories around them. This smell contaminated the people who worked in the factories and the clothes they wore. It was a smell on its own, which never seemed to diminish. Our Lil, Vi, Hilda and Arthur had this smell. It wasn't that they were dirty themselves, they weren't, but try as they may, they could not get rid of it. We left the bridge behind us, and there, as far as our young eyes could see was beautiful open countryside, fresh clean air, fields, trees, and a blue sky, that wasn't contaminated with smoke and grime from the factory chimneys.

We took all this scenery in, and saw what we had come all this way to see, for immediately in front of us, but quite a distance off were the guns.

Well it's not strictly true that we could see them, because naturally the soldiers had covered them with camouflage in the form of big nets. It was a little disappointing for us, but at least we had seen them. Around the outskirts of the gun site, to a considerable depth, they had let the grass grow tall and wild, presumably to deter anyone getting too near the site itself, until they built a more substantial fence later.

Naturally this wild grass was a wonderful place for us 'ockleyites' to play in, for it was quite hot, and the grass was dry, warm even. We must have been larking about for quite a while, going in and out of this tall grass, hiding and then frightening the life out of one another, when suddenly one of the lads ran to us and gathering us all together, with an index finger placed across his mouth, he told us to "Sh-h-h-h". Then he said in a quiet voice "keep ya' gobs shut, an' cum with me." So we followed stealthily, until he stopped and motioned us to all lie down, then we followed him as he squirmed his way further into the undergrowth. Suddenly we came to a halt at the lad's bidding and he turned to face us. With a grin like a Cheshire cat he pointed. We all looked in the direction of his outstretched arm and there some little way off we could see a man and a woman lying in the tall grass. Now at this point it should be known that unlike today the vast majority of kids at that time were brought up in a rather harsh Victorian fashion. So we were ignorant in many ways of life, and in this particular instance we thought that making love was kissing one another, and sometimes when you kissed too often the woman had a baby. Regarding any other aspect of sex, or birth, we were to everyone concerned, complete innocents, all of us. We stared at this sight for a few seconds, trying to fathom out what they were doing, and eventually came to the conclusion that they were doing something "dirty". I mean the bloke 'ad gorris trousas down, with 'is bare bum showin', an' 'e wus wrigglin' abaht eva sa much 'as well, burr 'e'd gorr all 'is other clo'es on, an' 'er, the woman, all we could see on 'er wus 'er legs, an' 'er clo'es wus in a 'eap lyin' in the grass by 'er, an' she wus moanin' summat bloody awful". We lay there for a few seconds, without a clue what they were doing, sniggering and making quiet gestures to one another, then we inevitably started to get fidgety. I looked around me and saw some tiny bibbles (stones), so I picked one up and took aim at the bloke's bare bum and the bibble hit it, but nothing, no re-action whatsoever. He must have been too busy with what he was doing, so l scraped a handful of these bibbles up, and getting more adventurous started to bombard his bum, one bibble at a time.

Finally after what seemed an eternity the bloke stopped what he was doing, and his hand reached backwards to swipe his own bum, perhaps thinking it was a fly or something. Anyway he settled down to his business again, with what I thought a little more fervour, but alas, the other lads had watched me and what I was doing with great interest, and thought what a good idea it was. So within a very short time, the bum was put under a very strong attack from showers of bibbles, which consequently brought the bum side operations to an abrupt halt, causing us to lie flat in the grass quietly. After a while we raised our heads in time to see the bloke tugging at his shirt tail, pulling it partly over his exposed bum, and after a short spell, the operations commenced all over again.

By this time we had become fed up with the situation anyway, so we prepared to creep away and resume playing games, but Ken said quietly "I'll 'ave one more gu at it, but this time the "rotton sod" picked a big smooth ducker (stone) up, and before we had time to stop him, he had taken aim and threw it. Time stood still, we were rooted to the spot, frozen, as we watched the missile speed through the air, praying that it would miss its intended target. Well our prayers were answered, it did miss the target it was intended for, the bloke's bum, but it *did* hit him; right on target it hit him in his vitals. Ouch!

The quiet country air was shattered with the most horrendous roar, as the bloke jumped up from whatever he was doing and turned, looking in our direction. Of course we kids had a very quick reaction to trouble situations, and this was a trouble situation with a capital "T", for the second the ducker hit the unintended target, we thought, as one man, "Goodbye countryside, 'ello 'ockley." So we stood up and all attempted to beat Sydney Wooderson's mile record, back to the bridge by the park exit. The bloke started to shout obscenities, which could have been dangerous to our little ears, including that old classic "COME BACK 'ERE YA' LITTLE B.......S, I WANT YA'."

He'd got about as much chance of us returning to him, as him flying to us without an aeroplane. Looking back over our shoulders as we ran, we saw that the bloke had stood up, with his shirt hanging down and his hand clutching between his groin, but the woman had only sat up and appeared to be talking to him. His next move had us all in creases, although we still kept running. Forgetting momentarily that his trousers were still round his ankles, in his anger he attempted to chase us. Naturally he went "arse over tip" and fell to the ground, and that we were pleased to say was the last we saw of him, because we then concentrated on putting as much distance between him and us in the shortest possible time. Consequently we must have got back to Walsall Road in a somewhat record time for kids of our age.

Once back amongst people, as we started our journey home through Perry Barr we nattered on, laughing about the incident, now that we were safe. One thing we hoped was that the "Ducker" hadn't broken any bones? I bet that bloke, whoever he was, would have broken some bones if he had caught us, and there's no doubt about that!

CHAPTER FIVE

"Saturdays and Arthur Crump"

AS A HAND gently shook me I awoke with a start. "Cum on Ron, gerup or yo'll 'ave Arthur 'ere, an' yo' wunt be ready fer 'im", the somewhat unfamiliar soft voice of our Mom stated.

Slowly I came round and rubbed my eyes to remove the sleep from them, wondering at the same time how quiet it was. No bawling and shouting, no sound from the outside, no bulls blowing then suddenly I realised why, "IT'S SATADEE!" The reason I hadn't heard any bawling was because it was too early for "The wenches" ta gurra werk, an' "Our Mom" dain't wanna wake 'em up yet.

I loved Saturdays. I knew I had to get out of bed earlier, but it wasn't to go to school. "Like I tol' ya', I dain't like school, any road up." It was to go and help our baker Arthur Crump on his bread deliveries, and was one thing I really liked to do, work. Helping to deliver the bread, meeting all those people I would never normally meet, if I didn't deliver their daily bread. Also I liked the money Arthur gave me. He paid me ninepence for helping him all day Saturday, but when I helped him all week, Monday till Saturday. "w'en I wus on 'oliday's, or playin' the wag", he would give me one and sixpence. Out of this princely sum I received, our Mom claimed half. At the time I used to think "twistin' sod", but I wondered later on in life if it wasn't a good thing, for it certainly introduced me into looking after the financial aspects of life a little earlier than one would anticipate.

A few of the customers, not many mind you, would give me 'a'penny sometimes, if they'd got it, but it was a rare thing. I used to keep this money in a separate pocket. "I dain't tell "Our Mom" of these extras, cus she'd a' took 'alf o' that as well, wouldn't she?" When I arrived home on completion of the day's work, I would scuttle off to hide this extra money. I'd put it away safe, so she wouldn't find it (I'd got a million hiding places she dain't know abaht), and then I would spend it later.

One very dear lady I will never forget was a Mrs King, who lived in Anglesley Street, in the first house up from the coffee house situated on the corner of Nursery Road. She gave me a penny nearly every Saturday. I shall never forget that kindness, not for the money itself but the thought and love that must have been within the lady, for giving it.

Arthur Crump arrived in my life "arter we moved from Gues' Street into Mrs 'ughe's 'ouse, at number two, two, eight, New John Street West. She moved further up New John Street West towards Summer Lane, into "The Dairy Shop", opposite Mrs Dutton's huxter's shop on the corner of Unett Street. The shop Mrs Hughes moved into "sold ev'rythin' from the country, like milk, butte, an' eggs."

"HOUSE" that was the understatement of the year, for anyone like us moving from "two up an' one down" into "four up four down" it was like moving into a "bloody mansion". There was also a long, but narrow garden. At the end of this garden was a wall, with trees in front of it. On the other side was a thirty foot drop into some back houses situated in Bridge Street West. "Nuncky" Collins lived in one of these houses. " 'e wus a great kid wus Nuncky, 'e could gob far'er 'an anybody ol' Nuncky cud."

What really fascinated "Our Kid" and me was that we had actually got a room to ourselves for sleeping in. For the first few days in the "Mansion" our Mom didn't have to tell us to go to bed, we were always ready.

But on Saturdays in Guest Street it meant getting up later, and after breakfast, "A birra bread an' scrape, an' a cuppa tea", "Our Kid" an' me nearly allis usta gu lookin' at trains in All Saints Road. "Our Kid" dain' like tekkin' me though, cus 'e'd gorris own mates, burr "Our Mom" sez 'e'd gorra tek me, an' that wus bloody that.

We usta scrap a lot, "Our Kid" an' me, burr I allis usta win, although 'e wus older an' bigger an' me. Sometimes I med 'im cry, an' I'd be sorry, an' I'd lay orf 'im. But sometimes the crafty sod wus on'y tendin', an' w'en I layed orf, 'e'd start beltin' me again. For all this though I loved "Our Kid," cus 'e wus ev'rythin' I worn't, e' wus quiet, an' wouldn't play rough games, an' 'e would neva dream o' 'avin' a bost up with enyone. He kep' 'imself to 'imself, which naturally, I couldn't understand.

Once w'en I wus cumin' 'um' from Burbury Street Infants School, one o' me mates siz me an' sez, "Ron, Tommy Froggit's got yowa kid in the school gateway, an' is thumpin' 'im". "Our Kid" at this period was attending Farm Street Junior School. Tommy Froggit lived in Bridge Street West, an' 'e wus a big kid, 'e wus, e' musta bin bigger 'an "Our Uncle Alf", 'oo wus small forra big bloke. Froggit 'ad nits as well, cus the School Lady 'ad shaved all 'is bloody 'air orf, 'ceptin' a little bit at the front, which 'ung down like an 'osses tail, 'e wus a bully as well, allis pickin' on the smalla kids, or weak big kids, like warr our Arthur wus. Anyway, I run as quick as I could alung Bridge Street West an' saw Froggit with "Our Kid" in the gateway, just past Villa Street. I rushed to them, graspin' a thick *Boys Own Annual* in my 'ands, which I 'ad took ta school that mornin', although I couldn't read it propa, I wus jus' showin' orf ta me mates, that I'd got one. On reachin' them I raised the book in the air an' walloped Froggit on top o' 'is bald 'ead with it, an' at the same time shouted to "Our Kid". "Cum on Arth, run forrit. "God I wus frightened as usual. On 'earin' me "Our Kid" run, an' I run arta 'im, an' we both run up 'um' forr owa dinna.

I dain't think enymore abourit arta, but w'en I went back ta school in the artanoon, I wus summoned to 'is Lordship's room (Mr Locker the Headmaster) and questioned about the Froggit incident. Some rotten sod 'ad tol' 'is Mom, an' she 'ad bin down the school. Poor ol' Tommy, I dain't realise it, but w'en I 'ad 'it 'im, I'd really 'it 'im fer six, an' 'e'd gone ta bloody sleep, an' (apparently) they'd 'ad ta tek 'im ta Dudley Road 'orspital, burr I don' think it wus too bad, cus they dain't keep 'im in. Burre'd gorra stay away frum school a bit, which I berr'e dain' mind, the crafty sod. His Lordship dain' cane me or enythin' though, which I thought wus funny, 'e jus' med me cry, an' promise I wudden do it agin. Sum broody 'ope 'e'd gorrof me keepin' that promise fer lung, with the rough arses we'd gorra roun' 'ockley.

"Our Kid" an' me usta gu ta 'ockley Brook an' cross ova, an' gu inta Icknield Street. We'd gu up there as far as the Lodge Road an' Key 'ill junction, turn right an' gu alung "The Flat", then turn left inta Piddock Street, alung there ta the end, turn right, an' then gu up the 'ill in All Saints Road. Up the 'ill we'd gu till we cum to a big wooden gateway, with a five barred gate across it. We'd jump onta this gate, an' tek our place with the other kids that wus already there. This gateway was the entrance to Hockley Goods Yard, which also housed the Passenger Station.

The railway blokes wus good to us kids, an' sometimes w'en it wus cold they'd lerrus gu inta their 'ut forra warm. They'd 'ave their fire guin' in one o' them fat stoves in the middle of the 'ut, an' the pipe frum this stove usta gu up through the

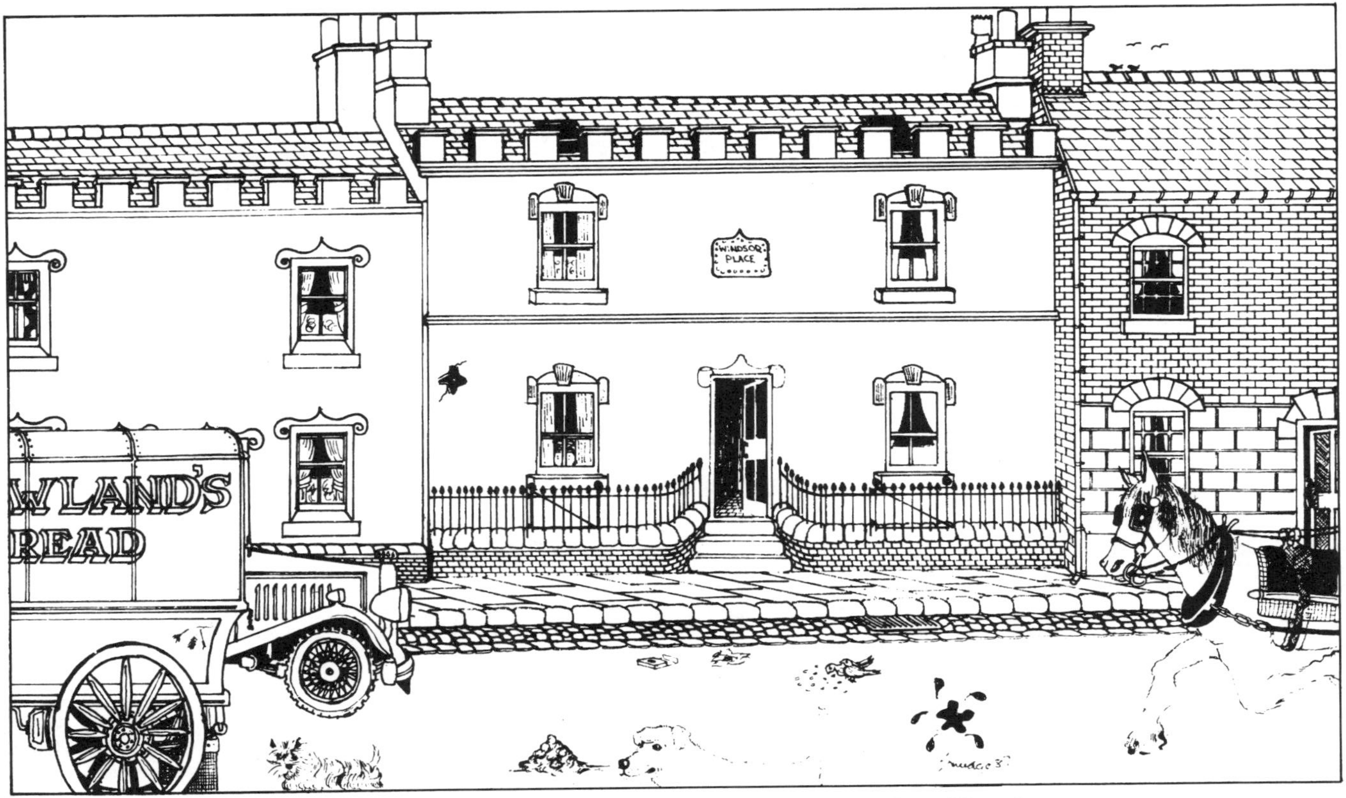

228 New John Street West (Right side of Windsor Place)

roof, an' let the smoke out. Sometimes they'd ge us a birra bread an' marge, or somethin'. The bloke wot drove the big shire 'osses would sometimes lerrus stroke 'em, an' I thought the 'osses smelt lovely.

The little shuntin' trains, the square tankers we usta call them, would move the goods trucks up an' down the lines, an' there usta be a bloke with a big lung stick 'oo usta mek 'em cum apart. Us kids usta play one game, an' that wus w'en one of these shuntin' trains wen' unda the bridge (which 'ad All Saints Street runnin' ova the top onnit, an' trams as well) with a stream of goods trucks trailin' behind it, yo' 'ad ta guess which line 'e'd cum back ouron. We 'ad a lorra fun with that game we did.

The big dark green trains with their brown and yellow coaches trailing behind them, thundered through the goods yard, white smoke blowing from their brass plated funnels, giving the occasional whistle as they went, which us kids usta believe wus the driver sayin' " 'ello." It might 'ave bin ya know, an' we usta wave enthusiastically back. We usta wonder "Where are they guin' or where 'ave they bin", the seaside, the country, or another big town like Brum.

Then there wus the fickle passenger trains that worn't guin' far. They'd pull up at the station, an' we'd watch people gerrof, but they dain't cum by us ta gu 'um', for the gate that we sat on wus on'y an entrance an' exit fer goods. They usta gu down some steps on the station which led to a yard, an' they'd gu through this yard out into Little Park Road. Then there'd be sum people gerrin' on the train, an' their luggage usta be purrin the wagon at the back o' the train. When everybody ad' gorron, a bloke usta wave 'is green flag, an' then 'e'd blow 'is w'istle, an' the train 'u'd blow 'is w'istle right back at 'im. There would be a roar from 'is boiler, an' the smoke usta blow out from the train like air from an 'osses nostrils on a cold day, on'y stronger. Then slowly it would chug, chug, chug, an' start ta move out o' the station. Then e'd get faster an' faster until e' passed us kids, an' he'd gu under the bridge, an' we'd watch an' wave, until the last coach disappeared in a cloud of white billowy smoke.

The smell of steam and oil, when the trains came near enough, and the smell of the big shire horses, the blowing through nostrils and stamping of their hooves, the gentle banter between the railway chaps, the aroma of real tobacco from the driver's pipes as they passed slowly and gently in and out of the entrance in All Saints Road, the smell of mixed chaff and oats for the big horses, a couple of nose bags full hanging from hooks under the rear end of the cart, with further supplies in herden sacks which the driver would place on the box seat in front. These sacks would make the seat a little more comfortable. Even the smell of "Hoss Muck" made the time us kids spent there so wonderful.

There were a few lorries, but not many, the biggest percentage of transport was horse and cart. One vehicle that was being introduced at this time was the "Mechanical Horse", consisting of a three wheel articulated lorry made by "Scammel". This introduction by The Great Western Railway was I imagine the start of speeding up and turn around of goods. I suppose the idea was that one man could back up to the deck, unhook his trailer, hook up to an empty trailer and away he would go on further pick ups, which would not only save manpower, horses and carts, but a lot of time as well.

Of course this was the beginning of phasing the horses out, but it was halted for a time due to the outbreak of the Second World War, when naturally petrol became short in supply, as also did oil, but war, politics, economic and commerce situations and the like did not intrude into us children's wonderful innocent world, thank God.

"Ron, gu an' arsk one o' them blokes the time" our kid suddenly stated. "Cus we don' wanner be late for the pitchers this afternoon do we?" I did as he requested and returned with the answer. "Our Kid" would decide whether we stayed a little while longer, or returned home, "Cus I dain't know abaht tellin' the time did I?" If it was time to return home we would wait until a cart came out of the yard and turn right down All Saints Road, and then run across the road and ask the driver "Ge us a ride ta 'ockley Mister please", and most times the driver would say "Okay kids, jump up", but if he refused, we used to wait for him to move off slowly down the hill and then run after the cart and hang on to the back. This hanging on to the back of the cart never lasted for very long though, cus some rotten bugger would warn the driver. He would pull up, and if he could 'ave copped us 'e would 'ave bossed us one roun' the ear'ole. I was very fortunate cus I never got copped, but some o' me mates did, an' w'en them drivers bosted ya one ya knew yowed 'ad it, for them buggers were right tough 'uns. Mind yo' it wus more bloody luck than judgement that I dain't get copped I cun tell ya. "Our Kid" would never join us on the back of the carts anyway, but 'e would allis snitch on me to "Our Mom" an' she'd belt me, burr I dain't mind, cus I wus ust to it, any road up.

Sometimes the driver would gu down Ford Street or 'eaton Street, inta W'itmore Street, by "The Tram Sheds", an' turn right up ta the "Brook", but sometimes e'd gu straight across the "Flat" an' turn left down Icknield Street, we're Bill Lewis 'ad gorra nuther Scrap Yard, an' 'arpers Shop wus down there as well on the right. Or the driver would gu straight up Key 'ill. If 'e went down Ford Street or 'eaton Street, we'd 'ave a longer ride, an' drop off at "The Brook", burr if 'e went over "The Flat" an' up Key 'ill, we'd 'ave ta drop orf at "Nortons" an' walk down Icknield Street to "The Brook". On reachin' there, one way or the other, we'd gu across an' up 'um' ferrour dinner, an' I wus nearly allis fust 'um' cus like I sez "Our Kid" 'e wouldn't gerron the back o' the carts, an' I usta beat 'im.

When I gorrin the 'ouse, I usta sometimes see "Our Dad" afower 'e went down ta "The Vic" or up ta "The Guest" forra drink, but most times 'e'd already gone. I usta like ta see me "Dad", cus I never sin 'im in the wick, cus w'en 'e usta gurra werk, I'd be out playin', an' w'en 'e cum 'um frum werk, we'd be on our way ta school. Saterdee wus the on'y day me "Dad" really 'ad orf, an' even then that worn't a full day. 'E'd cum 'um frum werk on Saterdee mornin', an' arter settlin' is wages up with "Our Mom", e'd 'ave 'is breakfast an' then gerru bed, but affor 'e went, 'e allis usta say, "Lil, if I ain't awake at twelve, geus a shout will ya?", an' 'e'd gerrup an' gu to the pub until two o'clock, an' then 'e'd cum 'um an' 'ave 'is dinner, an' then orf ta bed agen. Six o'clock at the very latest, an' 'e'd be up agen, but this time 'ed purris best suit on, which 'ad bin in the Pop Shop all the wick, an' leave 'is werkin' clo'es under the bed ready to gurra werk on Sunday Night. 'E'd tell "Our Mom" which pub 'e wus guin' to, so as she would know where 'e wus w'en she follard 'im later, w'en she'd gorrus mob orf ta bed. Sometimes we'd stay up a fickle bit, an' she'd gerr 'erself changed into 'er best frock, it wus a black one an' she looked luverley, an' she'd purrer gold bracelet on, with the 'eart shaped locket on it, an' she'd put sum scent on (Lavender) an' she smelt smashin'. Arter this she'd shoo us up the wooden 'ill ta Bedfordshire, say "Tarra" an' lower the gas, if it wus dark. One of the big wenches 'ad to stop in an' mind us, w'ile "Our Mom" went orf ta the pub to "Our Dad".

Arter dinner on a Saterdee "Our Mom" usta ge us tuppence each ta gu to the pitchers. We'd mek our way down to *The Palladium* on "The Brook", for our wickly escape from the real world. Sometimes we usta scrounge an' extra 'a'penny, for sommat ta eat at the arternoon matinee. "Greedy buggers" "Our Mom" 'ud say, but she'd sometimes ge it to us, any road up. I suppose it was accordin' to 'ow she felt, an' it worn't of'en that she felt generous. If we were successful in obtaining this extra money we usta gurra ol' mon Blackwells in Hunters Road, an' bein' the crafty lickle bugger I wus, I'd allis try an' wait for the ol' mon, not Mrs. Blackwell or 'is son Stan, ta serve me. "Can I 'ave 'a' 'peth o' specs Mr. Blackwell please" I'd ask, an' yo could bet a pound to a penny 'e'd say "ere yar son, 'eres a bag, gu an' 'elp ya self' an' 'e'd gi me a paper carrier bag, which 'ad gorris name on it, an' then 'e'd tek me' a'penny orf me.

I'd gu an' fill me bag ta the brim with specs, an' avin' dun this, I'd start ta mek me way outa the shop, but Mr. Blackwell nearly allis usta call out, "Yo gorrinuff there son" an' I'd say "Yes ta Mr. Blackwell" an' 'e would reply "come 'ere ya little bugger, 'ere ya are" and 'e'd gimme a couple o' oranges or apples, or sumfin that won't specked, an' I'd put these items away for meself, I worn't gunna ge'um our kid wus I? 'e wus a good bloke wus Mr. Blackwell.

When we went to these afternoon matinees's we dain't allis gu ta *The Palladium*. Sometimes we'd gu ta the tuppenny crush at "The Bughouse", which wus *The Metropole* at the bottom of Constitution 'ill, right opposite *The Salutation* pub on the corner of Snow 'ill and Summer Lane, some right rough arses down there I can tell ya. We 'ockleyites were bloody posh alongside some o' the 'Summer Lane Mob'. We went ta the "Bug'ouse" a lot w'en the serial called "The Wisperin' Shadow" wus on there. Then there wus *The Lozells* but we onne went there a couple a' times, cus it wus a bit too far ta walk up ta Wilton Street. An' sometimes, though agen not very often, we'd gu ta *The Villa Cross* on the corner of Villa Road an' 'eathfield Road. Mind yow it wus a bit too bloody posh forrus, an' we couldn't bawl an' play up, forrif we did we'd get throwed out by the big bully in a uniform.

Arter the pitchers we'd run 'um' to our tea, an' sometimes we'd 'ave Scribban's Choclat Junior Rolls, if somebody posh cum, like Auntie Vi from Doncaster, or "Our Auntie Kate," from Coventry, or somebody else 'oo we dain't know, but wus jus' as posh, or somebody speshul like one of "Our Big Wenches" chaps, but it dain't 'appen very oftern I can tell ya.

W'en we'd 'ad our tea, we usta gu out an' play forra bit, but not fa long on a Saturdee Night though, cus like I sez, that wus the night "Our Mom" an' "Dad" usta 'ave a knees up at the boozer.

That then was the usual routine on a Saturday whilst we lived in Guest Street, but a short time after we had moved into Two Two Eight, New John Street West, *My* Saturdays altered considerably.

In the beginning Violet Coleman, who shared the newsagents business in Hockley Hill on "The Brook" with her sister Elsie, offered me a job delivering newspapers for them, which I accepted after informing "Our Mom" of the offer, who naturally agreed, but with one stipulation. This was that I had to give her half of what I earned "Ta keep me in extra boot leather" as she put it. I thought about how I could get out of giving her this percentage because "I wouldn't 'ave used any more bloody boot leather, cus all that would 'ave 'appened wus "Our Dad" would 'ave put a bit more car'board in my boots, an' car'board dain't cost anythin' did it?" I soon came to the conclusion that it was an impossible task to fiddle anything from 'er, because it was uncanny how she found things out. Also we used to have all our newspapers from them then, until you-know-who went on the knock with them, and the

Colemans soon stopped the delivery, but "Our Mom" might have enquired what I was earning though.

My wages were two and sixpence per week, and for that I did a morning and evening round six days a week. Whichever sister was in the shop to see us delivery lads off, would give me a 'a'penny for the tram fare which would convey me to Handsworth Railway Station in Soho Road from "The Brook". The other sister in the meantime would be on "The Brook" by Tippers selling papers to the passers by, and people alighting from the trams or buses which had to stop there.

Off the tram I would jump at the station, with the canvas bag containing the morning's papers weighing heavily on my left shoulder. Remembering the instructions I had received from either Elsie or Violet, "Don' yo ferget ta keep that bloody flap over the top o'ya bag son, or else the perpers'll get wet, an' yow'll be docked forum outa ya wages". For the first one or two customers I followed their instructions, but then I would think 'sod the perpers, it's easier ta gerrem out, without lifting the bloody flap every time."

I crossed Soho Road from the tram stop, and after a final lingering look at the tram moving off on its journey to either Dudley, Wednesbury, "The Hawthorns", Oxhill Road, or wherever its terminus lay, turned right into Thornhill Road where my paper round commenced.

There was a note of sorrow a little later on for me when it was decided to phase out the trams on all the Hockley Depot routes. This happened in March 1939. I remember the Sunday morning the change over took place, I ran on to "The Brook" to watch for the first bus to arrive. It was with utter fascination that I witnessed, coming down Soho Hill, the arrival of the brand new "Leyland Cub". I stayed for a while, but then began to yearn for my old tramcars, and I came away from "The Brook" rather depressed about the whole situation, which still remains with me today.

Up Thornhill Road I would go, checking the board I had with me for the different papers and magazines to be delivered to these posh people, who would still be in bed at that time in the morning.

Along the road past the Police Station on the corner of Golds Hill Road, on down to the end where it met with Holly Road running across. It was at this site right opposite Thornhill Road, that one of the six entrances and exits to and from Handsworth Park was situated. On reaching this junction I turned right and went down Holly Road towards Hampstead Road. Just a few yards into Holly Road was a bridge which ran across the railway lines. I would, on occasions, stay a while and wait for a train to arrive and come steaming through the park from Handsworth Wood Station by *The Endwood* or from Soho Road Station going back to New Street Station, via Handsworth Wood, Perry Barr, and Aston. The billowing white and grey smoke emitting from its funnel, with an aroma all its own clouding the air, and leaving a trail floating about, like washing blowing in the breeze, to disappear only when the train was nearly out of sight on its way to destinations a small boy like me could only dream about at the time.

The livery of these engines was a deep maroon for the main structure, with the front part a deep shiny black. The linings, all hand painted around the boiler, window, and cab were in gold. The bumper grid was painted bright red with gold serial numbers on it, a black back up and white paraffin lamp perched on top completed the picture. On the tender which contained the tons of coal required for its journey was the inscription L.M.S., announcing to the world that this was "The London Midland and Scottish" railway system, these letters were signwritten in gold, and again with a black back up. This type of signwriting continued along the train on the coaches, indicating first and third class compartments, and various other numbers and figures. The engines on the goods trains were similar in their livery, although some were just a shiny black. The goods wagons with the different names painted on the sides, indicating which firm they were carrying merchandise for Palethorpes Sausages, Tangye's Pumps, British Petroleum, Ffyfes Bananas and a thousand others, but always at the end of these wagons was the familiar guard's wagon. If the guard happened to be standing in the open part of this wagon I would wave to him as the train disappeared out of sight.

After watching for the trains, or actually seeing one, I continued down Holly Road to Whitehall Road on the right, turn into there, delivering the papers as I went. Then first left into Broughton Road, and finally first right into Lansdowne Road, where I finished my round at the junction of Ivy Road, by Rose Hill Girl's Grammar School.

As my mailbag got lighter after the commencement of my round, I would play either trams or trains, running along the blue bricks nearest the grey kerbstones.

This row of bricks, unlike the rest of the bricks of the pavement, which were interlocked, ran end to end in a complete line and served as the tram or train lines to me, whichever game I chose to play.

With my round finished I would wander past Crick Lane, which ran from Rose Hill Road down across Broughton Road, then Holly Road, terminating in Hampstead Road. This lane consisted entirely of garages at the end of the "Posh" people's gardens. There was an abundance of apple and pear trees overhanging the fences between the garages, which was fair game for scrumping in the summer for us kids.

I would walk to the junction of Soho Road and Villa Road, Soho Hill and St. Michael's Hill and turn left which took me past The Dennison Watch Company and a little further on Mists Garage where I would ponder sometimes to look at the gleaming new motor cars in the showroom. I would dream of having one like that someday, and putting it into my Grandad Smith's shed, "Up 'is gardin', in Smerrick". On I would go past the R.S.P.C.A. we're they looked arter our dog w'en 'e wus bad" to *The Roebuck* on the corner of Hampstead Road, opposite Richmond Road. Some Chinese blokes lived down there an' yo daresn't gu down there arter dark cus they'd kill ya, an' tek yarroff to China, or we'n they gotcha there they'd sell ya, or torture ya". I used to run over the crossroads of Hampstead Road and Wretham Road, where Mr. Joseph w'o wus the vicar of St. Saviours, an' that big church where all the Irishmen usta gu. Past there and down the hill I ran, going by another church, then Adies to Naden Road, further on down was Elvins the builders and finally "The Brook" itself.

I handed my empty bag back to one of the sisters on reaching the shop, and with a brief "Tarra - see ya ternight", I'd run up 'um for me cuppa tea, an' piece o' bread, afor guin' ta school.

The evening paper round consisted of the same customers, and sometimes one of my mates would come with me. Never in the morning though, "It's too bloody early fer me Smithy" would be their comment. On the evening round *if* one of my mates came, the 'a'penny bus fare given to me wasn't enough for both of us to ride on either the bus or the tram, so we would walk quickly from "The Brook" to Thornhill Road, then spend the money on sweets at the shop opposite Handsworth Park in Holly

'The Guest' and Blacksmiths Shop

Road. Sometimes we'd run on the deliveries so that we kept on time for the customers, otherwise they complained, the rotton sods, "burr I usta think BUM to 'em, any road up."

Occasionally when the light nights were with us, I would nip into the park and look through the palings down the bank to the railway track, or play with my mate, if I 'ad one with me. But most times I would scurry back to "The Brook" to play with my mates down "Johnnie Kinghams openin' " or "Frankie Anderton's openin."

But on *Saturday Mornings*, the situation was completely different, our Mom would say to me when I left the house for my paper round, "Don't yo get dawdlin' our Ron, yo've gorra be back 'ere forr Arthur, an' yo' know 'e don't like ta be kep' waitin' ". "Are, oright Mom" I would reply, but she didn't really have to remind me of this, because I wouldn't have missed going with Arthur for the world.

The papers would be delivered in record time, and Arthur's Morrison electric van would be parked outside our house when I arrived back home. I can see that van now, dark blue, with gold lettering on both sides and the rear, with a red back up, advertising "Bradford's Bread and Cakes". In addition on the rear doors only was their Trade Mark, a red circle with gold dots on it representing the pimples on the bottom of their cottage loaves, small and torpedo loaves.

I would have a couple of pieces of toast wrapped in a newspaper to see me through the day. Arthur had his cup of tea Our Mom gave him and we would leave our house to start the day's work.

When I jumped into the van the smell of the hot bread was wonderful, but better still, especially in the cold weather, was when I handled this bread at the commencement of the deliveries. Little cold hands accepting the warmth of the bread, which certainly revived my circulation. Then when I felt a little peckish, and what small boy doesn't, I would gather some of the crumbs together, that lay on the clean wooden floor of the van, or on the wooden boards that divided the top and middle layers of bread, and pop them into my ever-hungry mouth. The cakes were kept in a separate compartment at the rear of the cab, and could only be opened by a spigot key, which Arthur always kept in a leather band on the strap of his leather money satchel. The round covered quite a big area. It started in Park Road, at Miss Jefferson's on the corner of Wharf Lane, a shop which was a mixture of greengrocery and grocers and quite close to the bakery in Norton Street, and extended into most of Hockley, Lozells, Handsworth, Perry Barr and Aston. From Miss Jefferson's in Park Road Arthur would make his way down to Whitmore Street, turn down there to "The Brook", across there to the right, and up New John Street West to our house. I did meet him at the bakery a couple of times when he was late, but this wasn't very often. The kids that helped the roundsmen were very useful at times. For instance, if the regular man was away, ill maybe, or when his annual week's holiday came round, we would prove invaluable to the man standing in for him temporarily, this man was usually his supervisor. The lad concerned, if he was a good lad, knew the different peculiarities of the round. He would know whether a customer was to be served at the rear entrance, or at the front door, where to leave the bread if they were out, and what their order was without looking at the book each time. Also he would know which way the round should be routed to the advantage of both the customer and the roundsman.

Such occasions arose when Arthur was on holiday, Mr. Fred Blake, who was his supervisor would do his round. I was more than keen to do my best, because Arthur had told Mr. Blake in front of me prior to going on his holiday, "Don't worry about anything Fred, the nipper 'll show yo all the ins an' outs, 'e knows the bloody round better 'an I do, don't cha Ron?"

Sometimes we would have a petrol van, a ten hundredweight Morris Commercial, which was always a great thrill for me. Electric vans were alright, but "they dain't gu very fast did they". But the decision between the two was rather difficult though, because the benefit of having the electric van was that Arthur let me drive it on occasions when we were in a quiet street or road, like St. Silas's Square, Hartington Road, Roland Road, or somewhere like that.

I liked it when Mr. Blake did the round though, for not only did he buy me some dinner and give me some cakes to eat, he would also pay me a shilling for all day Saturday, and if Arthur's holiday fell simultaneously to my school holiday which would result in my helping Mr. Blake all the week, he would pay me a whole half crown. "But I dain't tell "Our Mom" abaht that. Sod 'er I thought, why should I, but I nearly did it in my trousers each time it happened thinking that she might find out!"

It was during these absences of Arthur's that I began to realise, in my own little way, the extent of several possibilities of utilising my labour, for better returns. But I'm afraid that loyalty to him was prevalent so I stayed with him, until an helping hand in the shape of fate changed things.

Our days work on a Saturday would commence at about eight o'clock in the morning, that is, for me it would. Arthur would be at the bakery at five thirty to load his van, check it, and serve several customers before he arrived at our house to pick me up. On completion of the days work Arthur would drop me off at the house before he returned to the bakery. I told our Mom I was home, gave her four pence 'a'penny, and then raced straight down to Coleman's to do my evening paper round.

This then was the procedure until Arthur was called up for the Royal Air Force at the commencement of the war. He was disabled out after a short period and returned to work for Bradfords, but not on the same round. His new round consisted of all retail customers, and covered the area of Alum Rock, Washwood Heath, Stechford, and Bordesley Green. During his short absence I had been helping several other bread and milk roundsmen who worked for Scribban's, Price's, Midland Counties Dairies, Wathes Cattell and Gurden, Tommy Shaw's, Holt's Birmingham Dairy Company, and Ravenscroft's. The money these different men paid me for this help varied, but it was always without exception more than Arthur gave me.

However I remained loyal and went back with him on his return, until one Saturday he was late arriving at our house, so I proceeded to walk up to the bakery to meet him, somehow or other we must have passed one another.

On arrival at the bakery there was no sign of Arthur, so I enquired and I was told he had gone out. I was about to return home when a man named Harold Allen asked if I would like to go with him. I answered "Yer please" realising I should be without money if I didn't do something, and that would have upset "You know who" and I didn't fancy a belting on top of having no money. Harold said that if I went with him, he would require me on a regular basis, and that he would pay me four shillings for helping on a Saturday and more if I helped during the week. I readily agreed, for it was too good to turn down.

My period with Harold Allen was really good. He was a very kind man, and very generous. I remember one week he said "I'm sorry I can't pay yo' this wick nip, I ain't gorreny change, burr I'll ge ya double next wick, okay?" So I said "Oright 'arold", but I must admit I was terribly disappointed. "Our Mom" dain't believe me either, she thought I'd spent it or summat. Burr I turned me pockets out an' she said ta me "If yo don' bring double 'um next wick, it'll be a bloody whalin' fer yo', an' don't yo fergerrit". So I sez ta 'er, "Are, oright Mom".

I worried all the wick though, an' all day Saterdee right up 'till we went into the coffee house over the road from Bradfords, on the corner of Radnor Street, w'en we'd finished the round. We 'ad our cuppa tea an' 'arold said ta me "Yow'll wanna gerrof now nip wun ya', fer ya' perper round?" and I replied "Are I will please 'arold." 'e purris 'and into 'is pockit, and said "Let's see nip, I owe ya' fer larst wick don't I?" and with a sigh of relief I said "Are, thank yo'." 'e drew 'is 'and ourov 'is pockit, tuk summat out and put the contents into my warm sweaty palm, sayin' "There ya' are nip, an' that's fer bein' a good lad, now run along 'um', an I'll see ya' next wick okay?". I nearly widdled myself, as I said "Yer, okay 'arold, I'll see ya next wick, an' thank yo'." The contents he had placed into my hand were no coins, but paper. I ran down Norton Street and into Park Road by Wharf Street, and then stopped, opening my hand with caution. When I had extended my hand to the full, I was overcome with excitement, for there in the palm of it was my very first "Ten Bob Note." Course I had to give "You know who" five bob on it dain' I?." W'en I gid 'er the ten bob note, she wus bloody slow gein' me two 'alf crowns back an' all.

Just about this period I had packed Coleman's paper round up and was delivering newspapers for Mr Phelps, Dinky Phelp's Dad. But the round I did for him only consisted of an evening round, and Sunday morning round, and needless to say, the pay was more lucrative.

That part of my life spent with Arthur Crump was good and interesting, although not too profitable, but it taught me in my own little way an awful lot, including a sense of value, not only for money, but for life itself.

CHAPTER SIX

"Sweet Smell of Success at George Street West, and How I Made a Hit in Handsworth Park"

THIS INCIDENT comes easy to mind, like one of many, but this one would be difficult for *anyone* to forget. Donnie 'arbridge, Chubby Moseley, Frankie Anderton, a couple of other mates and myself were "messin' abaht down Johnnie Kingham's openin', w'en we wus orf school for some reason, not knowin' w'at we wus gunna do that day." Suggestions were made, but turned down, until Donnie sez, I know, let's gurra that Rec in George Street West, ya' know by Spring 'ill Lib'ry, a,?". Well 'as we 'adn't bin ta that one afor, it seemed like a good idea, so without further ado we trooped off along Icknield Street to the Rec.

We arrived there in no time at all, wanting to explore and try out the swings. As the concrete area was empty, we had a choice of all of them, which we used with great whoops and yells.

Well, there we wus, mindin' our own bizniss, playin' on the swings, an' generally enoyin' ousel's, w'en up come some o' the local mob, an' in no uncertain terms tol' us ta piss orf, an' if we dain't, they'd finish our donockin with a bost up the earole.

They were bigga 'an us, an' although frightened to death on 'um, we felt we should at least retaliate verbally, which of course we did in our own inimitable style. "Gu an' get stuffed, it ain't yower bloody park so mind it." But these George Street West blokes were "Gunna 'ave none of this orf bleedin' litle twots from 'ockley," and closed in to "Bash us up proper."

Our intention was to stand our ground, but that idea didn't last long when we saw the look on the big blokes faces. We hurriedly decided "we'd berra get the 'ell ourov 'ere, an' the quicka the berra, "thinking of course that we could out run them.

Unfortunately for me, my mates came to this conclusion rather more quickly than I did, and just left me standin'. To add to this misfortune, runnin' wus not one of my betta features. The biggest bloke of the George Street mob soon weighed this situation up, an' consequently, w'en I did start to run, 'e came arta me, seein' me as an easy target. I dashed out of the Rec, up Camden Street, turned right into George Street West in the direction of Hingestion Street, where the thirty-two trams ran, with this big bloke in hot pursuit. I realised after a very short time that he was gaining on me, an' he wus gunna get me an' do me, which med me very scared indeed. I was a born coward, that is until *after* the event, and if I'd won then the story changed. Here I would mention the fact that people in this area were absolutely sure of one thing, *Horse Muck* for their gardens. The amount deposited by the big shire horses of The Great Western Railway between Pitsford Street and Spring Hill, was phenominal, God it was everywhere, due to the fact the drivers used this route probably more than any other.

The tears started to well up at the thought of this kid "Gerrin 'olt o' me" and I had to make some decision quickly to prevent this from happening. God was good to me for he gave me an idea, the only problem was that if it didn't work, the consequences would have resulted in a very grave situation for me.

I stopped suddenly in the middle of the road, turned, and faced this big bully. But, I 'ad med sure that I 'ad stopped by a great dollop of steaming "Hoss Muck". I mentally thanked "The 'oss" that 'ad purrit there. I quickly scooped as much as I could 'old in both me 'ands (I'm afraid hygiene, at this particular moment, or for any other moment come to think of it, was way down on the list of words in my vocabulary) an' shoved it into this bloke's kisser, who not realising what was happening, was still running at full pelt. Consequently, with 'is runnin' an' my shovin, splosh the hoss muck made quite an impact, not only over 'is face but over 'is shoulders, an' everywhere, stoppin' 'im dead in 'is tracks. God 'e looked a bloody terrible mess.

Instantly I turned ta run agen, expectin' 'im ta gerrin a worse temper due ta the situation 'e now foun' 'imself in. Momentarily everythin' stopped, an' in that time I got me second wind, an' wus grateful. But to my great surprise, I nearly wee'ed meself with 'appiness, this big bully dropped to the floor in the middle of the road, an' began ta "Blaht". Seein' this spectacle 'is mates stopped also, looked at 'im with disgust, an' immediately turned an' went back up the road, leavin' 'im to 'is own peril. I weighed all this up, an' with me courage floodin' back, an' also me mates cheerin' me on, 'an' watchin' me, although I know if the tables had bin the other way about, yo wouldn' 'ave seen their arses fer dust, I went back to this muck laden bully, gathered some more 'oss muck up in me' ands, forr I couldn't stink any wuss could I, an' commenced to plaster 'im all over with it, which med 'im blaht all the more. I wus really beginnin' ta enjoy meself with this, w'en suddenly I 'ad ta start thinkin' abaht runnin' agen.

Some ole gels (they must have been all of twenty-five or so) cantin' on their doorsteps started ta come towards me menacingly, an' wus bawlin', "Ya dirty little sod, leave 'im alone, I'll gerra bloody copper ter ya, an' 'e'll tek ya ta Kenyon Street an' lock yarrup. We know ya, ya dirty little bugger, we'll remember ya, an' if we see ya roun' 'ere agin we'll tell owerole men an' they'll tan ya bloody arse 'til ya can't sit down". I shouted back at them with my courage at its height now, "Mind yarrown business, ya silly old bleeders, 'e wus gunna do me 'e wus, afor I dun 'im." But these ole gels kep' comin' so I thought I'd berra gu, so l ran like 'ell, an' caught my mates up, 'oo 'ad naturally started runnin, themselves, yet agen, bloody 'eroes they were.

Of course I had to remove the horse muck off myself, for my hand, arms and shirt were covered, "an' I dain't smell too bloody sweet either." So up Hingestion Street we went to the junction of Warstone Lane and Carver Street where there was a big horse trough situated in the middle of this junction, by the lavatories and R. Stoddards the wholesale butchers. I washed myself off as best I could and on completion of these rough ablutions my mates and me headed back towards 'ockley', with them singin' praises of my conquest of the George Street mob.

Another occasion not unsimilar to the one just told happened whilst we were playing the wag from metal work. Frank, Kenny, two other mates and myself have good reason to remember one afternoon visit to Handsworth Park.

It was another glorious day, with the sun shining beautifully as we left school for Vittoria Street, and all thoughts of metal work completely dismissed from our minds.

We said 'Tarra" as usual to the other lads, not knowing exactly what we were going to do that afternoon. After much argy bargy we decided on a visit to Handsworth Park, and maybe a little scrumping wouldn't go amiss either.

Off we went down Well Street again, as usual keeping clear of the school. This time we went straight up Wheeler Street to Lozells Road, turning left along there until we arrived at the top half of Wilton Street by "The Lozells Cinema" and Abbotts furniture store. Turning into Wilton Street we trudged down the hill, carried on over Johnstone Street into Lenoard Road to the end where it met up with Heathfield Road, where we turned right and then sharp left into Churchill Road, which took us up to the park in Hampstead Road. Up Hampstead Road we headed, past the old church to a small entrance to the park nearly opposite *The Endwood*. Into this entrance we piled and along the path which was adjacent to the entrance to Handsworth Wood Station, "where all the nobs caught the train fer werk in the wick."

Once inside the park we started messing about wondering what we could do. Not having quite decided, we climbed onto the bridge which crossed the railway lines, waiting for a train to chuff its way out of the tunnel from the direction of Perry Hall, or come speeding down the gradient from the Winson Green direction.

Having watched the arrival and departure of two or three trains we moved on further into the park, arguing whether or not to go scrumping then, or later.

Eventually we made our way to a part of the park near the Holly Road entrance. We were playing away merrily when we heard a posh voice call out "What do you lot think you are doing here". We stopped playing and turned to see who was addressing us, ready to give the person an apt 'ockley' reply, but what we saw kept our tongues firmly in our gobs, for there in a group were some toffs from Handsworth Grammar School in Grove Lane. In the first instance they were larger in number than we were, and in the second instance they were bigger than we were, and in the third instance, looking at them we wished that we hadn't bin there in the fust instance, any road up.

These grammer school kids must have been on holiday or somethings "cus posh kids dain't play the wag did they." They had their school uniform on, that was how we recognised which establishment they came from. The caps were in yellow and black triangles, with the school badge at the front. The coats were black with yellow piping around the lapels and a ring round the bottom of the sleeve, with the school badge again on the left top pocket. White shirt and black tie with yellow stripes running diagonally, grey short flannel trousers, black stockings, with two yellow hoops around the top, and to finish off, black polished shoes.

"I will not ask you again. What do you scruffy lot think you are doing here?" boomed the voice that had made the first request. We stared at them for a few seconds, they were about eight in number - one was a coloured lad, which to us in those days was as rare as the proverbial "Do Do bird". " 'e must 'ave bin a Prince or summat." Well, they were always a Prince or Rajah in *The Wizard*, *The Hotspur, The Dandy* or other schoolboy comics or books we read sometimes, "So 'e must 'ave bin".

On receiving no answer to their last request these grammar school kids moved towards us menacingly. "We ain't doin' nuthin' mate, an' we ain't causin' yo no bother, we're on'y playin' 'ere, an' thats all". Automatically we started to retreat. But on came these "posh kids", intent on giving us a bashing, and the voice proclaiming "I am not your mate you riffy little sod, and I do not wish to be your mate, and further, we do not require a scruffy lot like you cluttering up this park, do you follow me?" Before we had time to answer they had caught up with us. They grabbed two of my mates first and then me. The bloke that caught me dain't talk, he just thumped me in the kisser and the stars I saw wus jus like a firework show as I landed on me arse in the grass.

I sat on the grass for a few seconds dazed. Then I felt my face and found my nose was bleeding profusely and I started to "Blaht". But this kid didn't show any pity, he just said, "Come on you snivelling little scruff, get up off the floor and fight." As I started to rise, not to fight mind you, I was intent on running, he kicked me up "the arse" and this really got my dander up. This kid was towering over me, telling me in his posh voice again "Come on you scruffy little devil, stand up and fight." I stood up alright, and took a boot at 'im, but I missed and nearly landed on my bum again. In the process he gave me another punch, up the ear'ole this time, which caused a singin' sensation. This made me "Blaht" even more and my tormentor started jeering at me. I thought to myself, "Christ I don' wan too much o' this, I'll 'ave no bleedin' brains left, the way 'e's 'ittin' me 'ead", so I made another swipe at him with my boot. This time it connected right on his thigh, and this knocked the wind out of his sails for a while. I took advantage of this short respite and jumped up and ran. The big kid wasn't expecting this, he was too busy nursing his thigh, so I did have a little advantage, at the beginning, but unfortunately not for long. The boot in the thigh hadn't helped matters, so he was soon in pursuit, and gaining on me. I thought to myself as I ran "God, if 'e gets olt on me now I'll be forrit, 'e wus mad enough afor I booted 'im, so 'e's bound ta be wuss now, so l gorra do somethin' quick". Like the George Street West incident, God was definately on my side again. Lying on the grass I spotted a thick bough which had broken off a nearby tree, so grabbing this I turned on the kid and shouted "If yo come any closer mate I'm gonna bost ya with this" hoping against hope it would frighten him off, but I'm afraid it didn't " 'e must think 'e's Errol Flynn or somethin' ".

Give him his due, he never stooped, but came right up to me and drew his fist back ready ta bost me again. So I let fly with the tree branch. I didn't care any more, I was so mad. I just didn't care what happened. The branch hit him full in the face, although I did not intend that it should, I tried to hit him on the body. Everything went quiet for a couple of seconds, and even the fighting between the others ceased for a moment when this kid let out an almighty scream and dropped to the floor like a sack of "spuds", with his nose pouring and spurting blood and a thick angry looking welt across his face. It was his turn to start "blahtin" then, and I was so mad at him that all I could say was, "Well, I bloodywell warned ya mate", I tol' ya not ta come any closer dain't I, so its yarrown bleedin' fault, an' it serves ya right". By this time the war had stopped altogether, and us 'ockleyites thought as a man, "let's get the hell ourra 'ere", so the mob onus ran speedily towards the location of Grove Lane Baths, because we didn't know what reaction these "posh kids" would have with one of their troops badly injured, and we certainly didn't intend to find out.

The last we saw of The Handsworth Grammer School bunch they were swarmed around the injured kid like bees round a honey pot, while we agreed between ourselves he had got what he deserved. We climbed through the railings surrounding the baths by Hinstock Road and not wishing to tempt fate, thought we'll keep well clear of Holly Road.

So we crossed Grove Lane and went down Herbert Road as far as the right hand bend. Then we turned left, which led us to Brunswick Gardens. We did not enter "The Gardens" however, but took another sharp left and cut through the gulley, which ran from Oxhill Road right through to Douglas Road, which is where we eventually emerged. Up Grove Lane to Soho Road, we turned left putting us in the right direction of Hockley and the safety of our own patch again. On our journey back we laughingly commented that "We've bin that busy thumpin', we fergot ta do any scrumpin"!

Although my nose was still sore, it had by this time stopped bleeding and I remember thinking, "I berrit ain't as sore as 'is, enyway it wus wuth it ta see a big kid like 'im blaht."

CHAPTER SEVEN

"Mr. Kingham, and the Tulips from Uplands Farm"

MR. KINGHAM was the father of one of my friends, Johnnie. To my young eyes he was without doubt a most distinguished and interesting man.

A tall, well built, big boned man with a sallow complexion. His blue eyes never seemed to stop twinkling, with a large nose and biggish mouth with a perpetual smile. Mr. Kingham was bald on top of his head but around the sides and back was an abundance of thick curly dark hair streaked with grey. A kindly, quiet, generous man with a general air of calmness about him. If I close my eyes I can see him wearing his dark blue suit, white shirt with a stiff starched collar, a tie, always neatly in place, polished boots, waistcoat, with his silver watch and chain strung across the front, and last, but not least, his billy cock (bowler hat) placed firmly and straight on his head.

Mr. Kingham was by trade a boot and shoe repairer, but he extended this craft by repairing anything made of leather. Women brought their handbags, purses etc., whilst the men would bring money satchels, wallets, coin pouches, and even the smaller parts of horse harness for him to repair. He had many activities outside his working trade, singing being the most predominant I should think. Well, not just singing, for he was very professional. He used to teach others this art, in the evening for a fee. Playing the piano was another accomplishment and I would listen to him with awe.

Gardening was another of his pursuits, his allotments at the Uplands a sight to be seen. It was full of all types of flowers and vegetables, some he would sell, the rest would be kept for his family and close friends.

Conversation after a day's work was a usual thing for him, and he could debate on practically any subject, be it topical, the past, or the future.

Mr. Kingham used the front room to teach his pupils the art of singing. When he was in the process of a lesson with one of these pupils, my mates and myself would sneak up and crouch under the window sill to listen. Naturally this did not include Johnnie. The room would be in darkness usually. I didn't know why he did this, but I could hardly go and ask, could I? "Anyroad up I dain't ge a toss anyway."

With Mr. Kingham on the piano, the pupil and he would commence the lesson, practising the scales. First the Master, 'Ah, ah, ah, ah, ah, ah, ah, ah,' (Do, ray, me, fah, so, lah, te, doh) and then the pupil - 'Ah, ah, ah, ah, ah, ah, ah, ah.' On completion of this first part, there was a short conversation and an intermittent note struck on the piano, the Master giving an emphatic, Ah, ah, ah, to correct and give advice to the pupil where she or he were going wrong. Off they would start again with the scales and this would be repeated time and time again, until presumably the pupil satisfied the Master. This satisfaction at last attained, they would move onto something more adventurous, using the scales they had been rehearsing.

Finally they would sing a song, first the Master and then the pupil. Again on completion there would be corrective advice given. They would then repeat this until satisfaction was acquired. To round the lesson off, there would be a series of songs sung by the Master, the pupil, and sometimes, both together.

Many beautiful songs were sung, *Deliah, Roses of Picardy, We'll gather Lilacs, On the Road to Burgundy, Springtime, The Continental, Sweetheart, Molly Malone,* and many more.

We kids under the windowsill would listen attentively right to the end of the lesson - *sometimes*? But on other occasions, when we wanted to have a bit of "donnuck", or if as kids running true to form do, we got bored with the whole proceedings, we waited until it was the pupils turn to sing up and down the scale, or to sing a song solo, and we would join in, with the most horrendous yells and catawauls.

'Ah, ah, ah, ah,' the pupil sang, and we'd join in with 'Ar, ar, ar, ar,' or join them in the song, with a 'Dah, dah, dah, dah' (Well, we dain't know the bloody werds did we?) until the pupil had to give it best and stop.

We waited giggling to ourselves, knowing what was going to happen next. After a few seconds there would be a sudden movement of the curtains in the dark and Mr. Kingham's face would appear looking stern. No shouting at us, or rapping on the window, his severe appearance would be quite sufficient and off we ran into the night.

Sometimes though I'm almost sure the stern look on his face would suddenly change to a smile. On reflection, I think, he was thinking the particular pupil's ability for singing was somewhat less than ours, and consequently appreciated this timely intervention, slight though it may have been, from us "little buggers."

Occasionally, with his mother's permission, Johnnie would invite me home in the evening to play. The most popular game we played, was trams. John had three or four model tramcars made by Dinky Toys, although not in the Birmingham corporation Tramway livery. The colours of his models were cream and light green, as per the Blackpool Tramcars. The preparation for this game was quite an ordeal. First the table had to be cleared, leaving the green coloured thin gingham linoleum exposed, after all the older members of the Kingham family had finished their evening meal. This linoleum was wiped over with a damp cloth and then John would get his tramcars from the cupboard, also some huge balls of plasticine.

The first job was to roll the plasticine into long thin strips ("jus' like snakes they wus") until we had enough to start laying the tram lines. I was never allowed to lay the tracks however. John always did this, but I must admit he did this job with the precision of an engineer. Starting at the City in Colmore Row, outside Snow Hill railway station, he laid the lines down for Snow Hill, Constitution Hill, Gt. Hampton Street, to Hockley Hill, and then onwards to the number twenty-six tramcar terminus in Oxhill Road, by Rookery Road and Stockwell Road. All the junctions, turns and crossovers were carefully placed out. The passenger stops were indicated by one blob of plasticine for a regular stop, and two blobs for a request stop.

We always used the twenty-six route for this game, simply because the table was not large enough to accomodate the Dudley, Wednesbury and West Bromwich routes, and secondly, we couldn't lay these routes out anyway "cus we 'adn't bin on 'em 'ad we!"

When it was all laid out, with the return track running up Livery Street, John and I commenced to play, one from Rookery Road, inward bound for the City, and the other from the City outward bound. By God there's been some miles driven through those plasticine lines. Cussings for the passengers and other vehicles committing some misdemeanour or other. Kind acts performed, like waiting for some old lady, laden down with shopping bags, for her to get on board, or waiting for others we saw running to the various stops. The "Billy Can" of tea which the conductor picked up at the coffee house situated between *The Trees* and *The Duke of York* in Hockley Hill, the drivers' comments to one another as we passed en route, of certain track repairs, or road repairs, or maybe an accident or something. We played happily, oblivious of time, until the table was required by "The Big 'uns" again, or if I was called to go to bed. It was with much regret we took "The Oxhill Road Tramway System" up and rolled it into its original state and John would stow everything back into the cupboard.

It was during these invitations to play at Johnnie's house in the evening, that a debate of some kind would develop, usually when Cissie's or Moira's boyfriends, Ernie and Frank, were there. (I worked with Moira's boyfriend, Frank Baynham, years later on The Birmingham Fire and Ambulance Service. He was by then of course Moira's husband). Mr. Kingham would be drawing peacefully on his pipe, with questions and answers passing to and fro, until the respective girls came in, stating they were ready to go out for the evening.

I listened in between playing trams, to the conversation, although naturally not understanding it, but never the less liking to hear it. Quietly spoken, but never the less determined when emphasising a particular subject, he would bring a quiet serenity and peace to the room, discussing the latest topic, whether politics, the imminence of war, sport, finance, or the local news.

The Kingham family, like most families of this period, was a large one. Mrs. Kingham had, on reflection, an Italian appearance, with her jet black hair, naturally with grey streaks, big brown eyes, and skin that looked light brown the whole year round. Cissie the eldest daughter had similar characteristics to her mother. She was breathtakingly beautiful (W'en I fust met 'a, I fell in love with 'er, moran I wus with Mrs. Tyne, down our entry, I did). Arthur followed his mother too. He worked for Fattorini's, who had their business premises in Barr Street, at the junction of Harford Street. Moira definitely followed her dad, with fair skin and blue eyes. Then there was Frank, Barbara, and last "The Babby" John all having mom's features. They were a lovely family, whom I greatly respected.

Mr. Kingham put a proposition to John one day, just before the commencement of the Summer Holidays. He asked John if he and one friend would like to earn some extra money. John readily agreed, and apparently had me in mind to help him.

The proposition was that John, with whoever he chose, would go to the allotment on a Friday afternoon, during the main school holidays. Mr. Kingham would provide the penny each for the tramcar fare to the Oxhill Road terminus.

From the terminus we walked to his allotment, situated just past Camp Lane, down Oxhill Road, and a dirt track on the right hand side, with a brook running alongside it, turned right and the allotment was about a quarter of a mile up there on the left hand side. The brook itself provided the allotment holders with all the water they required, for domestic use as well as for their gardens.

On arrival at the allotment, we were expected to help Mr. Kingham with little jobs (but I must admit that we played around more than we helped, or we watched him create wonderful bouquets of flowers, tying them with raffia tape.) On completing the bouquets he hung them on brass screws situated on a framework of wood, ascending from the well of a strong, sturdy, well made four wheeled barrow. When this task was completed, John and his friend would push the barrow and its contents back to Guest Street, selling the flowers on their journey. The financial reward from this venture was "A tanner each fer ev'ry poun's wuth of flowas we sol'."

When John related this plan his father had put to him and offered me the chance to be his partner, I jumped at it. Naturally this job would not last for long, so it was a golden opportunity to get a little cash for myself, besides the tuppence "Our Mom" gid me fer *The Pallerdidalum* on a Sat'dee arternoon". This period naturally was before the coming of Arthur Crump and the paper rounds.

The first Friday of the job arrived, and I "golluped" me dinner down me, and washed it down with the inevitable cuppa tea, and I shouted "Tarrar" to "Our Mom" and ran up Guest Street to Johnnie's house.

Both of us were excited as we waited for the number twenty-six tram to arrive at the tramcar enclosure on "The Brook" by *The Watt*. First a seventy-three, then a twenty-three, and with excitement mounting the twenty-six came. On its arrival, we rushed up the stairs to the front, happy to see that no one occupied the seats, the tram being partially empty due to the time of day.

I had not travelled on a tramcar right to the end of the line before, so I was most probably more excited about the journey than John, who had been on several journeys like this before. Nevertheless we both enjoyed this journey, noting extra items on the way to include in our next game of trams on the gingham linoleum.

When we arrived at long last at Stockwell Road we were indeed two very happy lads.

On we went looking across the vast amount of countryside just past Friary Road on this warm sunny afternoon, chattering and playing until we reached the allotment.

Mr. Kingham was busy as usual, but on seeing us arrive he stopped what he was doing immediately, came over to us and shepherded us into his shed. When we entered the shed I was amazed, "It wus berra than our 'ouse it wus". A table was situated in the middle of the room, with a couch running up the one side. Chairs round the table and still plenty of room for all his garden tools, even the barrow we were to use, and a wheel barrow as well. He sat us down, put a kettle onto the fat bellied stove and said "I'll soon 'ave a cuppa tea ready fer yo' lads, this kettle wunt tek lung ta boil". Then he gave us some sandwiches he had made, cutting the bread thick and piling the butter on. After we had finished this meal Mr. Kingham settled himself into a comfortable armchair and indicated for us to sit on the couch. He filled his pipe slowly, then lit it, the smoke floating around the interior of the shed, giving off a most beautiful aroma. Everything was quiet and peaceful for a moment, then he softly explained what he wanted us to do.

After he had finished the explanation, we set about our tasks. Filling the wooden buckets with water from the rain barrel, a natural well, or from the brook, whichever part of the garden Mr. Kingham required it. Gathering the weeds he had put at the end of the row of whatever he was hoeing and taking them to place onto the huge compost heap at the far end of the allotment, by some bushes and trees which divided it from the next allotment. We worked diligently this first day, so the time went quickly. Mr. Kingham called us and we went to the shed. On arrival we found that the framework on the barrow was completely covered with bouquets of flowers in different sizes and styles, looking very much like a float from a carnival. These bouquets were hung from the brass screws with raffia tape, in a most artistic way. He explained to John the prices of these bouquets; half a crown was the top of the range, running downwards in "tanners". So the complete price list read "half of a dolla," two bob, one an' a tanna, a bob, an' the lowest a tanna". He had arranged them on the framework like that, the dearest at the top, coming down to the cheapest at the bottom. Next he explained the route he wanted us to take, which I now realise was a very wise thing to do "cus there wus some rotton buggerous about in them times there wus". He warned us *not* to alter this route, saying that he would follow us on his bike later, after he had finished his work at the allotment. He also said "If yo' gu orf the route I ge ya', I'll worry abaht ya'". John and I listened intently to the directions he gave, which were straight along Oxhill Road to Grove Lane, by *The Grove* pub, turn right down Grove Lane as far as Holly Road, turn left up there to Whitehall Road on the right, just before Lansdowne Road and Crick Lane, along Whitehall Road to Broughton Road, where we were to turn left, go down there to Welford Road, which led us to Hall Road, Hampstead Road, and finally, Soho Hill to "The Brook". When he had finished giving us the directions he said quietly "D' ya' undastand me?" and we said "Yere", but he made us repeat them to him and did not interrupt, then he made us repeat them again, before he was fully satisfied. Then he said to us "Don' ferget w'en yo' talk ta the customers, yo' allis call the Gentlemen, Sir, and the Ladies, Ma'mm. Now 'ave yo' got that?" We both said together "Yus Sir."

Then he told us "Orf ya' gu lads, an' the besta luck ta ya', tarrar," and Johnnie said "Tarrar Dad" and I said "Tarrar Mr. Kingham" and off John and I trundled, with him holding the barrow handles and me pushing on the wooden framework.

We never veered from the route Mr. Kingham gave us on those journeys we made, until the nights started to close in, as autumn was giving way to winter, when we stopped altogether.

John and I had lots of fun during these trips, and people that bought the flowers off the barrow were so kind, "How much are these lads?" "Two an' sixpence Sir". They're a bit dear aren't they?" "I don't know Sir, that's w'at me Dad sez they are, 'onest." "Don't tease the lads dear, give them the half crown". 'Thank ya' Ma'am, an' thank ya' sir". "Be careful how you go now won't you?" "Yes we will, thank you Sir." Old couples, middle aged people, courting couples, gentlemen on their own, would stop us en route to "The Brook". We even had people call us from their houses on occasions to buy our flowers.

When we finally arrived at Guest Street, we pushed the barrow up the opening, through the door leading to the communal back yard of the first four houses down Guest Street, excluding Sid Webbs Fruit and Vegetable Shop, from New John Street West.

John would fetch his Dad, who would have arrived home before us, and we would remove the flowers' we hadn't sold, off the hooks, and put them into containers of water in the brewhouse. When the barrow was stripped we would then stand it on its end, also in the brewhouse. Mr. Kingham locked the door, and we all went up the alley to the backdoor of the house, where he would settle up with us. He would of course check the value of the flowers before despatching us from the allotment, then count the amount of flowers we had put into the water containers. He would know before we reached the house how much John should have in his pocket, for *I* was *never* allowed to handle any cash, which was perfectly natural. I wasn't real family was I?

Mr. Kingham was very good to us. For instance if we sold seven and sixpence worth of flowers, that would give us tuppence farthing commission, to be divided, he would always make it up to say threepence, which would give us a final total of three 'a'pence each.

Off we went to spend our money on our favourite bar of "Milky Way" which cost us 'a' penny each, from the shop on the opposite corner, or if we had done "a little bit berra", maybe a "Mars" bar at a penny each. But business was pretty stable for us, we only achieved the "giddy heights" of a tanner between us once.

The flowers that remained in the brewhouse over night were put on display on Saturday morning, still in their containers, outside the front door, under the windowsill to be sold, and the barrow was returned to "The Uplands" on Sunday morning tied to the rear of Mr. Kingham's New Hudson bicycle ready for us two on the following Friday.

CHAPTER EIGHT

"Sundays and Mr. Phelps"

AMIDST deep and continual coughing "Our Dad" searched for one of his numerous nub ends situated on a small wooden foot stool, much scarred with the burns of previous cigarettes placed there, alongside his part of the double bed.

This coughing would go on until the scratch of a "Swan Vestas" occurred and the bedroom momentarily came awake from its dinginess, giving a flickering, fluorescent glow, like fairy lights.

Dad would draw deeply on his "Gold Flake" and magically his coughing would cease, and a quiet conversation would ensue between Mom and himself. Dad's coughing would wake us four up in the single bed; it even woke us up when we moved to "Two Two Eight" and were in a separate room, just "Our Kid" and me.

We would listen, but wouldn't murmur, trying to get the gist of their conversation, but we never did, because we were too young to understand, but we would listen "any road up", for it brought a certain comfort and security just knowing "Our Dad" "wus at 'um".

Suddenly there would be the inevitable creak of the bed as Dad started to rise, and he would say "I'll gu an' mek us a cuppa tea Lil" and there would be a rustling as Dad put his trousers and socks on which he had reached from under the bed, by his "poe", and then you would hear the creak of the wooden stairs as he descended.

This then was the pattern that heralded *Sunday* to us kids.

After Dad had gone down "The Dancers" we would snuggle down again to wait for the tinkle of cups telling us that Dad had made the tea and was bringing it upstairs. First mom would have hers and she would give "The Babby" a drop, then Dad would take the "big uns" - Lil, Vi and 'ilda's in, and finally it would be our turn.

We would receive this tea in cracked cups, with grime in the cracks. The reason for this was because if you tried to wash, or scour the grime out, the cup would disintegrate, so it was a quick swill under the cold water tap - was there any other tap? - and that was your lot. Nevertheless that cup of tea was like nectar and it would be sipped slowly to obtain the full enjoyment of it.

When the tea was drunk, "Our Dad" would collect the cups and put them on the "Mackintosh's" toffee lid that served as a tray and off he would go down the stairs again. Down us kids would go, snuggling under the coarse blankets - "Mom, Ronnie's pulled the coat off us" - "Ge 'em the bloody coat back ya little bugger, or I'll be over ta ye," - a quick *accidental* kick on one of the wenches legs and quietness would reign once more.

Of course this routine altered later when I entered the world of business - the newspaper round, first for Colemans and then Mr. Phelps, or helping various milkmen on Wacaden, Midland Counties, Marsdens or Shaws.

Immediately I had finished my tea, up I would get and Dad gave me my breakfast, then I'd be off about whatever business I was doing that day.

After a while the aroma of bacon would find its way up the stairs to our young noses and that would be the incentive for one of us to say "Can we gerrup in a minnit

Mom?" "Yo'll wert fa ya fertha ta call ya, oright, yo wunt be sa bloody keen tomorra mornin' will ya, so bloody lie still, an' keep quiet furra bit."

The chime of bells calling the congregation to Holy Communion would then commence, the nearest St. Saviours, and then further away St. Francis, St. Mathias, St. Georges, All Saints, St. Michael's, and also the various chapels with their bells would in a way, although not intentionally, harmonise beautifully.

Dad's voice up the stairs would announce "Cum on yo lot, I ain't gunna keep this breakfast warm for ever. I'm puttin' it out now." "Our Mom" would stir, and tell us lot in the single bed, "Yo cun gerrup now, an' be quick abarit, cus I gorra get me an' the babby ready, so mek it quick, da yo 'ear me". "Are, we 'eard ya Mom, weam gerrin out now". We'd be out like a shot, putting on our clothes from under the bed, then we'd race down the stairs.

On arrival below it never surprised us to find a new aunt, or uncle, or sometimes, aunts and uncles. "Say Gu Mornin' ta Aunty 'azel, an' Uncle Charlie", or whatever their particular names were, Dad would instruct us, "Gu Mornin' Auntie ...., Gu Morning Uncle ...." and there might be a kiss, but "We dain't care any road up, whether there wus or not". We were more interested in having our breakfast "than kissin' an' luvin'."

Of course these aunts and uncles were people mom and dad had met in *The Guest*, *The Vic* or *The Turk* the night before, or dad would invite a friend and his wife to " 'ave a drink with 'im", then when "The Gaffer" called "Time Gentlemen please", "Our Dad" would invariably say to them "Cum on up 'um, an' 'ave another drink, an' summat to eat, it's early yet, an' yo ain't gorra gerrup in the mornin' 'ave ya?" "Are orr right Arther, ta" they would probably answer and equally probable they would miss the last tramcar, or bus home, so "Our Dad" would just tell them "Mek yaselves at 'um 'ere, we'll stoke the fire rup, so as yo wunt get cold", and so they would settle down where they were until the following morning.

We sat on the sofa "Cus there worn't enough room roun' the table" and dad would bring our breakfast in. I would look at the bacon, sausage, eggs, and tomatoes on the plate, savouring the moment before diving in like a vulture, with the help of several slices of dry bread. Then to finish it off, another cuppa tea to wash it all down with. Having demolished the food, I would think about what I had eaten, wishing I could have it again.

This meal was reserved for *Sunday Mornings* only, with just one exception, and that was Christmas Morning. That is, if we didn't go to St. Saviours Church Hall in Farm Street for the "Scouts Breakfast".

After everyone had eaten "Our Mom" would bustle us "little uns" into the pantry and give us a quick "slosh over" with soap, and the inevitable cold water. Then she would change us, in front of all and sundry, from our "wick day clo'es" into "our Sunday best" recovered from "The Pop Shop" on Saturday morning, after dad had come home from Bradfords with his wages, settled up with her and gone off to bed for a couple of hours before going to his local on the dinner time.

Hair would be brushed with a drop of water to hold it in position (not for long though with me), a final inspection, then mom would bawl upstairs to whichever 'wenches' had been allocated "ta tek us lot." "'ow lung am yo gunna be up thaya, the bloody kids am ready, an' if yo don' 'urry up, it'll soon be bloody time fer yo ta cum back an' serve ya the time guin' in the fust plerce." "Ar a'right mom we'm cumin now" they would reply. They didn't like to take us though, they'd have sooner been going out with their friends, or "guin' chap 'untin' ", which is probably why they were so 'finicky' and gave us a couple of back handers, or shouted at us.

When the 'wenches' finally came down, after putting their best frocks on, we were despatched either to "Grandad Smiths," "Auntie Berths" or "Auntie Nells."

In later years of course I would already be out on my paper round, or helping the milkman, and there was a short period when I was pushed into joining the choir at St. Saviours, but I'm afraid that singing was *not* one of my best abilities.

I had to be down in the vestry for ten fifteen for Morning Service, to don my cassock, surplus, and stiff white collar, with a black dicky bow put on with a press clip. Mr. Wrenshaw inspected us when we had put this gear on prior to entering the church in front of the adult choristers. During practice on a Wednesday night, one of us choirboys would be selected to man the pump situated on the side of the organ in a little passage, to pump air into the pipes serving the organ, and he, on the Sunday would wear just a cassock to carry out this operation. It was very hard work indeed, for you would have to pump continuously throughout the service, whenever Mr. Wrenshaw was playing. It was only when prayers, the lessons, or the sermon were in progress that you really had a break.

Lennie Hunt, Arthur Osbourne and the others seemed to take it in turns, but I was only requested to operate this pump once, it was a complete mystery to me why I wasn't asked again. It couldn't have been anything to do with the sound of the music when I had a rest "cus me arms wus achin' summat bloody 'orrible", going funny, could it?

The payment for this time consuming singing at St. Saviours was pretty poor, "us werkin' fer God an' all." We would be paid half a crown a quarter in little brown pay packets by Mr. Wrenshaw, which when "Our Mom" had her fifty per cent didn't leave me a lot to spend.

For this grand payment you would have to go to choir practice twice a week (I "played the wag" from there a few times, and "you know who" never "fount me art' "). Morning service and Evensong on a Sunday, and other special services like Easter, Whitsuntide, Christmas, etc., and other functions like weddings and the like, all for the one price.

I talked "Our Mom" out of me being in the choir when I went to work for Mr. Phelps at a lot more money, and more still for the Sunday morning, "well I couldn't rush the paper round could I"? I knew the way to me Mom's heart I did, crafty little, bugger, wasn't I?

Working for Arthur Phelps was another good period of my life. He wasn't unlike "Our Dad" in looks and build which is probably why I took the job when it was offered, for I really loved my dad.

Mr. Phelps was a fair man, he paid all his newspaper kids very good money, much better than others we spoke to. Our rates for week day deliveries, which consisted of a night round only, was a "half dollar", but Sunday mornings deliveries he paid us "One an' a tanner", if we did one round, but if we helped out, when one of the lads, or chaps didn't turn up, he would pay us an extra "tanner".

My paper round on a Sunday started in Nursery Road, from Hunters Road down to the junction with Villa Street, then I'd turn round and come back to Brougham Street. Up there I'd go to the top, serving Alexandra Terrace and Albert Cottages on the way, to Wills Street. I'd turn left up Wills Street to Hunters Road, cross over and return right down as far as Villa Street, at the junction with George Street, then I'd turn right and go down Villa Street, passing Olive Shellis's house, whom I loved when I was in the Infants School, to Nursery Road once again, where my round finished.

In the week I started in Icknield Street and went right along delivering until I reached Prescott Street, up there I would go to Crabtree Road, passing Coralie Street, Rosalie Street, and crossing over Clissold Street in the process. I bought my first bike for two bob, at thre' pence a "wick" from a lady who lived at the back of the first house on the left past Clissold Street. On reaching Crabtree Road, I crossed over and served down Brookfields Road which housed the old Heinz Fifty Seven warehouse. On completion of my deliveries in Brookfield Road I would return to Crabtree Road, serve down there to the bottom where I would turn left into All Saints Street to deliver my last papers to a few houses right by the church.

Whilst on the night round two or three of my customers would pay me for the paper as I delivered it, a penny for *The Birmingham Mail* or *The Evening Despatch* which I would tuck into my pockets if they didn't have any holes in them, but if that was the case I would drop the coppers into my canvas paper bag itself. The normal procedure was the customers gave me a tanner "for the wick's perpers" on a Saturday night, "an' sometimes, 'erp'ny fer meself."

On the week nights when I was walking down Crabtree Road I would pass Blackhams the Bakers and Confectioner, and there would be a beautiful smell coming from the bakery situated at the rear of the shop, which I'm afraid often tempted me, so much sometimes that I would succumb, and with the coppers I had received from the customers I would spend one on a couple of hot dripping cakes, currant buns, or perhaps another time I'd go into the sweet shop just below Blackhams and buy two ounce of "Blue Bird Chocolate Caramels fer a' 'erp'ny.

Now this spending in the week was alright providing you put it back, but we always thought we were clever buggers when we were kids didn't we?

On Saturday night when we had finished our round, we used to go to a house up a back yard in Bridge Street West to pay in the money we had collected from all our customers, instead of returning to "The Brook" by the Municipal Bank in "The Gulley" to hand our canvas bags back, and give Mr. Phelps any money from the rightly papers.

In the dim gas lit room, of the one down, two up house in Bridge Street Mr. Phelps would count the cash you gave him, which was nearly all "tanners', take the addresses of people who weren't in, or who had 'knocked you', and enter them into a ledger, which contained all the information pertaining to your round. He would then add this to the money you had paid him during the week, and total it up. In another column he would total the amount of papers you had delivered, turn this into cash, and then add last week's debts to it to give another total. Naturally the two totals *should* have been the same, but I'm afraid mine never were, I was always tuppence or sometimes even thre'pence short. I was never over, and Mr. Phelps would look stern at me and say "Yo'm bloody short agen nip, 'ave a look in ya bag, or ya trousis, an' see if yo' cun fin' it". I would look knowing full well that it wasn't there, and he knew too. I'd say, "tain't 'ere Mr. Phelps" and he would reply "Ar should tek it outa ya wages ya know nip, yo cum this bloody germe every wick, don't cha? I think yo're 'avin' me on", and then his blue eyes would twinkle, a smile would appear. He would ruffle my hair and reach into his money satchel, bring out a half crown, push it into my hand and say "Gu on ya little bugger, clear orf, an' don't be lert in the mornin'." I used to clutch the coin in my fist and say, "Thank you Mr.

Sunday Afternoon

Phelps, I wunt be lert tamorra, tarra" and off I would run out of the house. I can see his smile even now, and he knew what we were up to, God Bless him.

Sunday morning deliveries was a strictly cash on the nail basis, so there was no "I diddle diddle" there. It's funny though I was never short when I paid in a Sunday, very funny.

Customers on both the Sunday round and the night round would give us the occasional tip of an 'erp'ny", not many though, but again I "dain't tell 'er". I kept that to myself and hid it up in the attic amongst the few toys I had managed to buy for myself.

After I had finished my Sunday paper round, I would pay in to Mr. Phelps at one of the entrances of Tippers on "The Brook". He would reckon it up as per the same system as a Saturday night, and on completion of this he would give me my "One an' a tanner". I'd say "Tarra" and off I would run, but not home. I ran up Icknield Street just past Bill Lewis's other scrap yard to meet a milkman who worked for Harry Marsden.

Invariably his horse and float would be parked outside his house. I waited by the float for him to emerge. Sometimes his float would not be there, and I would wait for his arrival from the direction of Key Hill and "The Flat." I never did find out what his name was, for quite simply he never told me, but one thing about him I knew, he had a wonderful singing voice, and he certainly used it whilst driving his horse and cart between his customers. It's funny isn't it how you associate periods of your life sometimes with a particular tune? This milkman I should imagine, with the amount of times he sang it was "Am Appola", and whenever I hear it I think of him.

He would finish the deliveries, straighten the float up and return to the dairy in Heathfield Road just below *The Villa Cross* public house, and the cinema of the same name, where we would unload. The supervisor would check the returns and empties and I would help to take them off the float and place them by the huge stacks nearby. On completion of this we would drive out of the dairy and turn right down Heathfield Road in the Direction of Villa Park, past Mayfield Road to Gordon Road on the right. Up there we would go, and then turn left down Finch Road, where on the left just before Archibald Road the stables were situated. I helped remove the horses harness and whilst the milkman put the float away I would give the horse a drink out of the trough in the yard, then return him to the stable.

The milkman gave me a "tanner" and said "See ya next wick then nip". "Are, okay" I'd tell him, and then off home I'd run to my dinner.

Sunday Dinner - that was the epithet of British tradition. No matter what happened those days, sickness, bad news, even a shortage of money, nothing prevented that Sunday tradition in our home. I know there were folks a lot worse off than us Smiths, but to balance that channel of thought, there were an awful lot of people that were a sight better off than us.

The joint of beef with a nob of fat on it, potatoes around it, in the deep meat tray were put into the oven on the left hand side of the fire. Potatoes and cabbage prepared and put into their respective big black iron pots on either side of the fire, on the black leaded shelves. The mixture for the Yorkshire Pudding in a bowl ready for mixing. Rice grains, sugar, butter, and whatever in another deep tray. "Our Mom's" stern warning to the "Big Wenches", "Keep ya eye on things w'ile I'm up at the "Guest" with ya fertha, an' if yo ain't sure of anythin' cum an' tell me, da yo un'erstan', alright", and off she would go up Guest Street to dad to have a *few* halves!

"Our Dad" would go to the pub at about half past eleven as part of the "Sunday tradition", and join the others waiting for the doors to open at twelve. They would stand there in small groups smoking and discussing the fate or glory of "Brummejam City, Aston Villa, or The Baggies", and making quips about the team they followed or other relevant conversation. These regulars would stand there every Sunday morning, after the front of the pub and the pavement had been washed down with a hose earlier by one of the barmen, or some old chap doing it to earn himself a few pints.

Pubs in those days were kept spotless. "The Gaffer and his Lady Wife" were always dressed correctly and you would never see them unkempt. The bar staff and cleaners did their job with real care, it was a matter of pride with them.

You would see "The Gaffer", not his wife, pull an occasional pint, but not very often. Normally his wife and him would hold a conversation with the customers and attend to any queries that may arise, keeping an eye on everything and everyone, and the largest percentage of these pubs would have the same "Gaffer" and "Missus" for donkeys years, proving beyond a shadow of doubt, efficiency.

"Mom" would return from the pub at about half one to prepare the dinner for "Dad's" arrival at quarter past two, or thereabout. When he finally arrived, "the big uns" and "Mom an' Dad" would sit round the table, an' us little 'uns would have ours on tin plates on the sofa. "Yo 'ad ta be careful yo dain't gu down some of the 'oles in the sofa as well, an' spill ya dinner."

After dinner was eaten, "yo 'ad a dollop of rice puddin' ta folla" and always an argument ensued about the amount of skin off the top of the puddin' given to you, but a bang up the ear'ole from "you know who" soon brought quietness to the 'ouse again.

"The big wenches" an' "Our Mom" 'ud wash the crocks, - crocks, that was a bloody laugh. Most on 'em warn't crocks, they wus tin plates, but we called 'em crocks any road up. After that Dad 'ud gurra bed, cus 'e'd gorra gurra werk at five, an' sometimes Mom usta gurra bed with 'im, but she dain't tek "The Babby", wich wus funny, very funny, cus she allis took "The Babby" with 'er w'erever she went, burrit wus on'y sometimes she went ta bed on the Sunday arternoon.

Us "little uns" 'ud troop orf ta Sunday School, "outa the bloody road" the "big wenches" 'ud say, down at the Mission 'all in Farm Street. The teachers useta tell us abaht God, an' Jesus an' ev'rythin', but we dain't tek much notice on 'er, well, she couldn't cane us like they did at proper school could she?

W'en we wus lerrouta Sundee School we'd wann gu an' play, but we 'ad ta be careful cus we'd gorrour bes' clo'es on, 'adn't we?

"Penny winks, penny winks, warrercress, all fresh, lettis's, cue cumbers, radishes, cel'ry, spring onions, nice an' 'ot, com' an' gerrem afor they all gu yo lucky lerdies, jus' in time fer tea", would be the shout on a Sunday afternoon from numerous street traders with probably not a trading licence between them. "Com' an' gerrit w'ile its still fresh an' don' run away" they'd shout. The items for sale were situated on flat handcarts, with brass scales, and weights. These carts were hired out to traders at the cost of a tanner for the weekend.

The usual price, which was charged predominantly to "Rag and Bone Men" during the week, was a tanner a day. The cut in cost to hire the carts during the weekend encouraged more people to use them for "Freelancing", people who had a regular job during the week, but wanted to earn a little extra on a Sunday. It also brought extra income into the pockets of the people who hired them out, for without these freelancers their carts would be stacked doing nothing. Two of the most notable cart hirers of the day were Parkers in Heath Street, or Kellys from up town.

The fruit or vegetables etc. that these freelancers were selling, would be bought, presumably at very knock down prices, from the markets in Jamaica Row, Moat Lane, Moat Row, Upper Dean Street, all by the "Bull Ring", on a Saturday night when the official trading finished.

Also on a Sunday afternoon "Mr. Verrachia" from up Spring Hill, by Dudley Road Hospital would arrive in his decorative float pulled by a donkey. "Ica creama" he would call in his wonderful Italian accent. It was not very often that we could have a cornet, but when we did "Mr. Verrachia" would serve us in his beautiful white coat, using a spotless scoop and spatula. His brown eyes twinkling, with creases around them, a hooked nose, and beautiful mexican-type moustache which veered upwards when he laughed, and he did laugh a lot showing snowy white big teeth, and always the straw boater on his head. Also there would be the Eldorado or Walls blokes on their three wheel tricycles shouting "Stop me an' buy one". Snowfruit ices from the Walls bloke, and Cream Triangles from Eldorado, our mouths watering when we hadn't got the 'erp'ny required for these goodies. The "Pop" man would call down Guest Street sometimes, not very often though, I don't think he did much trade. His big green flat wagon, with gold lettering along the backboard, indicating Rothwell's Pure Mineral Drinks, Sandwell Road, West Bromwich, Staffordshire.

The big shire horses pulling this float, sometimes munched from their feed bags, or received a bucket of water from one of the houses. Rothwells served their pop in two pint earthenware jars, with a screw top. I can only remember the "Smith household" having any of this pop once, for I remember undoing the stopper and "'avin' a good guzzle ourovit" when no one was about.

Sunday was 'The Day" for food in "our 'ouse". Teatime produced tinned fruit, salmon sandwiches, cake, and loads of bread and butter, and more of it if one of our aunties, uncles, and cousins honoured us with a visit. During tea time "Our Mom" would keep an eagle eye on us lot though, "Ay, yo've 'ad one salmon san'wich a'ready, now put that bugger back, ya greedy little sod". Or, "I'm watchin' yo, that's the secon' lump o' cerk yo've 'ad, an' if yo gu forra 'nother I'll ge yarra dab 'and."

One of the rare occasions when these relatives came, it was Auntie Vi and Cousin Vic from Kirk Sandell close to Doncaster. They finished their tea and everyone paraded across the yard to our Auntie Berth's, leaving me in the house on my own, which was a silly thing to do. On the table was a huge glass bowl of pineapple squares, besides the other goodies. Well, how often did kids have pineapple squares? I'll tell you - once in a blue moon. I stared at them for a while, ignoring the other food, then I went to the door "Ta mek sure it wus all clear" came back and thought, 'The ol' gel wunt miss one on 'um, she wun even know one 'as gone." I picked one of the squares up and sucked all the juice off first, thinking, "Ner, I wunt tek it, I'll 'ave a good suck an' then I'll stick it back". Unfortunately the thought was dismissed and I decided to eat it. It tasted so nice I ate another and another until the bowl was half empty. Suddenly I heard somebody talking in the yard, so I stopped eating (it's a good job I did or I would probably have eaten the bowl full) and peeped through the cardboard which served as a temporary pane of glass until Dad could mend it, (you don't win a prize for guessing who broke it in the first place) and there was my Cousin Vic talking to our little Bertha. I thought that possibly a strategic withdrawal was in order, for if those two had come outside, it was more likely the rest would follow, and in the process return to "Our 'ouse" and discover the missing pineapple squares.

So out of the house I shot, down the entry passed Bertha and Vic, who were completely oblivious of me, they were so intent on the conversation they were having. I stayed out playing for a while, and then I was called in "Ta gurra bed". Whilst playing I had felt the odd pain or two in my "belly" but chose to ignore it, but when I returned home with one of the "Big Wenches", I suddenly had 'Ta gu ta the lavie" quick, or "I'd a dun it in me trousis".

God was I glad to get sat on the big wooden seat, and see the whitewashed walls and piles of newspaper in the outside lavatory. It absolutely poured from me. I had got diarrhoea and no doubt about that. After a good while I returned to the house. "I dain't feel like any supper, norreven a cuppa tea" and went off up to bed, with you-know-who looking very queer at me. It wasn't long before I shouted down the stairs, "Mom, can I cum down quick, I wanna gu ta the lavie agen" and the reply, "Whacha bin up ta ya little sod, if yo think I'm gunna keep yarraway from school tamorra', ya gorra, 'nother bloody think cumin', cus yome guin', now cum on down, an' be sharp abourit."

I rushed down and out to the lavatory again. On completion I returned and naturally my "bum" was sore, so I walked very precariously. I dare not tell you-know-who, she gave me enough funny looks as it was. I had to run down once more that evening, very fortunately "she " had gone up to the pub with the relatives (not dad though, he'd had to go to work). I'm sure "Our Mom", with the remarks and looks from the wenches knew something about the disappearing pineapple, luckily she never made an accusation for once, which was strange, and for which I was relieved.

I rushed to the "lavie" again first thing in the morning, but I didn't make a fuss about it, for I didn't want to revive any thoughts about the matter, and anyway after that the diarrhoea seemed to subside, and eventually stopped.

I didn't have any problem regarding eating pineapple squares for a very long time after, due to the fact "We dain't 'ave the bloody pineapple squares to cause the problem, did we!"

Sunday was no exception to kids getting into trouble, even big kids and blokes. I remember football being played in the Little King Street on a Sunday afternoon, which of course was strictly forbidden. "The Watch Committee" ruled these laws they had laid down for the people of Birmingham with an iron fist, and anyone caught breaking them would suffer the full consequences, whatever your circumstances were.

After Sunday dinner the blokes would gather in Little King Street by Coopers, the felt makers and George Davies the Bookie, pick sides and put a wager on. There would be look-outs posted at the corner of Guest Street and Great King Street, scouting for the local beat copper, who they all knew by sight and name. Coats would be put down and the match would begin, with quite a few spectators may I add, who also had bets on the outcome of the match.

Rules were stuck to as far as humanly possible, I mean it was a bit impossible to ascertain a goal without a crossbar, but it did not deter them, both sides with the assistance of the referee were always as fair as they could be under the circumstances with one another. If one of the look-outs gave a warning signal that a copper was coming, the players and spectators would disappear down a dozen different entries, into a dozen different hiding places, or if the copper was too near and followed the culprits down the entries, they had their own routes of escape into Bridge Street West, with the full knowledge and help of the residents. They did get caught occasionally though. I think Kenyon Street Police got a bit wise and sent a 'dick' down to catch them, although in all fairness to the police I don't think they were too harsh unless of course the blokes tried to ignore, argue, or be funny with them. I might add that some very fine players emerged from these Hockley Street matches.

One Sunday afternoon a bloke came to paint "Arthur Young's" name on his coal yard gate. Us kids had noticed the gate being painted green on the Saturday, but didn't take a great deal of interest in that, but when this bloke started measuring up and drawing lines, then letters in chalk on the freshly painted gate our curiosity was definately aroused. There we stood watching with the bloke talking to us amicably. We had all got our "Sunday Best" on, with the usual warning from our Moms "Don't yo gu an' get playin' rough, or gerrin in the dirt with them best clo'es on, or else it'll be a bloody whalin' fer ya w'en yo gerrin, da ya 'ear me". "Are Mom, tarra" the reply would be to her, but the thought would be "She's alis bleedin' moanin' she is, if she guz on moanin' like this all the time, 'er tongue 'll drop out".

I remember I had a grey blazer, with a yellow badge on the left top pocket, grey short flannels, grey socks with two yellow hoops round the top, a grey cap with a badge like the one on my blazer at the front, shirt, tie, and black shoes completed my outfit. All this outfit was obtained from Foster Brothers on the Soho Road, Handsworth, in the "nobs" district, with a "Provident Cheque". The reason "Our Mom" had to go so far afield this time, from "The Brook" was simply because she had probably 'knocked' all the other drapers and outfitters, or hadn't kept the payments up on the various didleum clubs and was consequently either in debt, or out of benefit, and so naturally they wouldn't let her have any more credit. Mind you the system she'd got for the local grocers and huxters was pretty good. She would have all her groceries, cigarettes and other things, which amounted to quite a lot due to the size of our "mob", eight kids and "Our Mom and Dad", from "Duttons" on the corner of Unett Street and New John Street West for a good while, on the book of course, and she would pay up religiously every Saturday without fail.Then suddenly "POW" she would build up a hefty bill all 'the wick' and when Saturday came she would knock them giving some ridiculous excuse, which they of course did not believe, but couldn't do anything about. On the Monday she would probably go along to Mrs. Cross's in Little King Street where she would be welcomed on the book, due again to the size of the family. Mom would again stay with Mrs. Cross until it was necessary, due to shortage of money, which probably arose through her incompetence of handling money anyway, when she would "knock" her, and go to the Co-Op on "The Brook", but this time for a short period only, for at the Co-Op it was strictly a cash only for goods basis. Mom would stay there for a short time, until the money situation started to get dicey again, and then she would return to "Duttons", apologising and promising to pay something off the bad debt each week until it was cleared. Duttons stood about as much chance of "Our Mom" clearing the bad debt up as rain turning to gold on reaching the pavement. They knew this, but could not refuse the custom due to the profit they would make on the goods "Mom" did manage to pay for.

This was the normal procedure adopted not only by 'The Smith Family", but a large percentage of all big families in Hockley, although it would be fair to say they all had their own particular systems for dealing with this particular "Social Disease" of "The Thirties" - shortage of money - although on reflection I think it is a disease of anytime. I only ever remember "Me Dad" being involved in 'mom's' system once, and believe me, once was more than enough for "Our Mom". She made the fatal mistake of knocking the baker Arthur Crump. He came late one Saturday. Not very late, but just a little later than usual, and as usual I was waiting for him, but the tragedy was that "Our Dad" had arrived home a little early. "Mom" was out the back yard somewhere, so Dad said to Arthur, "Serve ya wertin I'll pay fer the bread, an' the ol' 'oman can ge it me back w'en I settle up we 'er lerter". Arthur looked into his book and reckoned the bill up, and must have thought", I'll reckon the bad debt on as well, perhaps the "ol' mon wunt know the diff'rence", But when he told Dad how much the bill was "Our Dad" said " 'ow bloody much, we ain't 'ad that much bread an' cerk this wick 'ave we, are yo sure yo've reckoned it up right, it seems a bloody lot ta me. Will ya tell me w'at we've 'ad fer that amount of money Arthur?" All these questions off Dad and him waiting for a satisfactory reply must have been too much for Arthur, and he had to admit that "Our Mom" had indeed 'knocked' him. All the thought of Arthur getting off because he was late went out of "Dad's" mind as he strode to the back yard gate and bawled, "Lil, are yo out thea?" - and on the positive reply, he continued, "Well bloody well get yerself in 'ere, I've gorra bone ta pick with yo, an' yo ain't gonna like the soddin' taste on it". Then he came back into the middle room where Arthur and I were waiting, and he said to me in his usual quiet, gentle voice, "Yu gu an' wert fer Arthur in the van son, there's a good lad". I replied, "Yes Dad", but I really didn't want to go out because I knew "Our Mom" was "in fer it" and I would have preferred to witness 'er' gerrin a good tellin' orf ferra change". I don't know what ensued, but Arthur came out a few minutes later looking a lot redder than his normal complexion was. I mean, can you imagine the scene at "Bradfords". Dad was the Foreman baker, and if I may say he was held in high esteem, by both Management and Staff alike, and they, at least some of them, knew that "Our mom" had got a bad debt with them!

I bet there was a bit of back talk and tales running around, but I bet equally what "Our Dad" said that Saturday morning to both "Our Mom" and Arthur Crump whilst I sat in the van would have quashed any further loose talk, for Arthur was very quiet during the rest of that day which was *very unusual* indeed.

The bloke we were watching completed the markings in chalk on the green gates which read A YOUNG, COAL AND COKE MERCHANT. ORDERS DELIVERED. Then the bloke got some paint out of a big tin which was on his bike on the rear metal carrier, poured some of it into an old "Cadburys" cocoa tin, then he poured something else in, and stirred it. His stirring finished he got a long stick with a lump of leather on the end (a Maulstick) and a very thin paint brush from the wooden box on the carrier of his bike and commences to paint over his chalk marks. "e's good in 'e Smithy" said one of my mates, and I replied, "Are 'e is, 'e's real good". He completed painting the letters in a cream colour, and it was perfect. Then he cleared the cocoa tin out and threw the residue into the gutter. Having made sure that the cocoa tin was clean, he again returned to the wooden box on his bike and removed another tin of paint which was black. He put some of this into the cocoa tin, and added the something else and again he stirred it. Having done this he cleaned his brush with the something else and dried it. The bloke then started all over again putting the back-up paint to the cream letters. We were absolutely fascinated at the result on completion of the first letter. It looked beautiful and we remarked to the bloke our thoughts. He replied, "Tha's nice on ya lads, Ta", and we continued to watch with greater interest than before, almost willing the bloke to hurry, so that we could admire the completed job.

"Our mom ses would yo like a cuppa tea Mister?" a girl's voice suddenly interrupted. She was of course addressing the bloke not us. We all looked at this "little wench" with utter contempt, how dare she interrupt an artist at work with such a trivial request. We wanted to tell her to "Sod off an' leave the bloke alone", but it might have offended him, and that would never do, so we gave her some dirty looks and kept "our gobs shut". "Are, I wouldn't mind a cup luv thank yo, its bloody thirsty werk, standing' 'ere doin' this". "Well, come on over we'n yome ready, we live in tharr'ouse over there", and she pointed to the house where Jimmy Perry came to live, after these people left. The house was situated on the right side of Johnnie Kingham's opening, leading to Bill Lewis's scrap yard. "Are, okay ma wench, I'll just finish this one letter, an' then I'll be across, okay?" "Are, but don' leave it too lung cus it'll be cold". "I wunt be lung me wench, yo cun bet on that", and with that the little "wench" ran back over Guest Street to tell her mother that the bloke was coming. He completed the letter and then hurried off to a most welcome cuppa tea, and probably a piece of dripping. "The lucky sod" we thought.

We stood around admiring the bloke's work for a while and then one of my mates said "I'll bet yo could paint as good as 'im Smithy". "Nah, course I couldn't I replied. But nevertheless I felt proud he should hold me in such high esteem, not realising he was egging me on to do something for a bit of "donnuck". "Yo could Smithy, we've sin some of yower drawrins at school" they all chorused, naturally feeding my already inflated ego. "Why dontcha do some writin' on the shop back gert, an' show us w'at yo cun do?" they continued. The gate they were referring to was the entrance to the back yard of the General Stores situated on the corner of Guest Street and New John Street West, and was adjacent to Mr. Young's Coal Yard gates. "Are, okay, I'll 'ave a gu" I replied. I couldn't see it but they were all in on the joke now.

Having watched the bloke with rapt attention, I commenced to copy the motions he went through, and chalked, "A YOUNG" on the "ol' gel's" back gate, with a piece of the chalk the bloke had left by the coal yard gates. "W-o-o-o that's great Smithy" the mob shouted encouragingly. "Now gu on an' paint it, it'll be berra t'an the bloke's writin' wunnit?", and the rest of the mob shouted "Are, it will". I hesitated for a moment, but then pride got the better of me and I approached the bloke's bike cautiously, keeping an eye out on the house across the street where he had gone for his cuppa tea. I opened the wooden box on the carrier and saw the tin with the cream paint in it. I searched for and found an old nail in the bottom of the box with which to remove the lid. I began to attempt to prise the lid open, but to no avail, so l exerted more pressure - nothing. My mates didn't offer any assistance, they were too busy sniggering, but I didn't notice that. I put the tin horizontal on top of the wooden box, after closing the lid of course, got the head of the nail under the lid and *pulled*! The inevitable happened, the lid suddenly shot off with force, splattering cream paint everywhere, over the box, the bike, the road and worst of all, it went all over my *Sunday best blazer.* My mates just stood and looked for a few seconds, then roared with laughter and ran off, leaving me to my fate. I collected my thoughts together, and decided quickly that the best place for me was *not here*, I would have enough trouble with "Our ol' gel" without being caught here and have to face the bloke as well.

Off I ran, full pelt down Guest Street towards St. Saviours. I should have gone straight down to the church, maybe God would have helped me in this situation, but I didn't, I ducked into Little King Street and up there I went nearly to Great King Street, by Tommy Tandy's and Alfie Mobbs house, so the bloke wouldn't be able to find me. After a short interval to rest I walked slowly back a short distance and turned into one of several gateways of Coopers Felt Works to try to find some sort of solution to my grave situation. First I picked up a piece of discarded felt Iying about, which was the residue after the pattern the operator required was cut out, and tried to rub the paint off, but naturally it only spread it over a larger area. Next I thought I'll have to wet the felt first, to remove it, so off I went down to Burbury Street Recreation, where I knew there was a drinking tap just inside the gate by the "Parkies" house opposite Defford Road. I wet the felt and proceeded to attempt to remove the offending paint. What a bloody mess it made, for it spread it even further. By now I was completely at my wits end and just stood there and started to grizzle. This didn't do anything, no magic came and removed the paint, so I thought, "I'll have to 'gu and face the music", much against my will though, "cus I noo she'd gu bloody barmy w'en she saw this lot."

I strolled slowly along Farm Street trying to think up a story to tell "Our Mom". Well, I could hardly tell her the truth could I? Up Wellesley Street I went morbidly when suddenly I came up with a brilliant story. I would tell her that some kids had thrown it over me whilst I was playing in the "Rec". I must admit I felt a little better than I did having made up a story to put the blame on someone else, although it wouldn't stop the inevitable "whalin" I'd gerroff 'er I continued up Wellesley Street to Bridge Street West in a much better frame of mind. I turned right and went along Bridge Street as far as Copleys shop and stopped. I peeped round the corner up Guest Street but I couldn't see the bloke from this angle, so I rushed across the street to *The Vic* on the opposite corner. I peered cautiously from behind the pub doorway and saw the bloke working industriously on Mr. Young's gates again, so I crept up Guest Street past Spurrels and ducked up our entry without him seeing me.

Across the yard I went and opened our door quietly. I entered not daring to breathe and when I got in I could have jumped for joy, for it was silent and empty, which gave me a breathing space to try to think up some remedial treatment for my problem. Mom, Dad, and "The Babby" were in bed, and all the others were apparently out somewhere. I crept quietly into the pantry to have a scout round and see if there might be something to remove this "bloody paint" off my blazer.

I looked around for a while, being careful not to make any noise, when suddenly there on the top shelf over the sink was a bottle, "Like w'at the bloke 'ad got ta clean 'is paint brush with", with clear liquid in it (later I found out the bottle contained liniment for "Our Dad's" rheumatism!). My troubles were over, all I had to do was get the bottle. "What I'd do" I though, was "knacker the bottle, an' gu in the brew' us, where I'd mek the blerzer as good as noo, an' the ol' gel ud never fin' out - great." I commenced to climb onto the sink, for I had to stand in that in order to reach up to the top shelf and obtain the bottle. What I did *not* know was "Our Mom" had put the meat tin on the first shelf with the fat from the Sunday joint in it to cool off, and eventually coagulate into dripping. Now me being small I did not see this tin, and I had to lay hold of the first shelf in order to pull myself up onto the sink, so what did I get hold of - you're right - the tin. I pulled, naturally thinking it was the shelf I had hold of. I couldn't believe my eyes as I saw the tin topple towards me, and I was also falling backwards at the time.

I gave out a loud yell as I hit the pantry floor and the tin of partially coagulated dripping came tumbling down after me. It hit me, splashing its contents over me and then continued on its way clanging down the steps leading to the "bogey'ole", to its final resting place in the cellar, awakening them upstairs into the bargain. I looked at myself, I was covered in dripping, so I just broke down and started to grizzle again. Well, I couldn't do a lot else under the circumstances.

" 'oo the bleedin' 'ells down there kickin' up a rumpus?" - "you-know-who" screamed from the landing. I didn't reply, I was so scared. Down the stairs she came, "The Babby" started to cry, and "Our Dad" was shouting something, it was utter confusion. When she arrived in the downstairs room she took one look at me and without as much as a by or leave, no questions, she started to lay into me, with me attempting to ward off some of the blows by holding my arms across my face and body. "Yo little bleeder" she screamed "w'at 'ave ya bin up to now? Come on, let's 'ave it out on ya". She stopped walloping me momentarily and I blurted out, between grizzling, the story I had decided to fabricate, then I continued to explain why I had upset the meat tin, this time the truth though - "I wanned ta clean the paint orf Mom, so as yo wouldn't 'ave ta, I dain't know the tin wus thaya did I, else I wouldna done it."

By this time Dad had arrived, not very pleased either, his bleary eyes indicating too many hours at work, and the booze he'd supped at *The Guest* on the dinner time. He had also been disturbed from his short sleep prior to going to work at five o'clock. "W'at the bloody 'ells guin' on Lil, they cun 'ere yo screamin' the other side o' the "Brook", shet yersel' up a minnit an' tell me w'at's 'appened". Mom retold the story but painting a more ominous picture in order to gain Dad's confidence and support on the matter.

Having finished relating the story she went on, "Lookaris bloody new clo'es Arthur, 'e's bloody ruined 'em."

Of course what she was really worried about was that she couldn't send them to the "Pop" shop in their present state next morning, but of course she couldn't tell Dad this, for if she did somebody else would be "gerrin a whalin' ". Dad looked at me and said "Tek them clo'es orf, an' gu an' putcha ruthers on, gu on now an' be quick abarrit". I did as I was told, and went upstairs and got "me wick day clo'es" from under the bed, changed into them, and took my bedraggled "Sunday Best" back downstairs. Dad had apparently calmed Mom down a little, but she gave me a villanous look all the same, and I thought, "I'll be forrit agen w'en "Our Dad" guz ta werk tonight". He gathered the trousers, blazer and cap up and said to Mom, "Yo'll 'ave ta wash 'is socks, tie and shirt Mother, an' I'll gu across ta Twiggs, ar think 'e's got some stuff that'll shift this lot". With that he went out. Mom glared at me and said, "Gerrout o' me sight yo little bleeder afoa I ge yo some moa. I will, I'll bleedin' swing fer yo yet, they'll bloody top me at "The Green" they will. Gu on, bugger orf outa me bleedin' sight." Well, how could I refuse an offer like that? So I obeyed her request and went! I ran out of the house before she changed her mind and gave me another "Whalin'." At the bottom of the entry I stopped and peeped up Guest Street. The bloke was still there doing his painting, so I nipped rather quickly across into Little King Street again, where to my surprise I found my *mates* up Pat Wagstaff's yard playing, or were they hiding like me from the bloke, because strictly speaking this street was outside our area. They questioned me as to how I had got on and I told them, "Well, it's no bloody thanks ta yo, 'ow I gorron, butt I'll tell ya any road up". So I gave them the usual rose tinted version (all lies) of how I had confidently worked my way out of the situation. On completion of this pack of lies, they started to "pick flies" about me wearing "me wick day clo'es on a Sunday", referring to "Our Mom" tekin 'em ta the Pop Shop early cus she wanned some money fer booze", and the "I suppose it's yower kids turn ta wear the Sundies now ain't it Smithy?" I stood these sarky comments for a while, and then when "they kep' on abarrit" I saw red. I thought, well, I've got nothing to lose, I've already got me "wick day clo'es on, and they got their "Sundies" on, so "It don marrer if I get these a little dirtier". With those thoughts in my mind I piled into them. "I bosted a couple onnem, an' one onem started to blart, cus 'e'd got 'is Sundies dirty in the scrap", which brought an abrupt end to hostilities. "We'm sorry Ron, we wus onnee jokin' with ya, we dain't mean anythin' 'onest", one of them stated - "Oright". I said "let's be pals again" and this stopped the taunting immediately.

"Our wench" eventually called me in. I had my "bit of bubble an' squeak" and a cuppa tea, and went off to bed. "I dain't say anthin' and the ol gel dain't say anythin' " so I left it at that, not wishing for another "bost up the earole", but if looks could have killed "I'd a bin a dead un."

I presume everything was cleared, or should I say "cleaned" up, because two of the "wenches" were off early next morning to the "Pop Shop" in Farm Street, and the following Sunday my "best" was there ready for the trip to Grandad Smiths in "Smerrick", but *not* may I add without a threat from "you know who" of what would happen to me if I so much as got a bit of dust on them. "I wunt Mom 'onest I wunt, I wunt gerr anythin' on 'em 'onest" was my reply, and for once I really meant it, well - for the time being anyhow.

Hockley Tramcar Depot Whitmore Street (TheTram Sheds!)

CHAPTER NINE

"Hockley Nights"

Whatever did we find to do at night time in Hockley before the arrival of wireless, and well before the arrival of television and all the paraphernalia that goes with it? The answer is, we had plenty to do. I will not start quoting whether those days were any better than the present, but it's a certainty that in that generation we enjoyed ourselves equally as much as people enjoy themselves today.

Criticism comes easy to people who do nothing. I mean, does it really matter if a person has hair long or short, wears clothes that are different from what we might call normal, drives a car that's a disgrace, has a television in every room in the house, men painting their faces to look like women, women wearing clothes like, and acting like men, does it really matter? No! Providing they do not interfere with the way *you* want to run *your* life, by attempting to force their way of life on you.

Extroverts? Yes, we had them, as generations before did, and generations to come will no doubt have their fair share. All they do as far as I can see is attempt to exhibit what life should be like as *they* see it, so you can ignore it, like it, but not take part, or like it and then take part, everyone has that freedom of choice.

HOCKLEY at night in the winter months, cold biting, the rain lashing, and the snow, "med us kids 'appy" but was a nightmare for everyone else. We would play "I ackey" with the seeker standing under the gas lamp outside Donnie Harbridges house, half way down Guest Street, by the Cottons and Mitchells.

First we decided on a boundary, limited to a certain area, the hiders could hide in. Then of course we had to sort out who was on (seeker) first. "One potater, two potater, three potater, four; five potater, six potater, seven potater all, an' out guz yo". This was the system we used to eliminate all the hiders, and of course the last one was the seeker. What a system! We would sometimes "gu down the Tram Sheds" in Whitmore Street. There we waited patiently for the trams who were "Depot Only" to turn out of the "Brook" and into Whitmore Street to finish their journey, and be tucked up for the night in the long wide sheds, after being washed and cleaned, and any faults put right. The blue flashes from the overhead line, lighting up, then disappearing into the dark sky above, as the conducting poles ran over the cross wires. The hum of the traffic as it passed up and down "The Brook", horse and carts rumbling down Whitmore Street, passing us kids waiting at the entrance to the tram sheds, returning after their day's work, either to Scribban's in Goode Street, or Bradfords in Norton Street.

At last a tram would stop at the top of Whitmore Street with its front facing the city, and we waited excitedly to see whether the copper on point duty in the middle of "The Brook" had halted the tram until the traffic from the city had abated so that he could signal him to turn right for the depot, or whether the copper had halted him because he was allowing the flow of traffic across "The Brook" precedence. If it was the former the tram would turn slowly, with many blue flashes, and then rumble quickly down the gradient home.

On reaching the entrance to the depot, a man in uniform would tell the driver which shed he wanted the tram parked in and the driver would acknowledge. He would then enter the depot area. Once inside he would stop again, to allow his conductor to drop off, carrying his ticket tin, a black oblong box, with his supply of unused tickets, and also the day's takings in one hand and his ticket rack in the other. When he dropped off he would then shout to the driver for him to proceed, informing him that he was safely off the tram. On completion of this he would then walk off to the right to the paying-in office.

"O betcha 'e guz inta the fust shed", one of us would say. "Nay 'e wunt, 'e'll gu inta that 'un over theya" one of the others would cut in. We'd watch as the big cream and navy blue giant was put to bed gently by its driver. Many times when the Conductor dropped off the tram he would spot us kids by the entrance. He'd come across to us and say "ere yar nips, 'ere's a couple o' san'wiches me an' my mate dain't eat, get 'em stuffed down yarr 'odges." Or it would be some tea he had left in his billy can, a few sweets, or toffees. Sometimes he would take us to one of the trams already parked in the depot shed and he would open the used ticket box carefully via a flap at the bottom and let the used tickets drop into our hands. We shared these out and put them into our pockets ready for a game of buses and trams at a later date.

Some nights we would play "dares". The usual potato system was used to decide who the judicator of dares was. Having settled this part of the game the Master would then designate a dare to anyone of the mob and you could look out if you were, or had been in his bad books.

I vividly remember one dare I had to carry out. That was to knacker a loaf of bread off a George Baines van, whose driver was in the process of taking goods into one of their shops on the corner of Farm Street and Hunters Road. Now being the one who had to carry out the dare, you had the privilege of completing your dare whichever way you chose, which included using the rest of the mob, providing they were not called upon to actually assist personally in the act itself.

Flrst off I scouted the land, on the pretext that I was admiring the goods displayed in the window. After a few minutes, having decided how I was going to stage this dare, I nipped back across Farm Street to The Benyon and revealed my plan to the mob. When I gave the signal, we all went across the street towards the van, but according to my instructions, went boisterously, with me staying to the right side of the crowd. As we passed the back of the open van, I put my hand into it and quickly grabbed what I thought was a small loaf, just under a pound in weight. But when I picked the object up, I nearly fell into the van, with the weight of it. I had to decide quickly, let the object go and face the wrath of my mates, and also, which was worse, be designated another dare, or I could turn and grab the object with both hands, before the vanman came out of the shop. I looked quickly, for by this time my mates were casually strolling up Hunters Road, to see if the bloke was anywhere to be seen. No, he wasn't in sight, so up with the object and under my jersey it went. I hurried up Hunters Road in the wake of my mates. I eventually caught up with them opposite Charlie Kirby's and said "Yo'me a great lorra mates yo am, leavin' me in the lurch like that". They replied, "Wot's a marra with yo Smithy, da ya need all on us ta knacker a loaf a bread?" - "That's where yome wrung bloody clever dicks, cus I ain't knackered a loaf of bread, so there ya rotton sods".

At this statement they all looked at me suspiciously. After a few seconds one of them said, "Wotcha mean Smithy, yo ain't knackered a loaf of bread?" "Oi mean 'xact'ly warr I sez, I ain't knackered a loaf a bread, I got summet berra than that", I replied, hoping fervently that I had, because I had not removed the object, heavy though it was, from beneath my jersey for fear of someone seeing it and starting to make some enquiries. "Well ge us a look arrit then, an' let's see w'at yo got" they all chanted. "Wunt, not 'till we'em up past Nursery Road, where nobody cun see us". "Ar' roright" they replied, and we all hurried past Samuels and The Carnigie and were nearly at Naden Road before we stopped. Then they gathered around me in a circle, waiting with anticipation for me to bring the heavy object into sight. I sensed this anticipation and made them wait that little while longer, pretending to look around suspiciously for anyone coming. "'e's 'avin us on 'e is, I berr 'e ain't gorr anythin' under 'is ganzie, an' 'e's tryin' ta gerr ou' rov 'is dare, the twistin' bleeda", one of the gang suddenly said. This remark prompted me to withdraw the object abruptly and shove it under the speaker's nose. " 'ere ya are then big gob, 'ave a look at that, an' see if that's nuthin' then. Gu on 'ave a good look". There was a loud "Who-o-o-o, look at that it's the biggest we've ever sin in our lives, good ol' Smithy". When I took a closer look, because I had been too pre-occupied to do so before and not daring to look, hoping to deflate the speaker on his earlier remarks, but I was also equally apprehensive as to exactly what the object was. I removed the object from the offending speaker's nose to take a closer look for myself, being now full of confidence, due to the remarks of the mob. On closer inspection I saw it was the biggest pork pie I had ever seen. "Sorry Ron, (it was always Ron when they were wrong) I dain't mean it, I wus on'y jokin' with ya 'onest I wus", came the apology from the kid who had "Opened 'is big gob too soon". "Soright. I know ya dain't mean it anyway, so let's fergerrit", and with that we all set about devouring the pie. We all had our fill, but couldn't manage it all, so the remainder was thrown over a hedge into one of the "nobs" front gardens in between Charville Road and Weston Road. Later that night when I was in bed, I reflected on the happenings and felt sorry for the van man when he discovered the huge pork pie missing. Then I thought, "Well 'e shoulda shut 'is back doors, an' then I couldna knackered 'is rotton pork pie". I reflected with fors and againsts, until eventually I drifted off into an uneasy and restless sleep. But kids resilience is a wonderful equalizer, and when I woke up in the morning the whole incident was put to the back of my mind.

On other occasions when we played dares, it was surprising what ability and scheming was produced by us kids, although I suppose it is fair to say this about any youngsters, any time.

The "Blackwell" incident was one of the other plans instigated by one of the lads, but the end result meant we all had to participate for it to be carried out successfully. What was proposed was that approximately eight of us would play cowboys and indians, which meant the smaller lads in the gang would be situated on the backs of the bigger lads, as per horse and rider, then half the gang would be indians, with the other half being cowboys. Naturally the cowboys would inevitably be chasing the indians and according to plan, the chase would have to pass Blackwells in Hunters Road, with their fruit and vegetables stacked in neat rows on trestles in front of the shop itself. The plan was that one of the indians would be shot, just as we were passing Blackwells. This indian naturally being the lad whose dare it was. He would of course fall off his horse and quite accidently land on one of the neat stacks of apples, knocking them to the floor.

All of us would then be alarmed at this unfortunate accident and apologise most profusely to whoever came out of the shop to scathe us for the misdemeanour. Also we would *help*! to pick up the apples and return them to their rightful place on the trestle. Whilst in the process of this *assistance*! some of these apples would find their way into some of our pockets, accidently of course!

This plan went off successfully, the final score being Blackwells 0. Us Kids 7. But on reflection, in this particular instance, I think compassion played the biggest part. It was Stan Blackwell the son who came out of the shop when he heard the commotion outside and shouted "W'at the bloody 'ell's guin' on 'ere?" One of the gang briefly explained about the accident, and we were all apologising at the same time. On hearing the explanation Stan said, "I oughta fetch the coppa orf the "Brook" ta ya' little buggers, now put them bloody apples back up thaya, an' mek shure yo' don' miss any, put the lot on 'um back, cus I'm gunna watcha". And watch us he did, I feel sure he knew we had "knackered" some. I might have been wrong, but I don't think so, for on completion of this remedial work Stan said "Gu on one on ya', gu in the shop an' tell 'em in theya I sent ya', tell 'emta ge ya' a bag a specks, an' then bugger orf all on ya', or I will fetch the "Brook" coppa to ya'. One of the lads went into the shop and came out with a carrier bag full of specks. We thanked Stan and said "Tarrar". He replied, but we noticed that when he did he had the biggest smile we'd ever "sin on 'is ferce."

"Mr Vann the 'ot tata Mon" was certainly a notable character on cold dark nights. He was a small wizened man, his face thin and grossly wrinkled, his small eyes partially obscured with metal framed glasses, a slight but protruding nose, with a grey moustache lying beneath it. His mouth small and sunken, emphasised no doubt with a reluctance to wearing dentures. Swathed in a large overcoat, meant for a man three times his build he was always hunched forward with what we kids thought of as a permanent "charlie" on his back. Mr. Vann was always to be seen on winter nights, with his coke burning cart outside George Baines bread and cake shop on the corner of Farm Street and Hunters Road. His cart would be parked just inside Farm Street, with its black boiler-type shape and brass rings around it, the black funnel with one brass ring encircling it at the top, belching out smoke and acrid fumes. The canopy which housed Mr. Vann, the sack of potatoes, the supplies of white triangular bags hanging from a nail, the box of salt, and the tin drawers with long brass handles on them, where the potatoes were placed in to bake, was like the cab on the trains we watched on a Saturday Morning at Hockley Station. The metal chassis which held the boiler etc, gleaming black, with the two wooden cartwheels and axle surround painted bright red, with yellow lining and a brass piece circling each hub end. A brass candle lamp burned brightly either side and the red glow from the fire, when Mr. Vann opened up to feed its interior with more coke, coupled with the smell of potatoes being baked was one of life's better things on a winter's evening.

As we get older, we have pangs of remorse for some of the misdemeanours committed in earlier days, well, biggest majority of us do anyway. You committed these defaults through being thoughtless, through poverty, through ignorance, or as children through pure innocence of what you might bring about with your socalled games. I bet there are quite an amount of us who say, as I do, " I wish to God I had not done that, think of the trouble it probably caused. "Or" God, that was a rotten trick I played on so and so". But at the end of the day, I imagine it's half the battle squaring your conscience, by feeling a deep regret within yourself.

Some of the misdemeanours I have written about I now realise show that my mates and myself were "bad lots". But kids will, I hope, always be the same, providing the deed is not too acute in it's intensity.

"Can I 'ave 'apeth a' tatas please Mr. Vann?" would be the enquiry by one of us "little buggers" to this very nice old man. He would reach up slowly, very slowly, I suppose his rheumatics would be intense on these bitter cold nights, and pull one of the white triangular tissue bags of the piece of string which held them.

Then he would open the bottom drawer, naturally the one closest to the fire below, and feel the potatoes within, with his gnarled hands. Some he threw back into the

Mr. Vann with his potatoe cart on the corner of Farm Street

drawer, presumably they were not baked enough, others he put into the bag until it was full. "Do yo' wan any salt son?" he would say, "Are please" we would reply.

The salt would be put into the bag and he would hand them to us. As soon as we had them in our hands, we would belt off down Farm Street without paying, knowing full well he hadn't got a chance of catching us. Another time we climbed over the gate into Bill Lewis's scrap yard and scrounged around for some small chrome circles about the size of a "bob" he received on occasions from some metal stamping works, which in semi darkness would pass for a shilling coin. One of the lads presented Mr. Vann with this chrome disc with great trepidation, due to the other time we had run off with the "tatas". But like I said the old chap's eyes were not too good. He squinted at it for amoment, and the kid concerned got himself ready to nip away sharpish, back to us lot down by "Hodgson's bogey 'ole". After what seemed an eternity Mr. Van dropped the disc into his big overcoat pocket and gave the kid his " 'a' puth a tatas", and elevenpunce 'a'penny change. He grabbed both, so he told us later, refusing the salt Mr. Vann offered. "Silly bugger, w'at's the good a tatas without salt?" Then he ran to us as quickly as he could. We threw the "tatas" away telling him what a "nana" he was coming without the salt, but he was soon back in favour with the change he handed us. Off we went to Dudley's Fish and Chip Shop and bought a "pennuth" of chips each, with "scratchin's" Mr. Dudley piled on for us. I bet he'd have piled something else onto us if he had known where the money had come from for these chips. We tried the same trick again later on but Mr. Vann was wise to it and grabbed the kid, but fortunately for the kid in question he could not hold him due to his frail condition, and the kid ran off like a thunderbolt.

After that we decided not to try that gag again.

"Knackerin' " from sweet shops was a crime committed by most kids, and some adults too, I'm sorry to say, but the one bit of "knackerin' " by Harold Beardsmore has to be the most daring and cheeky I've ever heard of.

After the "Vann" incident we had to scout around for another dare for members of the mob to carry out, which would bring us "summat ta eat," for kids were always hungry in those days. Finally after much discussion we all agreed that the sweet shop on the "Brook", next to the fish and chip shop by the bus stop which served the 29, 29a, 16a and the 15a routes, would be our best bet. The shop had one of those warning bells, informing the shopkeeper of customers needing attention. Most shops had bells attached to a wall near the door frame, so that when the door was opened the top of the door struck the bell. In this shop however the contact to start the bell was underneath the floor, so that when you stepped into the shop you automatically started the bell ringing, and it kept on ringing until you moved further into the shop. So what we did on our first visit to the shop was to arrange for two of us to go in with 'a'penny. One stood on the contact location for the bell, whilst the other one skirted around quickly to locate where we could tread safely without bringing this bell into action. This was done and the two came out with the " 'a'the peth" of sweets purchased by pretence, and the kid that had reconnoitred the floor for a safe area explained to the rest of us exactly where we were to tread.

We gave it half an hour before two more of us ventured into the shop again, with a story already prearranged should the bell go off. " 'ave yo' gorreny em'ty boxes lady, or sir? (as the case may be). We'm mekkin' summat, an' we need some please", was the story. So off they went and within a few minutes they were back with 'a'penny block of "Aero". It was great, we had made it! We repeated this dare over a few weeks, with me taking part, naturally, on some occasions, and were only unsuccessful once.

One night it was Harold's turn to nick and Kenny Price's turn to look out, so off they went, whilst we waited in New John Street West by the second hand shop watching for them. Pricey opened the door for Harold and when he emerged we saw he had something big in his arms and naturally wondered what it could possibly be. They nipped across the "Brook" quickly and when they reached us and we saw what Harold had in his arms we ran away from them, being the *heroes* we were. Up New John Street West we ran, and didn't stop until we reached Barr Street by the Bandalasta Works. We then went into the goods gateway in Barr Street itself to hide. Harold and Ken soon caught us up, came into the gateway and started to tell us in no uncertain terms what they thought of us. But we retaliated with a weak argument, that due to what Harold had "knackered" it would definitely cease to be a safe place for our dares in the future. Anyway we were soon all pals again in a very short time and dived into the contents of what Harold and Pricey had "knackered". Oh yes, !,I forgot to mention what he had taken, well, it was the *whole bloody display case*! Yes, that's what he had nicked, the whole display case. What a bloody nerve. We again ate what we could, put some in our pockets and threw the rest, display case and all over the wall into the backyard of Fred's Cafe opposite.

Yes, we found plenty to do on nights in Hockley. When I was in the choir at St. Saviours, Mr. Wrenshaw, along with the vicar Mr. Joseph, would at Christmas arrange Carol Singing at the "nobs" houses in Claremont Road, Richmond Road, South Road, and other roads in that area, by prior appointment, the proceeds collected going to the church funds". Rotton lot, they dain't ge us anythin'." On reflection it was really nice. With the full choir, we would sing half a dozen carols, then march to the next house on the list. Mind you I have to admit I only took part in this singing once, for I didn't stay in the choir long, I was more interested in earning a bit more money. It was properly organised and carried out beautifully. Not a quick snatch of "Noel," and half a verse of "Good King Wenceslas" and then a babbled "We wish you a Merry Christmas", before knocking on your door. No, the residents knew what time we would be at their home and they also chose what carols they required us to sing. It was indeed a pleasant way to spend a night in Hockley, although for me it was only for a short period.

Later on when we were a little older there were always the "Monkey Runs", one in the Hockley area along the Lozells Road, and the other in the "nobs" area along Soho Road. These were the places we would show ourselves off like prize cockerels, and the girls would be shy, telling us to clear off, "an' don' be cheeky", but liking the attention "any road up". If you were lucky you'd get to hold hands, and if you were really blessed there would be a kiss in some dark entry, before she scurried off with her mates and you went back to yours to relate some fantastic story, which was naturally all lies. How you had a "French Kiss," (although you hadn't a "bloody clue" what a French Kiss was), how you held her close like they did in the pictures and she had promised that you were the only boy for her and you were going to see her again the next night. It was beautiful though, a most beautiful period of anyone's life, however it takes place.

Then, like many others lads, for it was the done thing, we'd occasionally "gerrin the pitchers". We waited by the long passageway alongside *The Palladium* adjacent to Abrahalls, then we would select one of us, with the usual "tata method" and he would sneak up the passage to the exit door at the very top. There was another exit door just on the left inside the passage, but that was exclusive for the patrons in the Stalls, "the ninepennies", as was the front foyer the exclusive exit for the gallery patrons, "the Gods bobs". We could not use either of these exits to enforce our illegal entry, but had to be satisfied with the pits, or "the tanna mana." On arrival at this exit door at the top the kid selected would wait for someone to come out when he would nip inside quickly before the bar doors locked. Sometimes the people coming out would see the lad and actually hold the door for him. "Gu on cock, gu an' enjoy the pitcher", and then once you had the door firmly in your hand, off they would go laughing, perhaps remembering when they did exactly the same thing in their youth. Once the door was in your hand you would whistle, or, if you couldn't whistle, give a call sign, or, just simply shout, and the rest of the mob would come running up the passage and you would all enter the cinema. Just inside this exit door on the right, was the gents toilet, and we initially barged in there. When we were settled inside the "lavie" we would wait a few moments and then two of us would enter the cinema itself. Fighting shy of the usherettes and positively shaking with terror of the doormen, their uniforms spelling "Kenyon Street" (police) to us kids. Whoever entered first would sort out some empty seats as close together as possible. On completion of this reconnoitre one of the kids would return to the "lavie "and guide the rest of us to the location of the empty seats and we would settle down to watch the film. Of course there were several things that could have gone wrong. For instance if it was a particularly good film and the cinema was packed inside, the doorman from within would pass a message via one of the usherettes to the front doorman that so many seats had become vacant, when confirmed by the patrons they were indeed leaving the cinema and not going to the toilet, or to fetch refreshments. Then the front doorman would shout out to the queue waiting "Two singles in the front stalls" or "Three together in the rear stalls" or wherever, and the people would enter the cinema through the foyer. Now if we had got in and occupied those seats in the meantime, we would certainly have been caught and in a lot of trouble. Another problem was if the cinema staff suspected you had sneaked in, they could demand to see your half ticket. It was no use saying, "Uv chucked it away" because they were quite within their rights to either eject you, or make you pay again, for it stated quite clearly on the tickets "Patrons must retain this half of the ticket throughout the performance". Sometimes we overcame the latter situation by the mere fact some people coming out of the cinema, whilst we were sneaking in, would give us their half tickets, thereby substantiating that we were law abiding, ticket paying patrons!

With reference to the former situation that could go wrong, our mob used to weigh it up and if the queue outside was too big "we'd nit it". We only ventured away from "sneakin' in" *The Palladium* once. That was when we thought we would try *The Lozells Cinema*. The reason for this venture was purely due to the fact they were showing an X rated film and naturally we thought it would be a bit of a giggle to have a look, although we realised it would mean we would have to throw caution to the wind, but nevertheless we did exactly that and set off on our dangerous mission. But alas it was never to be realised. When we arrived at the cinema there were naturally, huge queues, because the film they were showing was both new to the screen and very daring. Consequently everyone wanted to see it, for whatever reason, informative, sensationalism, or just pure sexual. These queues should have deterred us from even trying to enter the cinema illegally. Bearing in mind my earlier comments, we should have "nit it", but after walking all the way from " The Brook" we decided that on this occasion it wouldn't deter us. So we weighed the situation up. There was only one exit, besides the main foyer in Lozells Road, so we had to gain an entrance there somehow. We had another problem too. Due to the popularity of this film it meant the staff would fill the cinema before the show started, and once full they would allow no one else in, even if someone left the cinema before the film had finished, which they did on occasions, due to the daring and outspoken script, which in those days, and if you were of a nervous disposition, could cause you to leave. So the problem was that we had to gain entrance before the queue waiting outside entered, because naturally after they did there would be no vacant seats. In the normal way when the run-of-the-mill film was showing you could of course enter the cinema whenever you desired, and then you would stay until you reached the point were you had entered, or in some cases you would see the film right through to the end and then leave. But with this new film they adopted a different routine. Knowing that no one would be emerging from the exit in Wilton Street, well it was highly unlikely anyway, and we could not sneak in through the front main foyer, we decided we would have to make a forcible entrance at that exit. We weighed the situation up and finally decided that our only access was over the roof at this exit, which entailed us shinning up a drain pipe on the right hand side of these doors. Once on the roof, one of those flat tarpaulin affairs, we should have to investigate further on the possibility of gaining entrance from up there. We shinned up the drain pipe and when we had all reached the top, we looked around to check our bearings and for an easy access. After a few minutes Frankie Anderton spotted an open skylight. We all moved towards it and to our delight found it was the ventilator of "The Gents". All we had to do was drop down and we were in!

The first lad cocked his leg over the sill in readiness for his drop. That was as far as we got, and as it proved later on was lucky for us, because suddenly a uniformed figure appeared, a bit premature, for if he had waited a moment until we had all dropped down there would have been no escape for us, but on the other hand he must have been cocksure that he had us. He looked up from his position below and said "Right ya little sods, o' gottcha an' yo carn' gerraway". That's what he thought, for kids who are suddenly frightened don't wait around. They act, and act we did quickly. We all ran swiftly back across the flat roof to the edge leading into the passage some ten foot below, but we didn't stop to shin down the drain pipe, as we did on the ascent. This time we all jumped, not bothering about the drop, due to us being frightened of the bloke "coppin' us". Some of us fell, others landed alright, but we were *all* on our feet and half way up the passage before the exit doors burst open under the thrust of the irate doorman. He shouted for us to stop. He really had to be bloody joking! We reached the top of the passage and turned left into Wilton Street. A good job we did too, for had we turned right we would have bumped straight into the arms of another doorman who was running up Wilton Street to intercept us, presumably at the top of the passage. Possibly due to his stature (he was on the plump side) and "The ale an' fags" he wasn't as quick as he thought he might be. The sight of this second doorman and the run of luck we'd had so far spurted us to greater effort. We shot off up Wilton Street with extra zeal, leaving the two doormen in our wake.

We turned right into Gower Street and at the top turned left into Berners Street. Down there we went and didn't stop until we turned right into Clifford Street. Once in Clifford Street we stopped to get our breath back. Then in sheer relief of not getting caught we all had a fit of the giggles, which continued until we got into Burbury Street, where we started to weigh up what went wrong. We all agreed by the time we had reached Defford Road that "Some rotton sod 'ad sin us gerrin' on the roof" and told the doorman at the front of the cinema. I mean, one doorman catching us in the "lavie" was one thing, that was bad luck on our part, but to have another doorman coming up Wilton Street was a different kettle of fish altogether and must have been planned. Mind you, we had a bit of a titter again when we thought of the first doorman being so confident he had got us, knowing his pal was coming the other way to trap us. We thought of all the things he might have had to say to the second doorman and could not visualise any of them as being complimentary. 'Serves them both right' we thought. All was not lost though, for we all got into *The Palladium* and saw the Errol Flynn and, I think, Maureen O'Hara in *Robin Hood and his Merry Men*. 'Sod the Lozells' we thought, 'we'll stick to *The Palladium* in the future.

Bonfire Night was just one night in the year, and kids today probably enjoy it as much as we did then. Looking around you can't help but feel that these days things are a little too organised. Bonfire parties at clubs, pubs, parks and leisure centres, all possibly calling for admission charges. I realise that people are a little more safety conscious these days *maybe* but again it is debatable.

Weeks before the fifth, one of the neighbours would see Bill Lewis and tell him we were having a bonfire in between his scrap yard and the back garden walls of the houses in New John Street West. The Onions, Gilberts, Coopers and Bedfords, residents in these houses having already given their permission, Bill apparently always agreed. Us kids would set to and scrounge round for material for the bonfire. Shakeshafts on The Brook and Kirbys in Hunters Road, for old wooden or cardboard boxes. Crowder and Brown in South Road, or Mists in Hampstead Road for any old motor car tyres. Sid Webb or Wally Colley in Guest Street for any old sacks or rubbish they might want to get rid of. We would drag, carry, push or pull these items back to Johnnie Kingham's opening and stack them right at the end, because we did not want this bonfire material to prevent Mr. Gilbert getting his three wheeled Morgan into his garage. There was a garage at the top of the opening, but the Bedfords "'adn't gorra car, they 'adn't even gorra bike, so it dain' marra, anyway Mr. Bedford was a real gent."

When the big night arrived us kids would gather up the opening and watch as Messrs. Moseley, Kingham, Harbridge, and a few more men, gathered the material we had collected and stacked it in a big pyramid in the centre of the opening. "Our Dad" couldn't come "cus 'e wus on nights all the time, worn't 'e?" On completion of this, one of the men would fetch a can with something in it (petrol) and splash this around the base of the pyramid. Then he would get some rag, twist it into a long line and put one end of this rag into the material. The other end he ran along the dirt floor away from the pyramid. He then poured the "something" over this and instructed everyone to stand back, especially us kids. He made sure we all stood well back and when he saw all of us were outside the perimeter of the fire, he struck a match and lit the crude fuse. In a very short time the fire would be burning away merrily, with crackles, pops, and bangs, as fresh material caught light, other material burnt out, or more material was added, each time sending glowing orange, yellow, red, violet and blue sparks shooting upwards into the cold dark night.

When the fire really got going some of the wives of the men would arrive with a load of potatoes already scrubbed and dried, which they would place around the fire to bake. Then one of the men, normally Mr. Harbridge, would arrive with a big box of fireworks which he handed out to all the men present. Us kids were *never* allowed to handle them and we certainly could not buy any, even if we had any money, which we hadn't, because the shopkeepers wouldn't sell them to you. Oh! what a beautiful sight when the men let the fireworks off. Catherine wheels, rockets, jumping jacks, bangers, wheezers, and sparklers. It was pure magic for us lot, you might say it was one of the bright spots of our little lives. Sometimes, contrary to what I have just said, we might be given a sparkler to hold, but only under strict supervision by one of the men.

" 'ere ya' are son, get this down yar 'odge", one of the ladies would say and she would put a "tata" and a piece of bread into your hand, "Tar Ma'am" you'd say, then start juggling the red hot potato from one hand to the other until it was sufficiently cool to handle. Then you took a bite, first the "tata" then the bread, savouring every morsel. God, you would think you have never eaten before. It was all so wonderful; the warmth of the roaring fire, the fireworks setting the deep blue-black sky alight, the feeling of a full belly, perhaps overful if the ladies came round with seconds, the laughter and joviality between the men, women and children. This continued until the material for the fire ran out and consequently the fire would ebb, until just the glowing embers remained. We moved closer to look at the pictures in the glowing remains, wishing it would start all over again. Us kids would be shooed off home, if some of the older kids or wenches hadn't already called for us, moving, always slowly, trying to witness the fire completely dying, but always unsuccessful. One of the men would make sure that the remaining embers were safely put out, then all the men would retire to *The Guest* or *The Vic* for a drink, with some of the women going as well.

I went to sleep content on these nights.

In the winter, when it snowed, the caretaker at our school, Farm Street Junior, would let us stay in the playground for a short while after lessons had finished, playing on the slides we had made during the day. Naturally we had a lot of fun and it also stopped us making slides in the streets, which was of course always a potential danger to old people.

Sometimes I would be in Jackie Thornton's house in the evening. It was situated at the rear of the house on the corner of Little King Street, next door to Bernard Osbornes. "Jackie wus a great drawer 'e wus, an' sometimes 'e'd show me 'is bestist drawin' book, w'er 'e kep' all 'is best drawin's that' 'e'd done, an' they wus great, an' I wished with all me 'eart that I'd be able ta draw like w'at Jackie Thornton did". On occasions during these visits, Ivy, Jackie's sister, would be making herself up waiting for her current boyfriend to arrive. I was fascinated whilst she applied mascara, rouge, lipstick, pencilled her eyebrows, and finally applied her face powder and scent. God, she smelt beautiful. I used to reflect at what a waste all these cosmetics were, for in my opinion, and a child's opinion at that, she was beautiful before she started putting it on, women, huh! Her boyfriend arrived and off they went dancing, or to the pictures. I think they went to *The Palaise de Dance* a lot, on the corner of Monument Road and Ingelby Street, for it was very popular at this period. "I dain't fall in love with Ivy though, cus of all that stuff she purron 'er ferce."

When the summer came, and naturally the light nights with it, "Our Mom" usta lerrus stay out extra, which I thought wus good on 'er, and the days seemed to go on forever, in constant sunshine for "us kids. Sometimes we'd gu up the cut by "The Looney bin" in Lodge Road, forra swim, if we 'adn't got the 'a'penny' ta gurra Northwood Street Baths."

About eight of us went one hot summer night down to the tow path by "The Nurses Home". Amongst these eight was Gordon Hipkiss who lived in Farm Street, near to Jimmy McDonald by *The Benyon*. We took our clothes off and placed them up against the wall, along with some bits of rag to dry ourselves on and then jumped in. It was lovely and cool after the long trudge from "The Brook". We were enjoying ourselves splashing about when Gordon announced that "'e wus gunna 'ave a dive orf the bridge". This bridge being a low iron structure spanning the canal, we all naturally stopped to watch, "cus none on us could dive" at that time. He poised momentarily on the bridge, "like Tarzan 'e wu," and then suddenly he went," 'ead fust" into the canal, with arms and legs all over the place. Needless to say we were not very impressed with his diving ability and shouted our comments to one another with our usual Hockley etiquette. When Gordon emerged from the water expecting praise for his diving prowess, we were all dumbstruck with what we saw. We just stared at him and no word was said.

"Wasamarra with yo' bloody lot, 'ave ya' lost ya' tongues or summat" he said, "yo've gone bloody quiet, I'll ask yarragen, wasamarra?" We approached him to get a closer look and one of us said, "ave a look at yaself in the cut Gord, ya' do look a soddin' sight". He peered at his reflection in the water and exploded "O-h-h-h, bloody 'ell warram I gunna do?" "Don' wory Gord we'll gerrit orf ya."

Poor old Gordon, there was oil all over him. He must have gone into a slick which had been discharged by some factory. We set to and used all our rags, meant for drying us, until eventually he looked a little more presentable for the walk home, for by this time we had lost all desire to re-enter the cut. The rest of us had to get some reeds and grass to dry ourselves off with. We all agreed though, on the walk back home that "Gordon was sure a slick fella."

When we could afford the 'a'penny, we liked to go to Northwood Street to swim. It was a real old fashioned building just off Livery Street; it looked more like an oversized lavatory with all its tiling. The pool itself was very small, with three diving boards, but due to the smallness of the pool they were not at all high. Alongside the pool on either side were the changing cubicles.

When we did go swimming there I always had to borrow a "cossy", because I did not own one myself, but if I couldn't borrow one off my mates, I had to find another 'a'penny for a Birmingham Corporation Baths Department slip. This slip was something between a "babbies nappie" or "a wenche's rain 'at". It consisted of two triangles of rough material sewn together at the crutch with white tape, which you had to tie at the sides. The colour was two shades of blue, both "manky", with the words BIRMINGHAM CORPORATION BATHS DEPARTMENT printed on them. I suppose this was an effort on the Corporation's part to prevent them from being "knackered". They needn't have bothered, they weren't worth "knackerin'". In fact I don't think they could have given them away if they had tried. The sizes of these "babbie's nappies" were big, bigger, and bloody enormous. When I did have to hire one, which was more often than not, I could pull the side tapes around me fully, sometimes twice, and still tie them in the front, instead of at the side where they were supposed to be tied. Once you had been in the pool with one of these monstrosities on, then the fun really started. Once they were wet they would continually come adrift from the bather and you had to straighten them up rather sharpish or otherwise it would be "fronts bare all the way." Sometimes they would come adrift altogether and there was a mad scramble to retrieve them and put them back on, much to the amusement of the other bathers. On one occasion for me, when I had learnt the art of diving, I went off the board when I hit the water the slip came off. It floated merrily on top of the pool and the bathers in the near vicinity roared with laughter at my downfall. I mean downfall literally, but being a nipper "it dain't bother me none; what's different about one winkle or another?" I just went back, retrieved it and put it on.

Even at the swimming baths our mob had to work a fiddle. The routine the attendants were instructed to work was half hour sessions in the evening, but during the day, with the exception of school holidays, they weren't too particular. How they ran the system was that cubicles one side of the pool would be for the bathers coming in for their half an hour, whilst the other side would be for the bathers getting dried and dressed after having had their half an hour. What our mob did was two of us would go in, have the half an hour, then when the attendant blew his whistle to indicate the half hour was up they would go to their cubicle on the pretence of drying themselves; all they really did was to dry their hands and gather up their clothes.

Then they waited for the incoming bathers, which naturally included some more of the mob. They noted which cubicle they went into and kept an eye open for when the attendant wasn't looking. This was often, because he was kept busy having to receive hired towels and slips off the outgoing bathers, take tickets from incoming bathers, and make sure everyone was out of the water after blowing his whistle. He hadn't a minute to look around.

We grabbed our clothes, nipped smartly across to the other side of the pool and threw them into our incoming mates' cubicle. At the end of the session all it meant was there were four of us in the cubicle to change instead of two. When we went out the attendant wouldn't know, "Cus 'e on'y counted 'em cumin' in, not guin' out didn't 'e?" To sum up this caper, you might say "Us kids, although we weren't very old, were in the swim longer than anyone!

Earlier in this story I remarked on the kindness and understanding some people had for us kids in those days, as people do in all generations. I've had no doubts about that. This next event will explain this kindness and understanding to the full.

It started on a very hot summer day, late in the afternoon and went on into the late evening, whilst us kids were on "The Big 'oliday". I don't remember what had happened to most of my regular mates, Johnnie Kingham, Frankie Anderton, Donnie Harbridge, Dennis Clark and the others. I suppose they must have gone out for the day or something. Anyway the only mate available was Chubby Moseley. I never found out what his christian name was. He had instructions from 'is Mom to "look arter the babby, an' don' lerrim outa yo'er sight, cus if I 'ear yo 'ave I'll whale the bloody life outon ya". The "babby" was his younger brother David (I played football against David many years later when he was playing for a team called *Zodiac United* and I played for *Hockley Sports* in *The Festival* Sunday Morning League).

So there we were, not knowing what to do with ourselves, just messing around down Johnnie Kingham's opening. Chubby was allowed down there even when Johnnie was not available by the mere fact that the Moseley's lived next door to the Kinghams. I think what really started the events that followed was an old battered brown suitcase we saw through the locked wooden gates amongst the scrap metal in Bill Lewis's yard. We thought we would retrieve it and see whether it was good for anything. Chubby gave me a leg up to climb over the spiked iron railings, which were situated alongside the path leading to the rear of the Perrys, Harbridges, Cottons, Mitchells houses. I clambered over the scrap metal whilst Chubby and David, who was holding his big brother's hand, kept "dog" for anyone coming.

I arrived at the site where this suitcase lay and had a quick look. The result of this cursory investigation revealed a few holes in the case, the lock itself had no key, so that was useless, and the one catch was broken. Altogether it wasn't in too bad a condition, not for us kids it wasn't, but I couldn't see anyone turning up at "The Grand" (The Grand Hotel in Colmore Row) with it. I thought briefly whilst extracating it that we might be able to flog it "forra penny" which would enable us go to Northwood Street Baths. "Blimey, it wus just the day forrit, it wus bloody boilin'." But I soon dismissed that thought, "there worn't anybody we could flog it to, an' if they 'ad gorra penny, they'd already be in the baths themselves. I finally got the suitcase out and after many attempts I managed to throw it over the high wooden gates to the waiting Chubby. Then I started the return journey over the scrap metal the way I had come, finally jumping down onto the narrow path. We both gave the case a thorough examination, (well, we couldn't ask David could we? I mean, he wus too young, an' 'e worn't an expert like w'at me an' Chubbie wus, wus 'e?). Our final conclusion was, "It's a right load of bloody rubbish" and thought the best place for it was back in Bill Lewis's scrap yard. We didn't sling it back right away, we placed it by the wooden gates, whilst we had a think. After a "lot o' this thinkin' " we came to a final decision that we would go scrumping down Crick Lane, because by then we were all feeling peckish. Then we had a further brilliant idea, "well we thought it was, any road up". Why not take the suitcase with us, "knacker" a lot of apples, instead of just a few for us three, then bring them back to "The Brook" and flog them to anybody who wanted them, including our mates, who would presumably have returned from wherever they had been to by then.

Both of us brightened up at the prospect of this venture, and all of a sudden life had a new meaning to us, even though we had "got the babby to look arter". So off we set on our hopefully profitable venture, over "The Brook" and up Soho Hill until we reached Rose Hill Road, down there we went past the Girls' High School to the entrance to Crick Lane. We walked down the lane scouting for a tree low enough for us to gather our harvest in. The ones that were low enough had already been stripped of fruit (some greedy buggers 'ad bin there afoa us), the others that had fruit in abundance on their branches were too high for us to reach even by climbing. We gave this situation some thought and so not to be deterred we thought up a way of getting round it. We scrounged around for some sticks and then began throwing them upwards at the fruit, hoping it would dislodge the apples and knock them to the ground. All to no avail, for besides being very hot work throwing these sticks up, we'd never bring enough apples down this way to go into the business we had proposed. The final decision to push off from Crick Lane was not ours though, it came in the shape of a big red faced bloke and his rotton dog. "Hey you, you scruffy little buggers, clear orf, before I fetch a policeman to you", he said as he advanced towards us, and he didn't look very happy either. Perhaps it was something we had done. Whilst thinking this we were moving away fast! I think his dog was getting a little restless too, for he had started growling.

With me dragging the suitcase and Chubby dragging David we soon outpaced him. Off we went out of Crick Lane into Hampstead Road, where we decided to duck into Handsworth Park for a while, which we did. We wandered around the pool by the second set of tennis courts, the other set being situated up by Holly Road and Grove Lane. Up past the old church and churchyard, we carried on until we came across an opening in the railings, which had been erected to keep anyone from going into or falling into, the pool. Two of the iron bars of these railings were bent outwards and we squeezed through and tried our luck attempting to catch sticklebacks, but naturally they were too quick for us. After a while we heard "The Parkie" bawling something across from the other side of the pool, near the boathouse. Assuming he was bawling at us, for we could see no one else in the near vicinity, we retraced our steps back through the railings.

Off we went further round the pool, then turning right we moved on up to the railway bridge, staying there for a while, but as no trains came we carried on over the bridge into the field opposite and lay down in the grass to decide yet again what we were going to do. I tried to think where there was some other location that contained fruit trees. I lay sleepily in the hot afternoon sun, dreaming about this and that, when suddenly it came to me where there were a couple of trees, although on second thoughts the apples we "knackered" from up there the last time were "bloody terrible". They were sour. Then I had a third thought which told me I was "soddin' 'ungry" so they would have to do. The location of these trees was in a little lane that ran alongside the old pub which was now closed just below *The Endwood* public house. This lane ran from Hampstead Road opposite Handsworth old churchyard right down to the junction of Grosvenor Road and Wellington Road, and it was at this junction the apple trees were to be located. The left side of this lane, running from Hampstead Road, were fields that descended down to the London, Midland and Scottish Railway lines. On the right hand side were the rear gardens of the residents living in David Road, Hylda Road, and Maxwell Avenue, with a couple right at the bottom belonging to residents from Grosvenor Road. I discussed my thoughts with Chubby and he agreed whole heartedly that we should give these trees the benefit of a visit. So we got up from the grass, but instead of going directly to the lane, via Hampstead Road, we thought we would have a wander up Hinstock Road, then turn right and walk straight down Wellington Road to the junction with Grosvenor Road - well we had all the time in the world, didn't we? After playing around for a while, we continued on our quest for "summat ta eat".

Arriving at the top of Hinstock Road eventually, at the junction with Wellington Road, we happened to look left towards Oxhill Road direction and saw, a couple of hundred yards up on the right of Wellington Road, a lane running between these posh houses.

Chubby and I thought it was worth investigating, for anything would be better than the sour apples in Grosvenor Road. It was at that moment David decided to start "grizzling" and complaining he was feeling tired. So despite the warning from Chubby's Mom, we left him sat on the suitcase on the corner of Hinstock Road and Wellington Road whilst Chubby and I went off to investigate this "New Territory".

We went along Wellington Road cautiously and on reaching the lane we peeped round the corner of the wall. What we saw could hardly stop us from shouting out with joy, for there to our delight up on the left hand side of the lane was an abundance of apple trees all bearing big red fruit. With the upward gradient of this lane it would only necessitate Chubby getting up on my shoulders to pick as much fruit as we desired from the branches overhanging the lane. I said I would nip back for David and the suitcase, but Chubby looked back and saw that his brother was still there sitting on the suitcase quite content, so he said, "Nah, leave 'im be Ron, it'll be berra if we pick some apples an' then tek 'um to 'im an' purrem inta the case, then come back an' pick some mower". I agreed and said it was a great idea, but secretly wishing that "I'd thought on it". Anyway, as events turned out this inspiration of Chubby's saved our bacon later. So up the gradient of the lane we trudged, to the point where it levelled out. This revealed a slight set back, for we discoverd that the lane didn't go straight through to anywhere but ended where a garage was situated and beyond this garage was a high wire mesh construction containing a private tennis club with its only entrance situated in Handsworth Wood Road; the lane in fact was a dead end. We gave this some thought, because normally we liked to have an avenue of escape if we were in danger of being caught. But the apples hanging there on the trees proved too tempting and we decided to throw caution to the wind. Chubby and I set to like a couple of squirrels, plucking a few apples, then concealing them beneath our "Ganzies". Next we would creep cautiously back down the lane, shoot along Wellington Road to its junction with Hinstock Road and deposit our plunder into the suitcase, instructing David to keep the lid down and not to eat any until we said so.

Naturally the more we continued this mode of operation the less cautious we were, and of course, the inevitable happened. The suitcase was nearly full, and was honestly more than enough really for us to carry back to "The Brook", but we just had to have those extra few didn't we? Both of us raced back to the lane, running now to increase the production. Straight up the lane we went and on reaching the trees

Chubby got straight on to my shoulders to pick some more fruit. He had picked about three or four apples when we heard a deep stern voice announce, "Or right yo' young devils, an' w'at da ya think yo'me up to?" The few apples were dropped and Chubby practically fell off my shoulders, causing me to wobble and nearly lose my balance. On regaining some composure we turned slowly, to find "the biggest copper we 'ad ever sin, 'e must 'ave bin as 'igh as Lewis's in town, an' 'e blocked the 'ole of the lane". The sight of him made Chubby start to "grizzle" and with tears starting to well up in my eyes, I lost my voice for once in my life and couldn't answer. "Well yo' little devils, 'ave ya lost ya tongues, as well as ya senses, I ast a question an' I wan an answer, w'at are yo up to?" l thought to myself, even though I was frightened to death, " 'e must 'ave summat wrung with 'is eyes 'e must, anybody can see w'at we're up to, we're knackerin' some poor bloke's apples, that's w'at we're up to". But I didn't say anything naturally. I looked at the "copper". I knew Chubby was upset too for he was still "grizzlin' ", "so 'e worn't gunna say anythin', an' I wus older 'an 'im any road up". I was just about to answer when I saw for the first time this smartly dressed gentleman standing at the side slightly to the rear of this mountainous police officer. As I said, the copper was so big and us being so small it must have obliterated the gentleman from our view altogether. He had the kindest face, but I had learnt a long time ago that you can't judge peoples characters by their faces. Well, can you? But I must admit this gentleman did look extremely kind.

Was he really as kind as he looked? Afler all he must have fetched the policeman, why else would he be here? Anyway they weren't about to explain to me why they were here, were they, for it was they who wanted to know why us two were here. "I wun arsk yo' agen, w'at are yo' doing', an' let's 'ave it, let's 'ave an ansa, now". The deep voice of the 'copper' intruded into my thoughts, at this the tears fell copiously from my eyes as well as Chubby's and I stammered through my tears the first lie I could think of, as I hadn't had much time to think one up. "We dain't mean anythin' sir, 'onest we dain't, we wus jus' 'ungry, an' we saw the apples so we thought we'd tek a couple, tha's all, jus' a couple". Mind you, I was really scared because I knew I was lying, and they must have known as well, they must have watched Chubby and myself going to and fro to little David on the corner of Hinstock Road. This made me feel worse than ever, having fully committed myself to this lie, but I had to continue - "We're eva sa sorry, we wunt do it agen Sir, 'onest we wunt, please Sir, we wunt 'onest."

I had visions of the policeman taking us to the station and fetching "You-know-who", being locked up and then "guin' ta court in Corporashun Street in town, an' being' sent to reformatory". I was out of my mind with worry and it must have shown, because suddenly the gentleman stepped in front of the policeman and said in ever such a posh voice, "I think these lads have learnt their lesson officer, and I do not wish this matter to proceed any further. I apologise most sincerely for any inconvenience I might have caused you and will forward a letter to your superior with a full explanation of the matter. I thank you personally for your swift attendance". " A letta ta the stachun wunt be necess'ry Sir, if yo' ain't mekin a complaint agenst these kids, but thank ya' all the serm". "Well, it was only a couple of apples after all officer, hardly a world shattering crime would you say? So we'll forget all about it shall we?" "As yo' wish Sir, I'll see these two back ta the road, an' send 'em orf 'um. Yo' two say thank you to this gentleman, an' thank ya lucky stars it ain't somebody else, now gu on an' say thank you". We did as we were told and thanked the gentleman. Suddenly it came to me on listening to their conversation that they had not seen us running backwards and forwards to David with the other apples. They thought we had only 'knackered' what was on the floor in the grass. "Well goodnight Sir", said the officer. "Thank you once again officer." "Tha's a'right Sir, it's all part o' me werk." He then took Chubby and me by the collars and started to march us back down the lane, when a voice said, "What about these apples, it appears a pity to me to leave them here when they have been picked, and you did say you were hungry didn't you lads?" "Well, ansa the gentleman then ya' little devils, do ya want the apples, or dontcha?" "Yes Sir, an' thank ya' very much". I ran back and picked the apples up, then looked up into the gentleman's kind eyes and thanked him yet again. He replied, "That's alright my lad, you and your friend go and enjoy them, goodbye". His face was a picture of smiles. I returned to the policeman and he had apparently mellowed because he released his hold on Chubby's collar, then put his arms on our shoulders and gently ushered us back down the lane to Wellington Road.

My fears and troubles hadn't left me, for there was still David on the corner with the suitcase full of apples to contend with. "W'at if the copper sin 'im? worse still if 'e come with us down the road an' David shouted across to us?!

On reaching the bottom of the lane, the gentleman having disappeared into a gateway somewhere, the policeman gave us a good talking to and told us what would happen if we were caught doing anything wrong again. Then he asked us where we lived and I said, "We both live in Gues' Street Sir". "No", he replied, smiling for the first time, and looking quite nice, well, "forra coppa 'e looked quite nice anyway". "I mean where about da ya live, not w'at Street?" I said "In 'ockley by "The Brook" Sir". He smiled again and said, "Well, yo'ed berra gerrorf 'um 'an sharp, it's a lung way fer little 'uns like yo' ta 'ave ta gu, an' ya mothers'll be lookin' out fer ya', so tarrar then an' mind 'ow ya' gu". We said "Tarrar" to him and with a sigh of relief watched him march smartly up Wellington Road towards Oxhill Road and Grove Lane.

We dashed down to David, wiping our eyes and noses on our jersey sleeves as we went ("Well, we dain't want the babby to see we'd bin cryin' did we, it worn't on"). On reaching him we pushed him and the suitcase round the corner into Hinstock Road, opened the case and threw the few apples the gentleman had given us into it, shut it again, grabbed David and made off hastily to the entrance to Handsworth Park opposite Philip Victor Road. Once inside we veered off to the left across the field towards a line of trees and bushes which skirted it. Having attained the safety of these trees and bushes, and also getting over, slightly, our traumatic experience, we suddenly found we were still hungry. So open came the case and we dived into our plunder. For the next half hour we were busy "chobbling' our ill gotten gains, too busy to talk even, but after a while we were full, with the cores of the apples getting bigger as our bellies were getting fuller. We threw these cores into the undergrowth at the back of us. "Well, w'at shall we do now?" I said to Chubby, "we can't tek these apples back 'um' now can we, in case that copper siz us, an' if 'e duz, we'll really be in forrit". "O' dunno w'at we'm gunna do" said Chubby. "There's one thing we cun do Chub, leave 'em were they are, bloody case an' all, I don' wanna gurra reformat'ry do yo?" "Nah, are bloody don' " was Chubby's reply. So off we went, the three of us "back 'um ta the Brook" leaving a case full of surprise for some other kids if it were ever found.

I had a touch of diarrhoea again the next day and I think Chub did as well but that was nothing compared to what we might have had if that kind gentleman had not had compassion and love for the likes of us. I know I thanked him over and over again, until the torment of what might have happened gradually faded from my child's thoughts.

Yes, nights in Hockley in the Thirties, were good, because it was the people of Hockley in the Thirties who made them good.

CHAPTER TEN

"Out of Sadness comes Happiness, given Time"

MY DAD said to me on more than one occasion "We are put on this earth to serve a purpose, and when that purposc has been fulfilled the Good Lord will receive us back."

This was not an earth shattering statement and I believe the very simplicity of it has given me the strength and will to overcome certain trials and tribulations. For like "Our Dad" I have not been an ardent church goer, but I think in my own quiet, simple way, that I am and wish no harm to others including Gods creatures small and large; trying to help wherever possible is sufficient to guide one through the short time spent on this good earth. Utopia is real if you have a good clear conscience, because it is through this inner happiness and forgiveness that you will achieve it. Material things I agree are essential, they too bring happiness, but only for short periods I'm afraid, unless you achieve a contentment as well.

There are reasons for everything happening in life. Reasons for illness, death, hatred, happiness, which I'm afraid I haven't the ability to even try to explain, but I have hope and belief in what I do and I cherish these hopes and beliefs no matter how humble they appear. I mean, if you didn't have dark clouds how could you possibly appreciate the sunshine, or vice versa? Or if you frowned all the time you would think it strange if you met someone smiling. As much as we think it a good thing you cannot be liked by everyone all the time because you would not be able to distinguish anyone's real feeling would you? If I appear to be lecturing I assure you I am not, for I am not that clever. What I am doing is trying to explain how I feel about these events which took place in Hockley in the mid and late thirties.

I suppose on reflection the greatest heartbreaking tragedy in my young life was the fate of one of my dear schoolfriends Freddie Nicholls. Freddie was a tall, thin gangly lad, very quiet and inoffensive, again like my brother, quite the opposite to me. His complexion was always pale, in fact he looked as if he was continually ill, but I don't think he was. The face was small, with a crew cut hair style above, his features below almost screwed up, big blue eyes, a rather flat nose spreading a little, and below that a small mouth. He never did "dares" or "knackered" anything like the rest of us. He was, with the exception of a few of us, very much a loner. He lived in a back house on the left hand side of Little King Street, going from the Guest Street direction, just before Mrs. Cross's little shop. Being older than me he naturally left school earlier and I was surprised when I found out he had taken a job with a builder, whose yard was in Hampstead Road, because of his stature, gentle, nature etc. I must admit like all events in life, when it comes to parting for whatever reason, you make a lot of promises to continue to see one another, but for obvious reasons which are the normal running of your life, these promises do tend to wane, although not intentionally.

It was quite a shock when sometime affer he had started work I read the story in *The Birmingham Mail*. Of course by this time I had leff school at the age of fourteen and commenced work at Rowlands Bakery in New John Street, Aston, as a roundsman's mate.

According to the newspaper, Freddie's older workmates had made it a habit to give their racing bets to him to convey to the bookmaker. In those days it was illegal to gamble, so what you did was write your bets out on a piece of paper, then sign it with whatever code you and the bookmaker agreed upon, to protect your real name in the case of a raid by the police. You then put your money inside this paper, wrapped it up and gave it to one of the numerous touts or runners the bookmaker employed.

The Birmingham Mail continued with the events surrounding Freddie's tragedy. They stated he had continued taking these bets for the older staff, but that Freddie must have sometimes opened the paper containing the stake money, which would only amount to tuppence or thre'pence at the maximum, throw the paper away and spend the few pence. It is a thing my mates and I would have got up to, but unfortunately this lad was so meek and gentle he would not have known what action to adopt if he was caught. The newspaper went on to explain this. Apparently one of the men had a win, which mounted to roughly "four bob", but unfortunately Freddie had on that occasion taken and spent the money. Now if it had been any one of us lot, we would have owned up, or made up some ludicrous story such as "O'm sorry, but O dropped it down the suff 'ore, but O dain't like ta tell ya' " and then apologise profusely and offer to pay it back "a bit ev'ry wick". Evidently Freddie must have kept quiet and brooded all that night. The next morning when his workmates turned up for work at the small builders' yard they found Freddie hanging from some wooden beams. I do not know the exact circumstances as to how the suicide was linked with Freddie taking the money, but I should imagine he had confided in someone, or written a note. Of course there was an inquest and they recorded the verdict of "Death by Misadventure". It upset me considerably over the next few weeks, thinking how a life could be terminated over such a trivial thing.

I remember I used to take Mrs. Mitchell's bets along to George Davis's in Little King Street, by Cooper's the Felt Works, every dinner time when I came home from school. Mrs. Mitchell, what a nice lady, a manish type face, pale complexion, her mousy coloured hair swept upwards from the back of her neck, and then fashioned on the top, held in position by several large combs. The nose narrow but slightly flared at the nostrils, and above, two big blue eyes. Her mouth was generous, but gentle. She would always be dressed in a long black dress, covering her from high at the neck to below the ankles, where you would find a pair of highly polished boots peeping out. At the neck of the black dress would be a cameo encircled by a gold frame. Mrs Mitchell would give me a penny to run the bet to George Davis's every dinner time, and naturally I had to give "Our Mom" a 'a'penny of this, I spent the other 'a'penny on a Pegs Bar at the dairy shop by Pat Wagstaffes on the right hand side of Little King Street. Only once did "You-know-who" forget to ask me for the 'a'penny and I kept it in my pocket for a few days, just in case she did. Anyway I thought to myself "Ah bet the ol' gel's fergorrit" so I had two Pegs Bars instead of the usual one on that day. What a mistake! "Warrave yo' done with the 'a'penny yo' dain't gimme on (and she mentioned the exact day)"? "O dunno Mom, 'onest O thought I'd gid it ya". "Well yo' bloody think agen, ya twistin' little bugger, so w'en yo gu ta Davis's tomorra for Mrs. Mitchell, yo' cun bring the bloody 'ole penny 'um ta me, cus if yo' gerrup to any o' ya bleedin' tricks, an' yo' don't bring it 'um ta me, yo'll 'ave the biggest bleedin' w'alin' of yo'er life, d' yo' un'erstan' me". "Are oright Mom" I said, but I thought, "Ya rotton twistin' mean sod" and I kicked the door in mental protest on my way out to school, but all that did was to give me a pain in my toes for the rest of the afternoon.

Then there was the Rosebridge Bungalow business. This bungalow was situated alongside the top playground of Farm Street Junior School in Bridge Street West and on the other side was a row of terraced houses running down to Farm Street. The second house from Rosebridge Bungalow was where Kenny Hughes, one of my mates lived.

The bungalow was not what you might imagine. It was not a building with bedrooms, lounge, bathroom etc. It was a miniature hall. I suppose the name was originated by its owner and naturally it was all on one level, so the name was appropriate. On entering the building you walked directly into the hall itself. At the far end facing you was a raised stage with a few stairs on the left hand side leading up to it.

On the stage itself, at least on the few occasions I attended was a piano and a full kit of Premier drums. I had a bash on them one night, but got bo-o-o-ed off the stage - I was "bloody hopeless". To the right of the stage was a further set of stairs, this time descending to a small room, which I presume would serve as a changing room if a play, or whatever was put on. It served as a type of café when I went, serving tea, coffee, cakes, sandwiches etc. The owner of this place was a man known only as Bunny and I must admit, to all intent and purposes, he appeared a good man because he threw this Rosebridge Bungalow open to any youngsters who cared to attend. You could dance, if someone played the piano, or piano and drums, there was table tennis and various other games available, or you could just go and have a natter and some refreshments. Like I said I personally only went on a few occasions so my knowledge of the complete activities is limited, but I certainly enjoyed myself when I went, and Bunny was quite a nice, quiet, well spoken, likeable man. How wrong can you be!

It all blew up one day when one of the lads, naturally I will not divulge his name, gave some information to his mother about the other side of Bunnys character. His mother contacted the police and full enquiry was made, resulting in Bunny being sent to prison for interfering immorally with boys. It certainly was a shock to an awful lot of people that this man could have done such a thing.

I remember an incident which concerned me directly, with a man who lived in Ventnor Road. He was a small but plump man. Rather good looking really, with dark hair, brown sparkling eyes, a broad nose, a small mouth, with beautiful white teeth. His complexion was a deep tan, due I suppose to him working outside, and being dark he always had a dark shadow round his face, although he was clean shaven and immaculate. He worked for "Thomas Shaw" the Dairyman whose dairy was situated in Burbury Street at the back of some houses on the left hand side, halfway between Graham Street and Wills Street. I asked him if I could help with the deliveries one dinner time when school finished at twelve o'clock, and he replied "Yes, of course yo' cun son", so I jumped onto his float, with a beautiful small black pony drawing it, and after explaining to him that I had to be back at school for two o'clock, we set off. After a few deliveries which brought us to Claremont Road, I felt his hand on my bottom. So I said 'Watcha doin' that fer" and he said "I'll ge ya tuppence if yo'll let me put me 'and down yer trousis". I turned on the float and gave him a boot in the leg which nearly knocked him off the float. I jumped off immediately and shouted to him as the float moved away from me, 'Ya dirty ol' sod, um gunna tell me Mom about yo' ", then I ran back down to "The Brook" and home. I didn't tell "Our Mom" because I was really frightened and ignorant as to what the man wanted to do, I was also ashamed to tell Mom in case she got mad and gave me a w'alin'.

It is a terrible thing when youngsters are exposed to this type of person and atmosphere. I realise now that a person with these abnormalities has, to a slight degree, to be pitied, but it is no comfort to the parents of these children that are molested in this way, and it could be a life long nightmare to the children themselves. Also it could change and ruin their lives. I do not think that even today the medical or legal ruling bodies of this country have secured an answer to this continuing problem. If we are to believe the statistics of the present day media it has become more acute, or were these problems hushed up in earlier years?

Romance. The dictionaries tell us the meaning of the word is "fanciful story, a love affair" and how true this is. Young or old, healthy or poorly, human or animal, we all have romances, don't we? Like everyone else I suffered the pains of romance right from the age of about six or seven, when I was deeply in love with Olive Shellis who lived in Villa Street, and Joan Hardy whose father had the off licence on "The Brook". Yes I was deeply in love on and off right up to the day I met my wife Edythe in January 1947, when the real love of my life came into being. We married on the third of September 1949 at Bishop Latimer's Church, situated on the corner of Beeton Road and Handsworth New Road.

I loved her the first time I saw her, and I love her more each day I am with her. We often have a laugh and reminisce on our past romances, wondering what type of life we would be leading now if fate had led us different ways. But I'm glad it didn't, because we are both still very much in love with one another and God cannot give a man more happiness than that.

Jean Harvey lived in Nursery Road. The hours I must have spent just trying to catch a glimpse of her. When I had my new bike I used to ride around in the vicinity of the buses parked in Gordon Street, by Burbury Recreation Park at the beginning of the war, for that's where us kids would hang around sometimes. Playing on these buses, running upstairs, ringing the bells, until the watchman came round and cleared us all away. The first meeting when we said 'ello" shyly with our respective friends tittering to themselves, and then finally at a later date, after many messages passing to and fro via friends, we met alone! I blushed as well as she did, not knowing what to say. I was eleven at the time and she was thirteen. Eventually we went upstairs on one of the buses and chatted quietly, getting used to one another. Suddenly we kissed! Oh God, it was beautiful! Just one kiss and then she had to go home. My heart was full of joy as I rode home that night and although I eventually dropped off to sleep I was restless.

I went round those buses for hours over the next few weeks, but I never saw her again. I was heartbroken, it couldn't have been that she didn't love me too, because we had kissed.

Joan Hardy - I fell in love with Joan when I was about seven, but she didn't know it, I worshipped her from a distance. Well, I couldn't very well tell her my thoughts for she was too posh for me. " 'er Dad 'ad gorran outdoor on "The Brook", an' there wuz on'y 'er an' 'er young brother Alfie in the fam'ly worn't tha, but just look aroun' our tribe, ten on us. Nah, she wouldn't gi me a secon' look, she wouldn't". I would go to the outdoor for "Our Dad" to fetch his two or three pints of draught "Ansells Mild" in the bottles provided by Dad. Off I went clutching the ninepence tightly in my hand, hoping against hope that Joan would come into the shop whilst her mother or Father were serving me. I can see them now, Mrs. Hardy a beautiful woman, quietly spoken, and gentle, always dressed elegantly. Mr. Hardy was a big man, immaculate in dress and appearance. He would dip the sticky labels into the overflow of beer in the tray and then adhere them over the stoppers to keep within the law of that time when serving draught ale to minors, for naturally you had to break this paper seal if you wanted a swig. Equally naturally "us kids" got around this restriction! Sometimes I did get a glance of Joan and she would smile. What that smile did for me she will never know, or perhaps she might have, I probably will never know! I was also in love with Elsie Guest who lived in Tower Street by Cresswells and Lena Palmer out of Cowper Street by Holts the Dairyman. What a lover I have been; well, in my imagination anyway.

"I think Nunky Collins loved Renee Barnes as well, cuz w'en we went ta 'amstead Colliery one arternoon with 'im an' Julie Barnes, 'oo l think wuz some sorta relashun of Renee's, an' some other kids as well, they went orf somewhere together, arter we'd bin playin' some games forra bit, an' w'en we went to folla, they tol' us ta bugger orf cus they wanned ta gu somw'ere on their own. I think they wuz gunna play another game, an' they dain't wan any on us with 'em, an' also they wuz older 'an us, any road up, an' we might a gorra back 'ander if we played up."

The rest of us lay down in the grass and watched the big metal tubs full of waste from the colliery going across Hampstead Road on cables suspended by pylons, dropping their load on to a mountain of waste and then returning to the colliery empty. "Arter a w'ile Nunky an' Renee came back to us, an' Nunk wuz all red like, an' sweatin'. 'e must 'ave bin runnin' or summat in the game 'e'd bin playin' with Renee. She must 'ave liked the game they'd bin playin' as well cus she wuz smilin' an' eve sa nice, an' she said she an' Nunk wuz gunna tek us to the bluebell woods, which they did an' we all 'ad a smashin' time, until we had ta gu 'um ta "The Brook" agen.

Then there was another type of love. The love of something given to you, sometimes a pet dog or cat. The Smiths always had an abundance of these at two back of twenty-four and two two eight. I must admit that the latter address we seemed to extend our range of animals due to the fact we acquired quite a long, but narrow garden. "Our Dad" took advantage of this by obtaining some hens. and a couple of cockrells. I think he did moderately well with them, and what with the two cats and a dog, we weren't so much a family, we were more a pet shop.

One love of my life I will never forget was the day I received my first brand new cycle. I remember it was a Saturday when "Our Dad" fetched it from Len Waterhouse's shop; not the one situated by Higgs the Tabbacconist on "The Brook", it was from this other shop on the corner of Whitmore Street and Heaton Street opposite Rabones factory, I had been saving as hard as I could from my fifty per cent of the money I earned from helping Arthur Crump, the Marsden's milkman, and delivering papers nightly and Sunday mornings for Mr. Phelps, giving most of it to "Our Dad" until one day he said, "Yo ain't gorrinuff money served yet son, but yo've bin so good, an' the cost o' the bikes gunna be five guineas, burr I'll put the rest onit, an' yo cun pay me back a bit each wick a' right? - an' I'll gu an 'getcha bike on Saturday arternoon fer yo', 'ow's that do ya' a?" "Ta dad eva so much, I'll pay ya' back 'onest I will, I promise". "I know yo' will son, now don't yo' worry about it, yo' pay me back w'en yo' cue."

I really meant what I had said, but I don't think I ever did pay dad back, not because I didn't want to pay him back, but he said to me, "I think yo've paid me enuff now little 'un, yo've earnt ya' bike now so gu on an' enjoy it". Dad never said an awful lot, but I think he used to notice things and bear them in mind. In all probability he had noticed all the jobs I was doing and the money I was putting by in my little black box amongst my toy motor cars and lorries (all paid for by me) in the attic. He knew how I had yearned for a new bike, simply because I was always nattering on about it to anyone who would listen. On the Saturday dad was going to fetch it for me, I couldn't wait for Arthur and me to finish the bread round. When we did, I was practically pushing the electric van in my mind, to make it go a little faster on its journey from Alum Rock back to "The Brook". When at last we arrived at two two eight Arthur gave me my ninepence and I said "Tarrar, I'll see ya' next wick, and then I rushed up the entry to home, "I gid "Our Mom" 'er 'alf o' me money, but I'd on'y got pennies, so I gid 'er fivepunce, an' she gid me an 'a'penny change" and then I stood waiting. "Yo'd berra 'ave summat ta eat an' a cuppa tea quick afoa yo' gu on ya' perper roun' "said "Our Mom". "Ar oright Mom ar' will, tar" I replied, but I wasn't feeling hungry due to my excitement. I must have looked subdued as I stood at the table for my tea, because dad, who was up by then getting ready to go to The Turk said, "Dain't yo' see anythin' unusual in the 'all w'en yo' cum in Ron?" "Nah, o' dain't see anythin' Dad cus it's too dark in thaya". The hall which was facing the door from the entry was always in darkness, simply because there wasn't a gas lamp in there to light it. "Well we'd berra gu an' 'ave a look then 'adn't we, cus if there is anythin' there we don' wannit ta fall down the bogey 'ole do we?" "O-o-o-o no dad we don' wan' that ta 'appen". So dad went first and opened the door to the entry to throw some light into the hall. Then he went down this short hall where piles of coats of all descriptions were hung in the darkness. He was moving this and then moving that, when suddenly he said "Well, I don' remember this bein' 'ere this mornin' w'en I cum 'um from werk, I'll 'ave ta gerrit inta the entry an' see warrit is wun I Ron?" "Ar' dad" I replied, hardly being able to control my excitement. I knew he was teasing me, but I went into the entry whilst he manoeuvred "the mystery" from the dingy hall. When dad finally extricated it he backed it into the enclosed dark entry, then brought it forward and propped it against the whitewashed wall, a shaft of sunlight seeping through the open door at the end of the entry fell on my brand new cycle.

I just stared at it, I couldn't believe it was mine, it was so beautiful.

The name on the badge situated above the front forks proclaimed it was a Kingsway Cycle, but undeneath in smaller print was written The Hercules Cycle Company Limited, Rocky Lane, Aston, Birmingham 6. I touched the cycle gently, running my hands over the shiny metal, then opened the leather pouch attached to the rear of the saddle, just to make sure my tool kit was in there. Then I detached the pump to make sure it worked, and dad said, "It's oright Ron I've already put the right pressure in ya' tyres", thinking I was going to blow them up. "Nah I worn't gunna purreny airin dad, I wus jus' checkin' to see that the pump werked, tha's all". I stood back again admiring the bike, and then I asked dad "Can I keep me bike in the 'all please dad?" "Are as lung as yo' keep it clean, or else yo'll 'ave ya' Motha arta ya' " he replied. Then I continued, "Dad, cun ar tek it on me perper roun' ternight please?" "Look son" he said "it's yower bike an' yo' cun do w'at ya' like with it, but look arta it alwis, an' now we've done enough talkin' let's see if yo' cun ride it, cum on now." I pushed my new bike up the entry, down the three steps into the street and propped it in the gutter whilst I got aboard. It was great. Down went my foot on the right peddle to get me started and off I went, across Guest Street, past Barr Street and up to the island situated in front of *The White Horse* at the junction of Unett Street. I went round the slabbed island with its silver painted gas light in the middle and returned to "Our 'ouse" where dad was waiting for me. " 'ow wus it son, is it oright?" "Ar' it's lovely dad, are luv it". "Well yo'd berra cum an' 'ave ya' tea afower ya' gu an' do ya' perpers, else yo'll 'ave yo'-know-'ho arta ya' ". "Ar' oright dad, an' thanks". I scurried into the house taking my prized possession with me.

I used that cycle for years, even after I was demobbed from the Royal Navy in 1947. Of course I bought new items for it, a Miller dynamo set, a mileometer, a carrier and large saddle bag, mud flaps, even an extra battery powered front lamp in excess to the one attached to the dynamo, which I bolted to the right front fork, but nothing compared to that first Saturday my "Dad" presented me with it. I shall never forget that moment for as long as I live.

Whilst on the subject of money, with me putting my percentage in my little black box in the attic, brings out a very sad experience. Well, it was to a little chap like me at the time, although I do understand the situation a little better now than I did then, but I still do not condone fully what happened.

I had received a ten shilling note off Harold Allen the Bradford's roundsman I helped, but of course I had to give five bob of that to "Our Mom". She was reluctant to return my two half crowns at the time, after I had handed over this note to her, saying she would save it for me. "Burr I dain't fall fer that one, cus 'a'pennys an' pennies 'ad gone astray befowa, w'en she wus savin' 'em fer me", so I said "I'll serve it meself Mom ta", and after much grumbling she handed the two coins over to me. Since that Saturday after having a ten shilling note in my hand, I knew I had to have another, but this time one of my own not to be shared. So I strived towards this with a burning desire.

There were set backs, but of my own making, for I had one weakness I could not resist; cars. lorries, buses etc., toy ones that is. So I would get my savings up to, say seven and sixpence, then I would see some toy vehicle which caught my eye and up into the attic I would go to get the money required for this item. Although I didn't know it, you-know-who was watching these forays of mine with great interest. After much stopping and starting I found to my delight on counting the contents of my box (the little black one in the attic) that I had gone over the magic ten shillings I required, I had *eleven* shillings and a few coppers. Now people seeing a "little un" like me producing a load of three penny bits, tanners, an' bobs' and asking them "ta gimme ten bob note in exchange please" would to my way of thinking be highly suspicious, so I had to think. I thought long and hard and eventually came up with the solution.

On my Sunday morning round I had a gentleman who lived in Wills Street who nearly always gave me a ten bob note, so I decided what I would do was to take the ten bob's worth of change from my little black box on Sunday morning before going down to Mr. Phelps on "The Brook" by Tippers, and put it into a separate pocket to the one I put the money for the papers into. When I arrived at the gentlemans' house, I would take the ten bob note (if he gave me one) from him, give him his change and afterwards just change my silver for the note. And that was exactly how it turned out. I put my ten bob note, into my separate pocket after I had delivered the papers to the gentleman and every so often after that I kept feeling in this pocket to see if my ten bob note was still there - meticulously folded. On completion of my round at the bottom of Villa Street I ran like mad back to "The Brook", paid in to Mr. Phelps, and he gave me my one and a tanner which I put in with the note. Then I went along Icknield Street to meet the Marsden's milkman. We completed his round and I left him as usual in Finch Road, after he had given me my tanner, which I deposited in my "sky rocket", which gave me a grand total of twelve bob in all, but out of that I'd gorra give "Our Mom" 'er wack' which amounted to a bob, so it left me with eleven bob altogether. As I ran down the whole length of Burbury Street home for my dinner, I felt like a millionaire.

On reaching home I went straight up to the attic, put my ten bob note flat in the bottom of my black box and put the rest of my money on top of it, with the exception of you-know-who's shilling. I looked at it longingly and with pride. I'd done it, "I'd gorra ten bob note of me own."

"Are yo' comin' down fer this dinner, it'll be burnt to a cinder" - "Our Mom' interrrupted my thought with a start. "Ar' arm cumin' Mom" I shouted back down, the stairs. "Well mek it bloody lively then, else I'll ge it to the bloody dog". I ran down the stairs to eat my dinner, being a ten bob note owner made one hungry.

I gave "the 'ole gel" her percentage of the Sunday morning earnings and she took it and placed it into her purse, with no thank you, but a look of suspicion on her face, which I totally ignored because I did not understand why. After I had obtained this note, it encouraged me to save even more. I thought twice about buying any more cars etc., in fact I became a bit of a miser. As I added cash to my little black box, I used to look at my pride of possession, the ten bob note. I had just over thirty-five bob in my box when the incident occured!

I quickly ascended the two flights of stairs to the attic, it was during the week when we were on holiday from school. I hadn't any further cash to add to my box (for it was usually Saturday and Sunday when I was paid for helping on the bread and milk rounds, and delivering newspapers, and I would deposit this money into the box), I just wanted to have a look at my ten bob note again.

On reaching the attic I went to the left under the skylight, where a kind of raised platform was situated, due to the contour of the building, on which I used to store all my toys, and of course my savings box. I raised the lid of the box cautiously, savouring every moment, as I had done on dozens of occasions before. I suppose I could have obtained a nice green pound note, or two more red ten bob notes with the amount of cash I had now amassed, but I didn't. This ten bob note was really special to me, a young lad, I had earned it, it hadn't been given to me, not even a part of it, so it is understandable that in my child's mind this ten bob note was like a shrine.

When I had fully raised the lid and peered into the box, I thought at first that the silver and copper coins that lay on top of the note, had through the movement of the box completely covered it, or maybe it was a trick of the light. In a panic I started pushing the loose coins about thinking maybe that somehow the note had got crumpled and pushed to one corner, but no, it was not there. I tipped all the money out on to the top of the shelf, after clearing a space amongst my toys, and proceeded to count it, thinking in my child's mind that someone had removed the note for some purpose and put the equivalent amount in silver and copper back into my box. But on completion of the count it revealed to me that this was not so, somebody had "knackered" my ten bob note. I searched all round my toys, looking inside each one individually, thinking and fervently hoping that someone was having a joke with me. I exhausted every avenue in an attempt to recover my lost precious ten bob note. Then I just stared at the bare wall, thinking of all the hours of work it had taken me to attain that money, delivering papers, milk, and bread in all kinds of weather, and now it was gone. First I felt a great pity for myself, followed by anger, wishing all kinds of things on the person that might have taken it. Then I tried to figure out how I could find out who had taken it, and why.

A little lad with so many things to try to sort out on his own inevitably led to complete frustration. Finally I broke down and cried, long and bitterly. At last I realised the situation was hopeless, so I put my little box in a different location, hoping this person would not find it again, but knowing full well in my mind that they would if they had found it in the first place. I had no option but to leave it there, I couldn't carry it around with me, or put it into our bedroom, for it would be more vulnerable to the thief. So with tears in my eyes I came back down the stairs, slowly this time, trying hard to believe that the situation was not true, that it was a dream, and I would wake up at any moment to the real life. I entered the middle room on arriving downstairs, a very dejected little lad with tears still falling down my cheeks.

"Wasamara with yo' snivelin' an' grizzlin', an' look at yer bloody ferce, it's as lung as Livery Street, w'at ya' bin up to yo' ain't bin fightin' agen 'ave ya'?" This command came from "Our Mom" sat in her chair the other side of the table, immediately in front of the window looking out onto the back yard and garden. The sunlight flooding in through the window made Mom's bulky jet black figure look like a solid shadow to anyone opposite her, as was my position at the time. You could not see her face, so expressions were obliterated. I was too upset to answer. "I said wasamara with yo', an' w'en I ask ya' summat, I wanna bloody answer, now wasamarra with ya', an' be soddin' quick about tellin' me?" "Nuthin'" I replied, "Nuthin' " she repeated, "Nuthin', then w'at ya' bloody grizzlin' at?" "Nuthin' Mom 'onist" I said again. "I'll ge yo' a nuthin' bloody back 'anda in a minnit if yo' don' tell me w'at's wrung" she said. The creak of the chair told me she was raising her bulk from it so "a bloody back 'anda" was inevitable if I didn't explain why I was crying. "Some rotton sod's knackered a ten bob note out o' me box in the attic" I blurted out, fresh tears streaming down my face, with this harsh reminder. "BANG!" "Our Mom's" hand caught me straight across the side of the head. It knocked me off balance and nearly onto the floor, which brought more tears, I couldn't understand why she had hit me. "Watcha do that fer Mom?" "I'll tell ya' w'at I did that fer ya' little bleeda, I did that cus yo' swore at me, an' if yo' gu on, I'll ge yarra notha one."

Of course many years later I realised that this sudden anger of mom's was not that I swore, although she would normally not tolerate that anyway, I think maybe it was her conscience pricking her at the events that were to follow, of which she was fully aware. After I had recovered a little, she said, "W'at's all this bloody who-har ova a ten bob note?" "Somebody's took it outa me box up in the attic, an' I bin savin' it fer a lung time", and of course I naturally started to cry again. Now I don't know what made mom make the next statement, but what I think is purely hypothetical. Either she must have thought I might possibly turn to dad and tell him and Dad knowing "Our Mom" better than anyone would probably start enquiring - for as I have said before she was always "knockin" somebody, and dad probably knew more than mom thought he did - or someone in the family might have known she had made the trip up to the attic, which due to mom's size and slightly limited mobility at that time, was a very rare thing for her to do, and the story might have seeped out that way. Anyway, as I have said it's purely hypothetical why she made the statement, but she did, and I never obtained the answer to this mystery.

"It's me w'at's 'ad ya' bleedin' ten bob note" she suddenly blurted out. This really shook me and certainly stopped the flood of tears. "An' afoa ya' start blahtin' agen, I ony borrad it, an' think yasel' lucky I dain't borra the bloody lot. I'll ge it ya' back as soon as I cun, a bit ev'ry wick, so yo' cun shurrup an' gerrourra me bleedin' sight, gu on sod orf, afoa I ge yarra notha bloody beltin'." "But yo' shouldna took it, it's mine" I was going to continue further, but another "clout" on the opposite side of my head stopped any further conversation on my part. "I'll ge yo' cheekin' me, ya' little bleeder, yo' wert till yer fertha get's up, 'e'll ear all about this don' yo' fear, an' then there'll be anotha whalin' fer ya!"

I received another couple of back handers off her and then she continued, "Gerrourra me bloody sight, ya' little bleeda, afoa I kill ya'." I didn't require any further physical persuasion to realise I was not wanted, so I ran out of the house and down to "The Brook". I sat on Bendalls step to think about the events that had taken place. The ten bob note had gone, there was *no* chance of "'er" paying me that back, so I wrote that off in my mind. The thought proved right on the following Saturday and Sunday, for she still demanded the two shillings out of the four shillings I received off Harold, the one and thre'pence out of the two and sixpence I received off Mr. Phelps for my nightly paper deliveries, and on the Sunday she demanded the shilling from the two shillings I had earned, one and sixpence from Mr. Phelps for the Sunday paper round, and a tanner for helping the Marsden's milkman. Never once did she say "'e yar, 'ere's summat orf worr I owe ya'."

One thing I never informed her about though was the tips some of the customers gave me on all these deliveries, which was quite a few pence. After this incident it wasn't likely I was going to change *that* system. Then I thought to myself, "if she's borrowed the ten bob, she will naturally 'ave knowledge of and certainly 'ave counted the rest of the money in my tin, after 'er laborious journey up the stairs". I had moved the money temporarily, but if she'd a mind, and she had, I knew for certain, she would soon find it, "an' knowin' 'er, the bloody lot ud gu, serm as the ten bob note". So I had to move it, and soon. Suddenly I had what I thought was the answer. I had a big metal box van with Carter Pattison signwritten on the side. It was *metal*, all of it, with just one exception and that was the rubber tyres. The doors the back of this toy van *locked*, and I'd placed the key inside the driver's cab, which was naturally sealed off from the rear compartment. I felt that locking these back doors when I played with the van wasn't really necessary, due to the fact that there was a locking bar in addition to the key lock. This bar dropped across the back of both doors and secured it equally as well, so here was the perfect hiding place. I stayed out as late as I possibly could that night, in an attempt to evade seeing "Our Mom."

I refused my bread and lard and also a "cuppa tea" that was offered and went straight to bed. Mom was very quiet and didn't say anything, but she gave me some funny looks. That night it was impossible to carry out any preventative plan, due to there being no lights whatsoever in any of the upstairs rooms, and I could hardly ask Mom for a candle could I? So next morning I was out of bed bright and early, slipping my trousers and jersey on quietly so that no one, especially "Our Mom" who was already downstairs lighting the fire and preparing dad's breakfast for when he arrived home from Bradford's, would hear me. I didn't put my boots on, for that certainly would have made a noise on the bare wooden boards. I looked out of our bedroom across the landing to make sure no one was about. I knew where mom was for I could hear her cussing one of the animals. Off across the landing I went and started to climb the stairs to the attic stealthily, pausing, and listening each time the wood creaked, half expecting "Our Mom" to bawl something upstairs if she happened to hear. I attained the attic at last and removed the box from its new hiding place. Then I re-counted the money, just in case you-know-who had beaten me to the punch, and been "at it agen". With a sigh of relief I realised that this time all the money was there and thought "Thank God for that". Then I wrapped the money in sheets of newspaper, just in case she shook the toy van in an effort to "knacker" the rest of my money, stuffed it into the back of the van then filled the rest of the space with more newspaper. After I had completed this task, I extracted the key from the driver's cab and locked the back door securely.

I then put the key into some more newspaper and placed this inside one of my Dinky vans, hoping against all hope that this preventative measure would stop the pillage of my money in the future. I slipped quietly back down the stairs and back into bed to await the screaming announcement up the stairs from "Mom". "Cum on yo' kids, da yo' 'ear me, gerrup nowan' let's 'ave ya' ourra the way afoa yer Fertha get's 'um', an' I shan't call yarragen, I'll jus' be up an' w'ale yarr arses fer ya', so cum on an' gerrup."

In the days that followed I gave the ten bob note a lot of thought, which of course in turn made me miserable. I knew "Our Mom" wasn't going to pay me back, and even if I secured another note from my twenty five shillings in the van, it wouldn't be the same as my first one, of which I had no doubt had been spent by you-know-who already. Who could I turn to for help? Even if I had someone tackle Mom about my ten bob note, I would then be frightened at what she might do afterwards.

For the next couple of weeks my thoughts were fully occupied with this subject and in the process I was a right misery to everyone around me. Then one day me and my mates were passing Norton's on the corner of Icknield Street and Key Hill, and I saw advertised, real leather, twelve panel caseballs, only a few left, eight and sixpence each, on a big poster in their window in Icknield Street. I had bought rubber balls before, for a tanner or ninepence, but I'd never " 'ad a casa o' me own, eva". I looked longingly at the one displayed in the window, my mind all of a whirl. "Cum on Smithy, if we'em gunna gerra perch on the gert". We were on our way to watch trains at Hockley Goods yard in All Saints Road. "Wayrra bit yo' lot, um guin' in 'ere an' see 'em about one o' these casas". "Yo'm bloody daft yo' am, were am yo' gunna gerr eight an' six frum ferra bloody casa like that un'?" "Yo' mind yarrown soddin' business were I'm gunna gerr eight an' a tanna frum, or warr I got, an' warr I ain't got, now am yo' cumin' in wi' me or ain't cha, yo' cun please yaself, an' the other buggas to". With that I started to walk round the corner into Key Hill where the entrance to Norton's was. Despite the bit of jeering from my mates, they all, without exception, followed me, thinking I was pulling their legs and was going to make a right "nana" of myself, which I've no doubt they anticipated with great pleasure.

Through the glass doors we went into this posh shop, with carpets laid all over the floor, and all the ladies serving the customers "wus clean, eva so clean, an' smelled nice too". They were all dressed in black frocks with white collars and white cuffs and it was beautiful to us lot from "The Brook". "Yes lads, what can we do for you?" This request came from a beautiful and smart lady. "Tain't us miss, we don' wan anythin', it's 'im". A grubby finger was pointed at me. "Smithy, 'e wantsta buy a casa miss." The lady looked at me perplexed. "You want to buy a what, a case? I'm afraid I do not understand what you mean, can you tell me what a casa is, then I might be able to help you?" "'e means" I replied, referring to the lad who had first spoken, "one o' them footballs yo've gorrin yo'er winda in Icknield Street miss, thas worr 'e means. Tek no notice on 'im 'e's bloody daft 'e is." She smiled and showed a beautiful set of pure white teeth, which made her look even better. "Oh I see, what you lads want is the toy department. You will have to go down those stairs and when you reach the bottom, turn right and you will find ladies who will help you. You will be quiet won't you?" "Yus mis, we'll be eva sa quiet, we promise ya'", we replied, then headed for the stairs, which were ornately designed, descending from right opposite the glass doors we had entered the store by. On arrival downstairs we were met by another lady, equally as pretty as the lady upstairs and I explained to her what I wanted. She smiled at me and said "Have you enough money son?" I thought to myself, "Ya silly sod, o' course I gorrinuff money, or I wouldn't be 'ere would I". But I replied, whispering in her ear, (Well I dain't want that lot knowin' me bisniss did I?) "Yes miss, burr I ain't gorrit 'ere with me ya' know, could ya' save a casa fer me till tamorra please an' I'll cum and gerit frum ya' as soon as ya' open shop in the mornin', please miss?" "Alright then son, I'll save the best one for you and that's a promise from me to you, so I'll see you in the morning then?" I don't think she believed me though, because of her answer to my next question. "Could ya' blow it up fer me, an' lace it as well miss please, so it's ready ta play foota with?" "We'll do all of that for you tomorrow when you come with your eight and sixpence, all right son?" "Yes miss ta, tarrar then, I'll see ya', tomorra then early, okay?" "Yes son, all right nice and early then, goodbye."

Off we trooped out of the shop and across "The Flat" to watch the trains, with my mates still not believing me, I was sure of that. The next morning I was out of bed very early again and up to the attic I crept. First I removed the eight and sixpence for my football, then as an after thought, I took a further one and sixpence to spend on some sweets, or whatever, to share with my mates. I left the house early, with much suspicion and mumbling from you-know-who, which I ignored, to see if my pals were out of bed to come with me up to Nortons. But a series of "Nah 'e ain't up ourra bed yet Ronnie, cum back lerta forrim", left me mooching around "The Brook" for a while, because the shop didn't open until nine o'clock.

I watched with great interest as the trams went clanging by, the buses and other vehicles blowing petrol fumes out, and horse drawn vehicles of all descriptions rattling past over the blue bricks, with metal rims that covered the strong wooden wheels. I sat there on the steps of The National Provincial Bank thinking what we would do when I got my case from Norton's. Suddenly I heard the bolt of the big wooden doors being slipped, then the doors were opened by a bank messenger clad in his dark blue uniform. " 'allo son" he said to me " 'ave ya' brought us all ya' money ta purrin our big safe then, bein' as yome sa early?" "Nah, 'um jus' wertin' till nine a'clock, cus I'm gunna buy a casa from Norton's, an' I don' wanna be lert". "Well yo'd berra 'urry up if yo' ain't gunna be lert, cus it's jus' arter nine a'clock now". "Is it?" I replied excitedly, "thank yo' sir, I dain't think it was that time already, I'll gerrorf then, tarrar an' thank ya'." "Tarrar son I 'ope ya' enjoy ya' casa, see ya' w'en yome playin' fer the Villa, okay?" Off I ran towards Norton's up Icknield Street.

I arrived at the toy department rather out of breath and needless to say excited. It was a different lady who attended to me on this occasion. "Yes son what can I do for you?" "Please miss, I saw another lady yestadee, an' she sez she'd get me the best casa yo'ed got, an' she'd blow it up an' she'd lace it fer me, an' I got me eight an' a tanna 'ere look", I blurted out in a gabble of words, opening my grubby hand to show the woman my money. "Slow down son" she replied quietly, and with an understanding smile, realising my excitement, she then said, "Tell me what you want, only slowly this time so that I can understand". So I then re-told my story, and she said, "All right son, stay where you are", and off she went somewhere. When she returned she had the lady I had seen the day before with her and they were both laughing. "I dunno w'at they wus larffin at, but they looked nice, any road up". When they stood in front of me the lady I had seen this morning said, "Here you are (and she mentioned her name) then, here's your secret admirer." "Oh go on with you, teasing again, look, you have made him blush", my lady said, and I felt the colour rise in my cheeks. "So you have kept your promise and come back .to see me then young man?" she said, as the first lady went off still laughing, "l thought you were pulling my leg yesterday in front of all your friends, but I see I'm mistaken". "No miss I wouldn't do that ta yo', 'onist I wouldn't, I really wanna casa, 'onist I do, I wanna buy it, 'onist miss, yo've still got sum intcha? Yo' ain't sold 'em all, yo' did promise ta keep me the best casa fer me ya' did, look I got me money". I opened my fist again for the second time. "Calm down sunshine" she said, "of course we've still got some footballs left, come on, you come with me sunshine and I'll let you pick the one you want for yourself, how will that suit you?" "O-o-o-o-o, thanks miss, yo' will blow it up, an' lace it wuntcha? Cus me mates wanna play foota rirraway with it please". "Once you have selected which ball you want sunshine, I will see to everything for you, and that is a promise". Off we went together to another counter and the lady produced a big brown box from behind it, then she emptied the deflated leather balls onto the carpet in the aisle.

I studied the array of balls before me, then I chose the one I wanted. The lady put that one on the counter, put the rest back into the box and returned it to its former location. She then took a big shiny brass pump from beneath the counter, together with a tool that looked like a very large needle, but slightly bent at the end where the eye was situated. At the opposite end was a wooden handle, similar to the one on a screwdriver or chisel. This tool I found out very quickly was a lacer. The lady first took my eight and sixpence off me and put it into a metal box, along with a receipt she had made out. Then she screwed the top onto it and put it into a metal aperture which was fixed to one of the ornate stanchions, which was a part of the back shelving. She pressed something, there was a hissing sound and the metal capsule disappeared out of view, up a network of piping suspended from the ceiling of the shop. Once the capsule had been despatched she picked the ball I had chosen off the counter and put her index and second finger into the aperture in one of the "T" panels. Under the tongue her fingers went until she located the bladder inside, she then pulled this to the surface and moved it around until she found the long teat of the bladder. This she pulled out of the aperture, moving the leather tongue out of the way as well, very expertly, and I thought to myself, "This ain't the fus time she's done this" as I continued to watch with absolute interest. Cutting a length of very thin twine from a big reel, she placed it on the counter. She inserted a brass adaptor into the pump, put this into the teat and started blowing the ball up. When she had put what she thought was the correct pressure into the ball, she removed the pump and adaptor swiftly with one hand, whilst applying pressure further down the teat with the other to prevent the air escaping.

After laying the pump gently on the counter, she then bent the teat in half, which would automatically prevent the air from escaping. She picked the twine up off the counter and bound the bent teat up very expertly. "There" she said "that's the hard part of the job completed, now I'll sew it up for you sunshine. You will be playing football with it in no time at all". "Thanks miss" I said "Thanks very much, God ain'tcho cleva?" "Not really sunshine" she replied, "not when you do it as regular as I do". She then pushed the tied teat back inside the leather, then she pushed the tongue back with a small shoe horn, being very careful so as not to puncture the bladder, and situated it so that none of the bladder was exposed to the exterior.

At this point I heard another hissing sound, combined with a rattling, like a rat-tat-tat-tat of a railway carriage going along the lines. Suddenly these noises were stopped with an abrupt bump. The lady turned to the back of the counter, extracted the metal capsule from the aperture, then opened it and handed me an official Norton's receipt, for which I thanked her. She said to me, "Now don't you lose that note sunshine, because that will tell everyone that this ball belongs to you and that you have paid for it, now do you understand me?" "Yus miss, thank yo'." She continued, "Put it somewhere safe then sunshine before you leave the shop". So what

I did was to wrap my one and sixpence in it carefully, then place it back "inta me trousa pocket". The lady then picked the lacer up and threaded a brand new leather tape into it. She then pushed the metal end of the lacer through the first two lace holes of the ball. On completion of this action the tape was removed, then the lacer itself, leaving the leather tape in the ball. This was repeated right up the aperture. At the last two lace holes she pulled the whole tape up tight and threaded the rest of the tape over and under the crossed tapes, securing the whole lot. "There you are sunshine that didn't take long did it?" "Nah it dain't mis" I replied, but in my eagerness to get the ball and show off with it to my mates, I thought it had taken an eternity!

On replying I automatically looked at the clock displayed above another counter on the opposite side to the one I was standing at, and I was amazed that it had "on'y jus' gon' 'alf nine", so the whole operation right from me running from The National Provincial Bank on "The Brook", to my ball being paid for and ready to use, had taken only thirty-five minutes. The lady handed me the ball. "I don't suppose you want it wrapped up do you sunshine?" "Nah, thanks miss, I'll tek it as it is". I wanted to get out of the shop and show the whole world "I 'ad gorra branny nu casa". The lady continued as I went to move away from the counter, "Hang on a minute sunshine, I've got a little present for you". I waited whilst she bent under the counter and when emerging she said, "Put this under your jersey sunshine until you are out of the shop", and handed me a big round tin of dubbin, to keep the leather of "me casa" supple and clean. "Cor-r-r-r tar miss, tar eva sa much, I'll keep me ball nice an' clean now I will". "That's all right sunshine" she replied, "and don't forget that if your ball goes down at all, or if anything goes wrong, you bring it back to me and I'll see to it for you". "Thanks miss I will" I said and off I ran out of the shop, one very happy lad. I returned the ball on numerous occasions, when not only did she re-flate it for me, she put new leather laces in, applied new twine to the teat when necessary, and never, ever charged me. She must have loved kids very much indeed, she did not require a name, for she was in my eyes an angel. Back down Icknield Street I ran to "The Brook" and eventually found my mates, who scrutinized my new ball, and "wannid ta play foota straightaway with it". But I said, "Nah we ain't playin' 'ere with me nu casa, cus it'll get scratched on the road an' ev'rythin!" "Well w'ere we gunna play foota then Smithy?" they replied. "I'm guin up 'an'sa (Handsworth Park) an' play foota on the grass, yo'cun cum if ya' wanna, burrif ya' don't then sod ya', I'll gu on me own, so there". They groaned and mumbled at the idea of walking that far to play football, but when I told them "I'd got one an' a tanna ta spend on sweets, an' cerks forrus all" they suddenly agreed what a great idea it was "ta gurra 'an'sa" and we trooped off at great speed. First we called at George Baines in Hunters Road where I bought two big bags of stale cakes for "tuppence". Then we proceeded to the sweet shop on the corner of Hunters Road and Naden Road where I bought some sweets and a bottle of pop. What a day we had in the park! We played football until we tired ourselves out, then got stuck into the food and drink. We rested, then resumed playing "foota" again and eventually, towards evening, tired but very happy, we wended our way back through the park to the bus stop by Wellsbourne Road, just outside the park gates. I paid the fair home to "The Brook" for us all.

After the ten bob note incident and the initial intrusion into my black box for money to buy my football, I'm afraid I nibbled and nibbled into my savings until there was nothing left. This was mainly due to the fact that "Our Mom" never mentioned the re-payment of the ten shillings, and had I mentioned it, I know what I would have received, and it wouldn't have been money! Also I thought if I left the money in the house no matter where, she'd have probably found it and most likely have "borrowed" it! So I spent my money as I earned it, thinking to myself "well, I'da neva bin a millionaire any road up!"

I did have a brief spell of achievement in the upper sphere of soccer. I was suddenly picked to play for the school (Farm Street Junior School). I cannot remember how it came about, but I can tell you that the selectors couldn't have picked me for my ability on the field, so sufficient to say it must have been my size, for I was a big lad for my age. I had "two left feet" and the only dribbling I had done so far was down the front of my jersey. Mr. Warriner the sports master approached me one day and asked if I would like to play football for the school, to which I eagerly replied, "Yus sir". Then I remembered my manners and the consequences if I didn't, so I hastily added, "Yus sir, I would please". "Right then Smith, there will be a practise in the playground tonight when school has finished, all right?" "Yus sir, I'll be there, an' thank ya'."

After school a casa was brought in to the playground which had Farm Street running alongside, and practise commenced. The space between two of the five iron pillars supporting the playground shelter served as the goalposts and the practise session was one of attack versus defence, with Mr. Warriner standing in as the referee. I was slotted into the inside left position someone must have vacated through one reason or another, because the only skill I had in football was to kick the ball in the direction of the opposing goalkeeper, then rush after it and kick it again. The only two players I can remember from that team were Ray Izons the goalkeeper, who lived in New John Street West, on the right hand side, past John Wilson the Wholsesale Grocer in Well Street, before you reached Wheeler Street somewhere by Gwennie Bruetons, and Vic Hughes who lived in Burbury Street in a back house on the left hand side of the last entry, before the junction with Farm Street, running down from Bridge Street West. In this particular section of Burbury Street the whole right hand side consisted of Lucas's. Vic lived in the next yard to Roy Hayling who was another school friend of mine, but not a footballer, like me(?)! Ray Izons was a stocky lad, built for the position he commanded on the football field and also, like myself, had a fair talent for drawing and painting. Vic was a thin, pale gangly lad with blonde wavy hair. He played in the forward line, in fact I think he played centre forward. He was the captain of the team and I may add, a very talented football player.

After the practise session I went home wondering what my chances of getting a place in the team were. In the following days I waited anxiously for the team to be displayed on the notice board in the upstairs hall, for the forthcoming match on the Saturday morning. It was there on Friday, but one of my mates had seen it before I entered the school that morning and rushed up to me and said, "Yov'e bin picked fer the ge-erm on Sat'dy Ron, yo'me playin' inside left, great innit?" I acted nonchalant to this statement by one of my fans, but inside my tummy churned.

I proceeded to the hall upstairs to confirm this statement hoping it wasn't a joke, which would of course have caused acute internal agony, because I desperately wanted to be a Teddy Sandford of West Bromwich Albion or Ronnie Starling of the Villa, or even a Harry Hibbs of Brum, "cus I cud allis change me posishun cud'n I?" No, it wasn't a joke, there it was shining out like a beam from a lighthouse. SMITH. R. (Inside Left) for Saturday's away match against Wattville Road School, to be played at Oaklands Recreation Park, Rookery Road, Kick-Off 10.30 am. I could hardly get through the day. Naturally I went home to dinner that day and informed everyone of my success, but nobody was interested at two back-of-twenty four, which deflated me a little. However this was soon overcome when I returned to school, because the captain Vic Hughes came to see me, for I hadn't seen him that morning, and congratulated me on being selected (I bet he regretted the congratulations later). We had a short chat about the forthcoming game against Wattville Road, then Vic said it would be a good idea if I met him at his house and we could go to the ground together with his older brother, who gave up his Saturday mornings to come along with the team and assist generally, including buying the oranges for half time. I agreed to this and we arranged the time etc. The bell finally went for the termination of school for the week, but as instructed earlier the team, including the two reserves, stayed behind and met in Mr. Warriner's classroom.

He gave us a short pep talk, chain smoking during the whole process, which particularly fascinated me, it being the first time I had seen this done. On completion of the talk Mr. Warriner opened the big leather case and withdrew jerseys, knicks, and socks. The school colours were green jerseys, with a tie up at the top. Some of these jerseys had a hoop of lighter green at the top running around the neckband and were newer than the rest, although all of the jerseys could have been given to the rag and bone man without a second thought, and who, in all probability, due to their condition, would have refused them. The knicks and socks were no better.

The former were supposed to be navy blue, but I'm afraid the original colour had either faded or had been washed so often they now looked a light grey, also the elastic in them was suspect as well. The socks? Well, what can one say about holes being held together by strands of green, or green and yellow wool? Not a lot I'm afraid. A jersey, a pair of socks and knicks were handed out to the selected eleven players. When mine was handed to me I could hardly contain my excitement. I couldn't have experienced any better compliment than if I had been selected to play for The Villa. I definitely couldn't have felt more elated. I looked at my kit with pride, thinking of myself running up the tunnel, out on to the pitch, with the crowds screaming for me, the kick about before the whistle blew indicating the two captains to meet at the centre circle, toss the coin to select which direction we were going to play. The ball was kicked off by Vic Hughes, with me racing into position and then me sending a long ball onto the right wing, the winger beating two of the opposition's defence, then hitting the ball over into the middle of the penalty area. Vic Hughes trapped it, pushed it to me and I hit it on the run, giving the goalkeeper no chance as it thundered into the top right hand corner of the net from my trusty left boot, - boot, boot, boot? I quickly came out of my reverie. Boots? I hadn't got any football boots and there was no chance of "the ol' gel" buying me any, she couldn't afford to have my ordinary boots cobbled let alone buy me a pair of football boots, even a second hand pair from the "tatters". My world suddenly caved in, and Vic, who must have seen my glum expression said, "Wasamarra Ron?" "I don' think I'm gunna be able ta play tomorra Vic". "Why not Ron" was his surprised reply. "I ain't gorreny foota boots, tha's wasamarra." "O' is tharall, don' worry about that, I'll gu an' see sir" and off he went to Mr. Warriner. They talked for a while and there was a lot of head nodding and gesticulating. Finally Vic came back to me and said, "Sir's got sum foota boots at 'is 'ouse an' 'e'll bring 'um ta the ground tamorra, there's bound to be a pair that'll fit ya, okay Ron?" "Whoa-o-o-o, tha's great Vic, thanks eva sa much" I replied happily. "Don't ferget ta be at our 'ouse in the mornin', about 'alf nine, or earlier if yo' cun Ron, okay?" "Are okay Vic, I'll be there don' yo' worry". I ran home clutching my kit under my arm. When I got into the house I showed them my kit. Nobody was the slightest bit interested, but it didn't dampen my spirits. I went upstairs and in the darkness - I dare not ask mom for a candle, or light the gasmantle, because all I would have got would have been a back hander - I took my ordinary shirt off and shoved it under the bed, along with the knicks and socks of my kit, then slowly pulled on my football shirt. Oh! it felt great, and I started to day-dream again, this time playing for the "Baggies". "Ronnie, R-o-onnie, cun yo' bloody 'ear me, I know yo'me up there, warrar ya' doin'?" It was one of "The big wenches" bawling up the stairs, which again brought me back to reality. "I ain't doin' nuthin'." Well bloody get yasel' down 'ere, an' do bloody nuthin' down 'ere, were we cun see ya', an' w'at yo'me doin' a'right, an' be bloody quick abourit". I pulled my "ganzie" over my football shirt and went downstairs. In front of the fire was the half beer barrel and the big black kettle was hung over the fire suspended from a long black hinged bar, just starting to sing. I'd forgotten, it was "Friday Night", bath night! "The Babby" went in first, and whilst mom dried her, one of "the big uns" would be bathing Dorothy, the next youngest, then whilst she was being dried, "Our Ginge" would be dumped in, and then me. The last one in was "Our Kid", Arthur. The three "big uns", 'ilda, Vi an' Lil would bath after we were tucked up for the night. The Lifeboy Soap was in plentiful supply. You could smell it before you saw it, and the towel became wetter, and wetter, as it got nearer your turn. You would still be wet when you had been dried, even though desperate attempts were made to dry the one and only towel intermitently by the roaring fire. On completion of this Friday night ritual your shirt would be put back on, and you would have a cuppa cocoa, or tea, and a piece of bread and lard, and then off up the "wooden 'ill" ta Bedfordshire" you would be shoo-o-oed.

"W'ile yo'me wertin' ta gerrin the bath, yo' cun get them bottles frum under the sink in the bogey 'ole, an' gu down ta 'ardy's an' fetch Our Dad 'is beer, an' be quick abourrit" one of the "big uns" said. "Are, oright" I replied, not too anxious to get into the dirty water when it came to my turn, but there was no escaping the "Friday Night Sheep Dip". Our dad was out this evening, he wasn't at work for some reason or other, but why evades me. I was eager to go on this errand this particular night, because on "The Brook" I could look into one of the shop windows, "tek me ganzie orf, an' see 'ow I looked in me foota shirt". I did exactly that and oh how proud I was of myself as I looked at my reflection in Bendall's window, until I spotted the girls inside laughing and gesticulating at me. I hurriedly replaced my "ganzie", then stuck my tongue out at them, which unfortunately for me only caused more merriment for the girls. I fetched Dad's beer from Hardy's, had a quick swig out of each bottle, making sure that all three levels were the same, before I replaced the sticky labels back across the stoppers, then I returned to two back-of -twenty-four. I was just in time to get my clothes off and step into the sludge situated in the half beer barrel, with a little more hot water added from the big black kettle. After "The Bath"(!) I just put my football jersey back on looking around the room hoping someone would notice it and make a comment. Did they? Did they bloody hell. I put my ganzie, trousers, boots and socks at the door leading to the stairs. Well, it was no use putting them on again was it, to take off when I got up "the dancers".

I drank my tea and ate my bread and lard, then said "Tarrar" to anybody who was interested, but no one said anything, so I picked my gear up from the floor and said, "Bum to ya' then" under my breath and ran up the stairs to bed, where my two younger sisters, Dot and Ginge, were already snuggled up. I jumped into the bottom of the single bed, after throwing my gear under the bed by "The Piddle Pot" and manoeuvred my cold legs between "the wenches" warm legs to make myself comfortable, which caused a lot of grumbling from Dot and Ginge, but I "dain't care any road up". The gaslight was on now and would be until our Arthur was bathed and dried, and he came up and got into bed alongside me ("The Babby" was already asleep in the double bed). Mom would follow him up the stairs and turn the gas off, then she would whisper(?) to us in her endearing tone, "Now o don' wanna 'ear a bloody peep oura yo' lot, cus if o do, I'll be up an' tan ya' bloody arses 'til yo' can't sit". She would then stomp off down the stairs. The dreams I had that night were all football. I did score some goals with the crowds cheering madly.

At last the great morning arrived, the day I made my debut into The Farm Street Junior School Football team. It was cold as I jumped out of bed onto the wooden floor boards. I dressed hurriedly and put my football kit under my arm. After gobbling my bread and lard, followed by the inevitable "cuppa tea", I rushed out of the house to find quite a strong wind blowing, although the sun was shining. I thought it was "a smashin' day fer foota, spechly w'en yo' wus playin' ferra propa team, like w'at I wus". I arrived at Vic's house and knocked the door. His brother answered my knock and said, "Okay, we'm ready, we wunt be a minnit" and then shut the door again. After what seemed an eternity, Vic and his brother came out and Vic said, "Sorry we wus sutch a lung time Ron, but we've bin cuttin' the oranges fer 'alf time, an' gerrin the fust aid kit tergetha". "Soright Vic, it dain't mek any diff'rance, I dain't mind". We were well along Farm Street, nearly by Wellesley Street when suddenly I had a further shock. I remembered we had to catch the tram to Rookery Road (well the tram didn't stop actually at Rookery Road, it stopped at *The Regal* by Booth Street and you had to walk back to Rookery Road) and that "they dain't ge yo' free rides on the trams". So for the second time during this footballing incident I had to blurt out to Vic, "I ain't gorreny muney fer the tram Vic, waramy I gunna do", but Vic and his brother just burst out laughing and said, "Christ, yo' am a worry guts ain't cha, fust the boots an' now the tram fare. Don' worry Ron we got the muney fer ya' tram fare, Mr. Warriner giz it ta Vic an' 'e dishes it out to the players, burrov course 'e dain't 'ave ta ge yo' none, cus yo' wus meetin' us at our 'ouse, an' we've gotcha fare back agen, so don' worry about that either, okay?" "Yer're okay, I wunt worry no mowa."

This reply to my question made me feel even more elated, fancy being paid your tram fare for playing "foota", this was getting better every minute. We alighted from the tram after an exciting journey. Tram rides were always exciting for me, for these journeys were few and far between. After crossing Soho Road we walked back down to Rookery Road, turned left and on the left hand side just past Trafalgar Road was the lane leading to the entrance to Oaklands Recreation Park. When we arrived Mr. Warriner greeted us and showed us where we were to change. Once in the dressing room he opened up a bag which had several pairs of football boots inside and asked me what size I took. I stammered shamefully, "I dunno sir, our mom alis gets me shoes fer me", which brought a sudden outburst of tittering from my team mates, who naturally all had their own boots. One look from Mr. Warriner was enough to quell this outburst and once quietness was installed again he turned to me and said, "Right Smith, try these until you find a pair that fits you and don't forget to return them to me at the end of the match. Hopefully they will have scored a goal or two". "Yus sir, ah will", was my short reply. I rummaged through the assortment of old boots, but the only pair that came anywhere near to fitting me were too big, so we (Vic and I) scrounged around for some old newspaper and pushed it up into the toes of the boots until they felt a little more comfortable, but very definitely strange.

Eventually we were all ready to go out onto the pitch. We ran out and the home team were already kicking in. On seeing them I nearly ran back to the dressing room, I was so ashamed. Wattville Road were immaculate in their blue and white striped shirts, (not jerseys), they were spotless and pressed, with collars, and the school badge on the left side of the chest, their white shorts sparkingly laundered, with knife edge creases down the side. The goalkeeper, with his beautiful clean green jersey of pure wool looked like a giant, all the team had the same coloured socks on and without exception all of them pulled up to just below their knees. The boots they wore were dubbined and polished, and the laces in them were pure white. Oh God, what in heaven's name must they have thought of us as we poured out of the dressing room! Different shades and designs of green jerseys, knicks and socks that a rag and bone man would have turned his nose up at, and our boots? Forget it, I wouldn't even comment. Nevertheless we took the opposite end of the field and started to kick in. Out of a dozen passes to me I think I kicked the ball once, then I slipped on my "bum". Finally the referee blew his whistle for the two captains to go to the centre spot to toss the coin. This was done and the whistle sounded for the commencement of the match. At this point I would have liked to say that like the stories in *The Wizard*, *The Rover* or *The Hotspur* that we put two goals past Wattville Road in the first half, despite their immaculate turn out, with yours truly slamming one in from twenty yards out, then in the second half the home side recovering with a goal and putting a lot of pressure on us, until the last few minutes when I put it completely out of their reach with a beautifully timed header, brought cheers from the huge crowd and congratulations from my team mates. That is what I *would* have liked to say.

Truthfully it wasn't a bit like that! What a bloody nuisance I was to everyone. On our side that is, not on Wattville Road's. I was an extra man for them, helping them to beat us easily. Right from the kick-off I was useless. Vic must have thought, "I'll get him into the game as soon as I can, it'll help him to settle in", so he pushed the ball to me when the whistle blew (and I do remember this very well), I took a mighty swipe at the ball and missed it completely. With the momentum of my left foot in full swing, I went sailing into the air and finished up on my back in the soft grass. I got up rather ashamed and raced towards my own goal, which was where the play was and where it remained for nearly all of the seventy minutes play, largely due to my comic antics. What a disaster I was. I got in everybody's way and under their feet. When I did manage to kick the ball it was always in the wrong direction, or directly to the opposition. In a word, I was about as much use to Farm Street Junior School Football Team as a piano player with ten thumbs wearing wellingtons on his hands..

Of course we lost, that was a foregone conclusion, but fortunately due to the other ten lads, especially Ray Izons our goalkeeper who had a brilliant game, the score was kept respectful. I think the final outcome was four nil. Everyone was nice to me after the match, but I don't know what their real thoughts on the matter were. I said "Tarrar" to Vic and his brother when we got off the tram at "The Brook", promising to see Vic on Monday at school. I must admit I accepted the fact I was not going to make a Stanley Matthews or Tom Finney. I forgot about the fiasco at Oaklands Recreation Park and resigned myself to the fact that my career in top flight soccer was not to be.

On the Monday when I returned to school nothing was said, so I just went about my normal business. Tuesday was the same, but on the Wednesday Vic came to see me and reminded me that it was football practise after school. I thought, "well, they might just pick me as reserve this week-maybe! The practise match went off all right, I think. I was a little better, but again nothing was said. On the Friday I could hardly bring myself to look at the notice board, but finally when I did I couldn't believe my eyes, I thought I was dreaming, but no, there it was SMITH R. inside left. This time I didn't feel elated, because I knew what a "tunack" I'd been in the match against Wattville Road. I couldn't for the life of me understand why they had picked me. Still, who was I to object, but I did think to myself "they mus' be bloody 'ard up fer players".

The match that Saturday was another away match versus Boulton Road School, who incidentally were currently at the top of the division. We were to play them at Black Patch Park, which had Perrott Street, Woodburn Road and Foundry Lane located around it. This park played a big part in my life in later years, "wonderfully happy years". I met Vic and his brother again on the Saturday morning as pre-arranged and we travelled to Black Patch full of hope. But again I was useless, I just couldn't get it right and the lads in dark and light blue shirts had little trouble chalking up another win.

I was selected again the following week, when we were at home (Wood Lane Playing Fields) to Smith Street School. When they ran on to the pitch, they looked very smart, for they were wearing a brand new kit for the very first time. Red shirts and white collars and sleeves, white knicks and red and white hooped socks, and the goalkeeper had the new coloured jersey for the period, yellow. My, they did look grand, but unfortunately it did not match their playing ability, I think they were on par with us. It was naturally a scrappy affair which finished all square with neither side scoring.

I was never selected after that and consequently had no further aspirations regarding football. Then I entered the world of finance, with the help of bread and milk roundsmen, and paper rounds.

I have talked quite a lot about "Our Mom" and I'm afraid none of it very good, well for the most part anyway. But it was true, every bit of it, through the eyes of a small boy. She did however, on reflection, have an awful lot to put up with, with a family our size.

Love was shared the same as food, drink, clothing etc., and as I was nearly in the middle of the eight kids, love was there, but not often. So just to try to make amends, if only slightly, we must try to look at things from "Mom's" point of view, because I must admit "I wus a birrof a bugger at times", although not viciously intentional.

Like the "tata" in the oven story. It was Sunday morning in Guest Street and this particular day we weren't going to Gran and Grandad Smith's, Auntie Berth's, or Auntie Nell's, so I was playing in the yard whilst mom and dad and the "big wenches" got themselves togged up in their Sunday best. "Mom and Dad wer' guin' down "The Vic", Dad fust an' then Mom arta, an' the big uns wus guin' out with their mates until dinna". Now at this precise period I had an overwhelming desire for baked "spuds", and to bake them myself. I had already "knackered" a few puds from Colley's on the corner of Little King Street and Guest Street, and' 'id 'em in the brewus, opposite the middins, an' nex' doa ta the lavy". I watched as the big wenches, "w'en out fust', followed shortly by "Our Dad" dressed in his dark navy blue suit, highly polished boots, white shirt and smart tie, crowned by his black, well brushed "billy cock". He said, "Tarrar Nip" to me as he vanished down the entry heading for "The Vic" on the corner of Bridge Street West, opposite St. Saviours. I waited for "Our Mom" to poke her head out of the door and shout after Dad, "An' min' 'ow yo' gu with them Sunday best, don' get playin' in the bloody dirt with 'em, else yo'll gerra w'alin' w'en yo' bloody cum in!" Mom never spoke to Dad like that, she seemed only to bawl it out to me.

Her fear of us getting our Sunday Best dirty, was "cus they gorra gu ta the pop shop the nex' mornin'." But I suppose I was more prone to do this than any of the others. At long last "'er royal 'ighness" emerged, decked out in a long black frock, highly polished boots, to match her "highly polished turn of phrase" and perched precariously on the top of her head "The Hat". She spotted me immediately lurking near the "middins". "Gerraway frum theya ya little sod, ain'tcha gorreny moa bloody sense than that, yo'll gerra dizeze frum theya yo' will, an' if yo' get them Sunday best dirty there'll be a soddin' w'alin' fer ya', da yo' un'erstan' me?" "Are, okay mom" I answered, moving away from the "middin" just in case she "gid me a back 'ander any road up". I watched as she in turn stomped down the entry heading for "The Vic", and once she had turned left at the bottom of the entry and disappeared out of sight past Tynes, I dashed into the "brewus" and sorted the biggest "tata" out of the few lying under the boiler. I washed it under the tap, dried it on an old hessian sack and once this was done, I rushed into the house. "The Babby" was lying on the sofa asleep, and Ginge and Dot were playing some game. I couldn't see "Our Kid" so I assumed he was upstairs. I went over to the oven on the left hand side of the roaring fire and opened the door. "Watcha gunna do Ron?" our Ginge enquired. "Mindgeroan bizniss worrime gunna do" I replied, "I'll tell our mom w'en she cums 'um frum the boozer, if yo' don't tell me watcha doin'." "Gu on ya' rotton sod, an' twitta, I'll 'ave ta tell yarras s'ppose, I'm bakin' a tata, an' yo' ain't 'avin' any, so don' arsk." "Don' wan anya rotton tata anyway" she replied tartly.

I got the dish cloth and removed the Sunday joint of beef, cooking merrily in the oven, and placed it in the hearth. Then I carefully placed my "tata" in the oven and closed the door. Off I went into the yard again to play "till me tata wus dun". After what I thought was a reasonable amount of time I went back into the house and opened the oven door. Fortunately there was no one about this time, and I thought, "Great, I wun 'ave ta ge 'em any o' me tata" and smiled to myself. I felt the baking potato very gingerly, due to the heat and decided it was done, so I got a piece of newspaper (part of the tablecloth) and put my "spud" into it. I then closed the oven door, put the wrapped spud into my pocket and ran out of the house to play again. This time I did not stop in the yard I went and found some of my mates up Guest Street.

"Ronnie, Ronnie, w'ere are ya', our mom's sent me fer ya'," I heard one of "the big uns" calling. We were playing down Johnnie Kingham's "openin'" at the time and I thought, "I'd berra gu if it's the ol' gel arter me, an' it must be time fer me dinner any'ow", so I shouted back, "Ar' oright um comin' as quick as I cun". She replied, "Yo'ed berra be quick an' all, she's in a right bloody temper with yo' ova summat". At this statement my stomach turned over. "W'y, worrave I dun now?" I asked as I joined the "big un" and we started to walk down Guest Street. She replied, "she's in a flamin' temper, an' 'er an' dad 'ad a row, an' he's gone orf ta bed, burrit's summat to do with yo!" I started to concentrate on what I might have done; suddenly it came to me as we turned into our entry, "Ar neva put the Sunday joint back inta the oven w'en I took me tata out. Oh God, she'll bloody kill me for this". In an attempt to create an ally with the "big un" I blurted the whole story out as we walked up the entry, but all I got in return was, "serves ya' bloody right then, it'll teach ya' not ta play up in the futcha wunnit."

I had seen "Our Mom" angry on several occasions in the past, with different people, including myself, and on several different subjects. But I shall never forget her face when "the big un" and me entered the house on that Sunday lunch time. It was almost purple, I suppose with pent up rage, her eyes were almost bulging out of her head. Obviously the beer she had drunk at "The Vic" that lunch time didn't exactly enhance the situation.

"Gerrin 'ere ya little sod, da ya know the bleedin' trouble yo've caused, do ya?" "Um sorry mom, o, dain't mean anythin' 'onest I dain't." "Sorry, sorry, ya' little cow, I'll ge yo' summat ta be bleedin' sorry fer" and she moved quickly to the door where I was still standing, en route picking up a wooden rolling pin off the table. When she reached me she began to belabour me with it. I turned my back quickly on her and got as close as I could into the corner by the door jamb. I put both hands over the back of my head to protect it and naturally dropped lower and lower into this corner as mom continued to rain blows upon my hands and body. I could hear "the big uns" pleading with her to stop, but she didn't. Then the "babbies" started to scream and cry. Suddenly the door leading to the staircase burst open, "w'at the bleedin' 'ells guin' on down 'ere with all this racket?" It was "Our Dad". Then he must have spotted mom, who was still laying in to me. He rushed across to her and restrained her saying "Stop it Lil, stop it, yo'll kill the little bugga". "I will kill 'im one o' these bleedin' times, I will, I'll swing fer the little sod", and she attempted to get away from dad, but he held her tightly, took the rolling pin off her, put it back onto the table, then moved her gently away from me. Although I had taken a battering, I saw the opportunity to escape and took it, because this beating really frightened me. I was up like a shot and before anyone could say anything I had turned the brass door knob, wrenched the door open and ran straight down the entry and across Guest Street without looking. Mind you, traffic especially on a Sunday was very light in those days, but I was still lucky not to be knocked over. Into Little King Street I ran to freedom with "Our Mom's" voice ringing in my ears. "Yus, gu on ya little bleeder, run" she screeched. I didn't hear the rest of her ravings, because I had moved out of earshot so quickly. The tears were streaming down my cheeks and I could still feel where the rolling pin had caught me as I hurried along Little King Street. It was quite a nice day, weatherwise anyway, so I moved on down Great King Street into Burbury Street, where I slowed down to a walk, until I reached "The Rec", which I entered and went straight to the shelter on the right hand side, by Lucas's wall. I sat down on the wooden bench and looked out towards Gordon Street, Lozells Street and Berners Street, wondering what on earth I was going to do next. I was completely alone, there wasn't another soul in the park, I suppose they were all having their dinner. Finally I got up and wandered over to the swings. I had a go on the pancake, then the roundabout and finished up on the swings themselves. After a while other kids entered the park, which for me, made the afternoon a little brighter.

We played together on the swings, then a kid came in a with "rubba foota" and asked "Da ya' wanna gama foota?" "Ar'", I said, although I shouldn't have played football in my Sunday Best, but I thought, "I don't care", so I went and played. I passed the afternoon and early evening away pleasantly enough, with the memory of the lunch time incident flittering spasmodically through my mind, when I suddenly realised I had to make a choice. I could hardly stop out all night, where would I go? I really didn't want to go back home, because naturally I was dubious as to what reception I would receive, but basically, what real choice had I got? Eventually I started to wend my way, very slowly, towards Guest Street. On arrival in the street I was very reluctant to go up the entry, so I mooched about in the vicinity for a while. I was actually looking into Spurrels factory, through their grime covered windows, when I heard one of the "big wenches" shout "Ronnie, Ronnie." I turned and saw her approaching me from the direction of our entry. On reaching me she said, "W'ere rav ya' bin? We've bin lookin' fer ya' ev'ryw'ere, all ova bloody 'ockley we 'ave, we've bin worrid ta death about ya. Our dad's gone ta werk, 'e's 'ad ta, burr 'e's tol' us that w'en we fin' ya', one on us 'as gorra gu up ta the bak'ry an' tell 'im yo're a'right."

"I ain't comin' back evaragen, neva, neva", I yelled. "Yo' gorra come back, else they'll 'ave the coppas out fer ya', an' then yo'll really cop it, if they 'ave ta fetcha back, cus it'll be Kenyon Street fer yo', an' anyway "Our Dad" really rowed at "Our Mom" fer the way she 'itcha." I felt a little better knowing "Our Dad" had become involved, because I knew that if anything else happened I could at least turn to him for help. Whilst the "big un" was talking to me, we were joined by another one of the "big uns" and a "little un". "Yo' gorra cum 'um our Ron" said the second "big un", "else yo'me gunna be in trouble with dad w'en 'e cums 'um frum werk in the mornin', an' anyway the ol' gel wunt 'itcha agen, cus 'e's tol' 'er not ta lay another 'and on ya', or else there'll be trouble forr 'er, 'onest" (and I mentioned my sister's name, but I'm afraid I cannot remember which sister it was now), "yo' ain't 'avin' me yon am ya'?" "Nah, course we ain't now cum on let's gu up 'um' tergether, a'right?" "Ar'roright, but yo' wunt leave me will ya'?" I was still very frightened at what you-know-who might do to me even now. "Nah, course we wunt, anyway as I sez the ol' gel daresn't 'itcha agen cus 'e'll 'ave 'er guts fer gartas, so don' worry", the two "big uns" said, almost in unison. All four of us went up the entry and into the house, "We've found 'im mom" said one of the "big uns". "Our Mom" didn't answer for a few seconds, then she said rather quietly, well quietly for her, "'ere, get this down ya', w'ile I mek yarra cuppa tea, an' then it's up ta bed with ya', ya' little sod", and she pushed a plate of "bubble and squeak" across to me.

It was then I realised how hungry I was, and although it was cold I gobbled it down ravenously, with a couple of hunks of bread Mom had carved off the cottage loaf, whilst waiting for the big black kettle perched crazily on the fire itself to boil for the tea. Not another word was spoken as I finished my meal, drank my tea and made a hurried exit to the momentary security of my bed. Mom was very subdued for a few weeks after this incident and it was never mentioned again. Oh, she gave me a good hiding on the occasions when I deserved it at later misdemeanours I committed, but she always made sure that as few people were in attendance as possible, or got to know.

GOOD FRIDAY - now that is the most natural expression one could hear, just like Goodbye, actually meaning God be with you. It was the day that one man, according to the Bible, sacrificed his own life for mankind's happiness. It certainly brought some happiness to some of the men from "The Brook", well if you measure money with happiness, which had to be a must in the thirties, it certainly did that. On Good Friday these men would hire wicker three wheeled baskets, much like a pram, with a lid covering the interior, for about a "tanner" from Kelly's or Parker's. Having obtained this means of conveyance they would then proceed to some small bakery like Adams in New John Street West, Withers in Farm Street, Smiths in Lodge Road (The Flat), Blackhams in Crabtree Road, or others, and by previous arrangement regarding commission on the sale or profit on the amount they bought, these men would collect their load of Hot Cross Buns at a very early hour on this very special morning, and the buns would mean exactly what they were described as, HOT CROSS BUNS!

Once they had loaded their baskets they would surge onto the streets with their singing calls of "OT CROSS BUNS, 'OT CROSS BUNS, ONE A PENNY, TWO A PENNY, 'OT CROSS BUNS, IF YO'VE GOT NO DAUGHTERS, GE' 'EM TO YA' SONS, ONE A PENNY, TWO A PENNY 'OT CROSS BUNS."

As kids we would hear this chant throughout the morning, and sometimes well into the afternoon. The part of the call, "one a penny, two a penny" meant exactly that, you could have a large bun for a penny, or two small ones for the same price. But I'm afraid this was never verified by us kids due to a very simple fact, "Wid neva gorra bloody penny ta find out". Good Friday meant a little extra much needed cash for these men who took advantage of the situation, and consequently what it brought with it. For it brought happiness to a good many people, even though the period was short. On other occasions these men would walk the streets for hours to earn a few extra coppers, some of them employed at very low wages, and others that hadn't a job at all. They would hire their different conveyances and walk the streets selling almost anything, hoping the coppers would look kindly on them, which they did. These men would sell almost any range of goods: salt, pop, fruit and vegetables, they would move your furniture at any hour, which was a good service if you were doing a "moonlight flit" owing the unfortunate landlord weeks of rent money. They were certainly "characters" were these men with the different methods they used to sell their wares to the people, singing, playing an assortment of instruments, including a gramophone I well remember on one cart, or just calling out in a singing voice. "The rag and bone man" was special. He would blow his bugle, or sound his vehicle wind horn to call the people out of their houses, but at the end of the day, whatever or however, it certainly did one thing, it brought a lot of happiness.

Saturday and Sunday mornings before Arthur Crump, Harold Allen, Mr. Phelps, and Elsie and Violet Coleman came onto the scene, saw me with several other youngsters waiting at the gates of either Scribban's, Bradford's, or Wathes, Cattel and Gurdens, offering our help to any of the roundsmen willing to accept us. This believe it or not created a great deal of happiness and excitement to us kids. When one of the roundsmen selected us, that made us happy, very happy, then there was the excitement of wondering where the roundsman actually did his deliveries. Was it a long way out from the bakery, or dairy, or was it just in the local vicinity? For the ride on the horse and cart, or van, petrol or electric, was equally as important as the money the man gave us at the end of the day.

Of course some of these men abused this situation of offered help, by giving you a pittance at the end of a long and most times, gruelling period, and to add to this plight he most probably gave you nothing to eat or drink.

But fortunately this was adequately compensated by the men who did exactly the opposite, and consequently when us lads gathered around these various gates we would watch for the vehicles making their exit and shout to one another, "Don' gu with 'im, 'e's a rotten sod 'e is", or "If this bloke arsks ya' gu with 'im cus 'e's great". I experienced both these types before I attained a more permanent position with what I thought at the the time to be "good" with Arthur Crump, but as you know, eventually I went on to do even better after leaving him. To give you some idea of the vast difference of treatment these men dished out, I went with one man all day Saturday from around seven in the morning until eight in the evening, and when we returned to the bakery in Goode Street he said to me, 'Tarrar Nip, I ain't gorreny change now, I'll see ya' next wick". When I waited for him the next Saturday, he ignored me, even though I shouted to him "Da ya' wan any 'elp this wick mate" and drove by with his horse and cart, and a new lad with him. Then there was a man named Joe Fortnum who worked for Scribban's, he paid me well enough, but he pulled the dirtiest trick a man could ever pull on a young lad, not once, but every time we delivered bread to Lucas's canteen in Great King Street. This trick he pulled wasn't just your ordinary every day lark, it could have had very serious consequences for me personally, and further more, for a change, I was completely innocent! What happened was we would put the bread required for the canteen into the two baskets and Joe would cover them with two sacks, no matter what the weather was, "Ta keep any dirt frum the fact'ry guin' on the bread" was his excuse. I put the nose bag on "Gold", the beautiful black horse we had, because we knew we would be quite some time inside the factory. Into the main gate on the left hand side facing towards Hockley Hill we would go, Joe with one basket, me with the other, past the gate officers, after they had acknowledged us with a wave, and then presumably they would enter into their record book our time of arrival etc. We would then go through the gate and proceeded across the yard to a goods lift, which we operated ourselves to the required floor. After we had deposited the bread into a huge wooden bin, putting what bread was left over from the day before on top and the fresh bread at the bottom, Joe, but not me, would have a cup of tea. Whilst waiting for his tea to be poured by one of the canteen girls, he would slip a box or two of Cadburys chocolate bars (there were two dozen of these two ounce bars to a box, and the price was a penny each) into the basket, then cover them quickly with the sacks. If he had brought the baskets down himself with the ill gotten gains installed, he would have taken full responsibility for his actions, but he *didn't*, he used to say to me, "Gu on Nip, tek them baskets down ta the cart why I 'ave me cuppa tea, an' wait fer me there, I wunt be lung". Now in those days it was more than you dare do to answer yor elders back, it was more than you dare do to even challenge their word, or even give an opinion, for fear of the resulting consequences. So off I would go with the baskets containing the "knackered" chocolate in them. I wasn't that thick that I didn't know what was going on, but in the circumstances there wasn't much I could do about it. I suppose what was in Joe's mind, although fortunately it never had to be proved, was that if I got caught with the chocolates in the basket, it would have been me they would have accused, and not him, I couldn't see him with his rotten type character, coming forward and saying, "Hah, it worn't the nippa that knackered yer choclit, it wus me, an' I ony gorrim ta tek it down ta the cart fer me". But as I stated, this crime was never brought to light, but what made me madder about this whole situation was "The mingy sod neva evan gid me a slab o' the bleedin' choclit, arter me bringin' it down". However, I compensated these dirty tricks in the only way I knew later, when I had cottoned on to what this "rotten sod" was doing. I know two wrongs don't make a right, but it gave me a certain amount of satisfaction doing it, and more to the point it was profitable to me. What happened was that Joe got me to collect some of the money customers paid on a Saturday. Not much, but enough, and I would hand this money over to him when we had finished the round at the end of the day, but it was always minus a couple of bob, or more, and I used to think, "well, it meks up fer the dirty tricks 'e played on me". I wonder though if he knew what I did, for it didn't need a mathematician to reckon up the little money I collected, and accepted the fact?

Then there was the roundsman from Bradford's who asked me to help him whilst his regular lad was away for some reason or other. He paid me well, very well, (two and sixpence, and he gave me a "two bob" fruit cake as well) but unfortunately this situation only lasted a couple of weeks, more's the pity.

As a child I could only differentiate between two extremes, happiness and sadness, and consequently if I had been sad, through someone, or something, like the ten bob note incident, when happiness came again it was extremely enjoyable to me.

Another very happy event in my life was during the main holidays. It didn't happen often, maybe only once or twice at the most, and that was "the day out at 'an'sa". "Our Mom" would bake a cake (nearly always a caraway seed cake) the previous evening and the following morning she would prepare some bread and lard, or dripping sandwiches, and last but not least a milk bottle would be filled with tea, the milk and sugar already added and mixed, and a piece of newspaper would be screweed up and placed into the top aperture. All these items would be put into one of Blackwell's paper carriers (cus 'e gid 'em us fer nuthin 'e did) and with a final warning from "you-know-who" to the "big uns", "Nah, don' yo' upset the tea inta the bag, cus I wannit back, so 'old it up straight", off we would troop on our walk to 'an'sa". We would stay there all day enjoying the fresh countryside and it would be late evening before we returned to "The Brook", tired but happy. I remember one of these occasions when the "big wenches" were herding us "little uns" back towards home through the park after a very enjoyable day. We had just got out of the park gates and were walking up the hill of Hampsted Road in the direction of Villa Road, when suddenly the heavens opened up! It absolutely teemed down with rain. We ran for shelter under a tree at the bottom of some posh people's driveway and huddled together waiting for the storm to abate. There we were, all of us clad in just a few items of clothing, due to the time of year, and earlier the prospect of it being a brilliant sunny day, "any road up, we couldn' 'ave any raincoats, cus we 'adn' gorreny, an' we 'adn' gorreny muney ta buy any, so we couldn' wear 'em could we?" We had been huddled up together for some minutes when we heard a "C-o-o-e-e, I say thar, you children, you children down thar, c-o-o-e-e-e". We looked around and at first couldn't see anyone. "I say you children, ovar here, ovar here, (with a definite emphasis on the haitch)", it was then that one of the "big uns" spotted a lady calling from the house whose tree we were sheltering under. At first we thought she was going to reprimand us for "daring" to shelter under *her* tree, but then she called, on realising she had caught our attention and we had seen her at last, "Would one of you come up here for a moment please?" We were naturally reluctant, with past warnings of what happened to children who went to strangers, but with much apprehension, after the lady had assured us she meant no harm, one of the "big uns" made a run for it through the storm up the lady's drive to the house. There was a quick conversation between the lady and the "big un", then the lady disappeared into the house, shutting the front door after her, leaving the "big un" in the large verandah. Us lot under the tree waited expectantly, wondering what was going on, when suddenly the garage doors alongside the house opened, revealing the lady and an immaculate Austin Seven.

This lady was definitely a Margaret Rutherford type, with tweeds, strong manish style shoes, and a thick set figure. But as we kids were to find out, an angel in disguise. First "the big un" in the verandah ran into the garage and then this lady eased her bulk into the car behind the steering wheel. When she had made herself comfortable and closed the door, she then opened the passenger door to "our wench" who jumped in and deposited herself on the back seat. The lady then started the car, drove it out of the garage, then stopped it again, got out, walked back and locked both the garage and verandah doors and then re-entered the car. Once inside she drove it down the drive to "us lot" huddled under her tree, opened the passenger door once again and bade us four to enter it. "Come on my dears", I can hear her saying now, "poor little mites, don't worry about the car, you just get in out of this terrible weather". We crammed into the little car and were very excited, for this was "the fust time any on us 'ad bin in a car". Oh what a wonderful journey back to "The Brook" that was. The lady dropped us off right at the bottom of our entry and we all thanked her profusely, before she drove off down Guest Street in the direction of St. Saviour's Church.

By the time the lady had dropped us the rain had stopped and the sun was shining brilliantly again. We all ran up the entry, after the lady's car had disappeared out of sight, to tell "Our Mom" all about the adventure. She "med us a cuppa tea, an' gid us some doorsteps o' bread an' lard" and then told us "little uns" to "bugga rorf out an' play a bit, as we 'ad gorrome suna than we would 'ave, an' also it ud gi the "big uns" chance ta get themselves ready ta gu out lerta, cus they could stay out lerta, a lot lunga 'an us little uns, any road up". I was happy to go out for a while because I could go an' tell my friends that "I'd bin in a real car, an' mek 'em jealous, an' mek 'em more jealous by re'tellin' the 'ole "ventcha", instead of having to suppress this good news until the following morning.

Regrets! Yes, we all have regrets, I have regretted a hundred things, maybe more in my life, some serious, some not so serious, and others of no consequence at all, but if you have them, it does indicate one predominant thing about you, you have feelings!

I remember I went down Johnnie Kingham's opening one night to play. All my mates were there and after deciding what game we were going to play, I think it was "cowboys an' injuns", I was instructed by Johnnie to go and fetch Jessie. Now I don't know what came over me that particular evening, for I used to hold Johnnie in awe, he was my best friend and hero, and to be quite honest I was a little bit scared of him, because he was older than me, and naturally we all accepted the fact that to be older was indeed to be wiser. Anyway this particular night I must have had my "bum in my hand" over something, or I was just plain mardy, for I replied to Johnnie's instruction with "Wunt, if yo' wan 'er, yo' gu an' fetcha". Now this reply stopped everybody in their tracks, and naturally everything went quiet. After a few seconds of this deathly silence, I felt it was up to me to strengthen my position, now that I had made my initial move, so I continued glaring at Johnnie. "An' w'en Jessie cums, w'en *yo'* fetch 'er, *me*, or wanna these lot wanna be the 'ero forra change, yo're allis the 'ero, an' it's about bloody time we 'ad a change, so there." By the end of this vitriolic speech, Johnnie had recovered somewhat. He stepped up to me and put his face close to mine, and in a menacing voice said "Y-er-r-r-r, an' wore *yo'* gunna do abourrit Smithy?" At this point I couldn't back down, because I couldn't lose face in front of my mates, but even if I overode this factor, the "Smithy" bit would have eliminated any reconciliation taking place, because Johnnie always called me "Ron", and I had naturally always called him "John" or "Johnnie". Lads did call me "Smithy", and I called them by their surnames, but in those instances there was no malicious intent. "I'll do plen'y abourit if yo' wannu" I replied, and glared back at him. But I was sick inside, I didn't really want to do anything about it. I wished I had kept my big mouth shut in the first place. "Ya, wanna fight then Smithy?" Johnnie said, emphasising the "Smithy", knowing full well it would rankle me. "Ar' oright I'll 'ave a fight on ya', burr I wunt fight ya' 'ere, I'll fight ya' down Frankie Anderton's openin', if ya' wanna, an' ya' ain't scared ta fight anyw'ere else?" I was hoping he would refuse, when I could have withdrawn gracefully, but it wasn't to be. 'I'll fight ya' anyw'ere Smithy". "Well cum on then, let's gu an' 'ave a fight."

So off we trooped up Guest Street and down New John Street West, then down Frankie Anderton's "openin'" at the rear of Mr. Kavanagh's house, with Johnnie and his supporters glaring at me and my supporters, and vice versa. On arrival at the bottom of the entrance to the back houses, the lads of both sides formed a big circle. Johnnie took his jacket off and handed it to one of his cronies. I hadn't got a jacket to take off, so I just pushed my shirt sleeves up and then we faced one another. Johnnie took up a boxer's pose and started to move cautiously around the inner circle, in a series of hops and jumps, trying to imitate Tommy Farr I shouldn't wonder. I really didn't know what to do, so I just walked up to him "an' bosted 'im one in the gob". He looked at me for a few seconds, completely mesmerized. I mean, you don't do that when you have a fight do you? You don't just walk up to a bloke and plonk one on him. Well, I bloody well did and that was that, and there was great cheering from my supporters. Blood started to pour from Johnnie's nose, all down his clean shirt, I could see tears starting to well up in his eyes, so I did the only thing any decent "Hockley Kid" would have done, "I buggered orf with my mates, an' left 'im with 'is, an' bum ta 'im, 'e ast forrit an' 'e gorrit". But I wondered what the scene would have been had the position been reversed? My mates and I trooped off down to "The Brook" to play, with comments from them like "Bloody 'ell Ron, yo' ain't arf gid 'im a bashin' in ya', I berris mom "ll ge 'im anotha beltin w'en 'e guz 'um fer gerrin 'is shirt all buggered up wi' blood, mind yo' it's a good job it's 'is an' not yowers innit?" "I berr 'e wunt be sa cocky now, with 'is bloody broken nose." After a while when *my* confidence returned, I actually started to enjoy this adulation.

"An' w'at the bloody 'ell yo' bin up ta agen?" This is what greeted me when I finally returned home that evening to go to bed. "Nuthin' mom." "*Nuthin' mom*" she mimicked, "Well cun yo' tell me then w'at 'it Johnnie Kingham's nose then, a bloody seventy four tram, cus that's w'at kind o' a mess 'e's in. Well cum on then, let's 'ave it, w'at's 'it is nose?" "Well 'e started it mom 'onest 'e did, so I 'ad ta bash 'im, afoa 'e bashed me". "I've 'ad Mrs King'am down 'ere tellin' me orf, but I buggerd 'er orf bloody smartly, nobody tells me w'at ta do in me own 'ouse, cheeky bleeda, burr I'll see 'er agen in the mornin' an' fin' out warrit's all about, don't cho wory, now getcha cuppa tea an' suppa an' gerrorf ta bed."

I thought to myself, "Well, she ain't gid me a w'alin, so praps she likes me a bit berra now", but I didn't give out too much hope on that score", cus "Our Mom" dain't change that much anytime". So I ate my supper and had my cup of tea, then said "Tarrar" to anyone who was remotely interested and went off upstairs.

Once in bed I lay there quietly and thought about "Our Mom" for a while. One of these thoughts made me titter to myself under the rough blankets and numerous old coats that made up our "bed linen". That thought was aimed at the lunch times on a Wednesday or Thursday when mom had no money left in her purse. Mind you she never had much in her purse at anytime, she was always paying somebody or other a bit off what she owed them, then knocking somebody else to make up the deficit. When we arrived home from school, our dinner would be placed in front of us on *The Birmingham Mail* table cloth. The plates would be piled high with "tatas", carrots, or whatever vegetables mom had, and one of us would inevitably say to mom, "Mom w'er's the meat?" Her reply, as quick as a shot from a gun, and equally as inevitable, "Yo' dig deep enuff inta them tatas" ya' little buggers an' yo'll fin' it, an' if yo' don' fin' it yo'll 'ave e'ten it, so bloody shurrup an' gerron with ya' dinna." We knew this would be coming so it would start a fit of titters round the table, until mom intervened with, "There'll be bloody back 'anders all round if yo' lot don' shurrup, an' that'll ge ya' summat ta think about."

I didn't hear anymore about the Kingham incident from "Our Mom" so I assumed she had gone off into a huff with Mrs. Kingham trying to tell her off in her own house, which was, naturally, good news for me. Johnnie and I avoided one another for a short while, but like all kids we eventually made it up and were pals again. This happy situation remained until he left school and I lost contact with him. But I did meet his sister Moira in later years when I served on The Birmingham Fire and Ambulance service and was crewed up with her then husband Frank Baynham, and I asked to be remembered to the family.

Of course the most tragic thing by far to happen in the thirties was the war clouds brewing and with these warnings came intensified activities of all types. The call for civilians to enter the L.D.V. (Local Defence Volunteers) later to be renamed the Home

POPULAR CARTOONS IN THE THIRTIES

Guard, and A.R.P. Volunteers (Air Raid Precautions), Civil Defence, Special Constables, A.F.S. (Auxiliary Fire Service). Other civilians were filling sandbags, helping the aged to erect their Anderson shelters. Sections of all Parks and Recreation grounds were being commandeered for gun sites and barrage balloon operations. The call-up of the Territorials and eventually a National call-up was instituted. Issue of gas masks, air raid warning sirens erected on top of the tram poles, buildings etc., men being drilled in the parks and streets with broom stales serving as rifles. A call for Volunteers for all method of things, Red Cross, St. Johns, W.V.S., Air Raid Wardens. The issue of stirrup pumps, and how many of them were used for other purposes. It was intensified training for everyone including us kids. It was announced one morning in assembly that we had to have a practise on what to do in the eventuality of us being evacuated to the country. We were duly instructed by Mr. Locker that for one day only we would leave school earlier than normal at lunch time to enable us to inform our mothers to prepare our clothes, footwear, toiletries, personal items, not forgetting of course our gas masks and identity cards. I thought to myself whilst he was nattering on, "I know someone w'ose gunna be ova the moon w'en I tek 'er the list of things that our teecha wus gunna ge us forra muthers ta read."

We left Burbury Street at eleven o'clock, one hour earlier than normal and when I arrived home at Two Two Eight the first words from you-know-who was, "allo, watcha bin up ta now ya' little bugga, w'at brings yarrum at this time, yo' ain't bin playin' the wag 'ave ya?" "Nah mom, course I ain't, they've sent us 'um early cus weem guin on the evacuashun the sarta, an' they've sent yo' a list of things, an' they want yo' ta put these things ready fer me ta gu". "Yome guin we're?" she asked with agitation in her voice. "Weem guin on the evacuashun, we've all gorra gu inta the country cus o' the Germans comin'." "Yo ain't guin' now'ere, non' on ya' ain't, yome stoppin 'ere with ya' fertha an' me, weem all gunna stop tergetha, that's w'at weem gunna do, so yo' cun fergerrit fer a start off."

I hadn't up until then given mom the written list, which also gave the necessary instructions and explained that it was a trial, not the real thing. I handed her the documentation and she read it quietly, then she said, "Ya' stupid little sod, ya' nearly gid me a 'eart attack, yo' ain't gorra gu the sarta, yome on'y gunna pretend ta gu". I nearly "piddled meself" with laughter because I already knew this, but I dare not let her see me laughing or else "I'da bin in fera w'alin' ", so I ran off into the garden and had good old giggle. I sat on the tree right at the bottom of the garden overlooking Bridge Street West and I thought, "'Ows the ol' gel gunna pack me a case o' clo'es? Me Sunday Best's in the Pop Shop up in Icknield Street, along with me boots, socks, shert, an' tie, the on'y other clo'es I got, um wearin, I ain't gorreny personal things, 'ceptin' me lorries an' cars an' that, an' o' carn't tek them, an' w'at wus tharotha thing they said, tolitris?" I think it means soap or somethin', well the ol' gel ain' gorrinuff soap ov 'er own, so she wunt giv me any. Still, we'll 'ave ta wait an' see w'at she does, cus she wunt stand any nonsense orf anybody, she wunt."

I messed about for a while and then I heard one of the wenches bawl "Ronnie, Ronnie, cum an' 'ave ya' dinner, an' cum now, an' don' lerrit get cold."

"Ar' roright um comin" I replied, and up the garden I ran. After I had finished my dinner I asked mom about "the evacuashun" and she replied, "I've dun all the packin' yome likely ta want, an' I've purrit in thaya" and she pointed to a cardboard gas mask case with a string attached to it. This was to put round your neck whilst you were walking. One of the new laws was that you had to carry your gas mask wherever you went, which in most cases was completely ignored. I said, "Tar Mom", I picked the case up and slung it around my neck and then ran off to school. I met some of my mates en route, carrying all types of suitcases, canvas bags, paper carriers etc. I felt a little bit stupid with just the gas mask case round my shoulder. "Still" I thought "it's on'y a praktis, so it don' marra any road up". We arrived at school at the normal time and waited for the bell to sound for us to line up in our different classes. This duly happened, but instead of filing into the school as normal, each teacher went round their respective classes to inspect what the children had brought in preparation for the practice evacuation. My teacher went round my classmates looking at the items they had brought, making comments and writing something in a big book. Inevitably he arrived in front of me. "Well Smith, where's you luggage?" " 'Ere it is sir, in 'ere" I replied. "Is that all you have got lad, you won't be able to go far on that will you?" "Our mom sez we ain't guin anyw'ere, any road up, we've gorra stop at 'um with 'er an' dad, an' we've all gorra stop tergetha, all onus". He looked at me for a few seconds, with what I now realise as despair in his eyes, utter despair, and utter sympathy. "Well let's have a look at what you have got, although it won't be a lot will it, because of your gas mask being in there as well."

"Mom don' believe in gas masks sir, she sez they ain't natchrul, an' she wunt lerus 'ave 'em". "Oh I see", more looks of despair and then he started to write furiously in his book. On completion of this I think he must have been as curious as the rest of my classmates, who had closed in around me, to see exactly what indeed, if anything, "Our Mom" had put into the gas mask case, that was supposed to put me in good stead for this journey into the unknown. "Well, open the case up Smith and let's see what we have inside please". I fumbled around for a while, trying to avoid the actual opening of the box, but as the teacher didn't tell me not to bother, it was inevitable. I pulled the lid up and there it lay, up in one corner, quite on its own, its teeth broken and half missing. It was dirty and looked as though it had been buried in the garden for years. It had evidently been used, and used a lot, but what for? Certainly not for what it was originally meant for. There it lay, quietly minding its own business A BROKEN AND BATTERED OLD BLUE COMB. There was an awesome silence when this item, which was going to accompany me, serve me, clothe and clean me during my journey to, and my probably lengthy stay in the country, came into view. The silence didn't last long however, first there was the tittering, which grew into out and out laughter, and this went on until the teacher brought order again. "All right Smith, you can close your case now". I would like to believe by the look he had on his face when he said that, that he wished he had not requested me to open it in the first instance, but in all fairness he had to make some kind of assessment, to establish a kind of plan if the real thing happened, which unfortunately it did. Although the Smith kids did not, as "Our Mom" stated, participate, "we all stayed at 'um with 'er an' fertha."

To quote "Our Mom's" actual words, she said, "Yo' ain't guin' now'ere, non' on ya' ain't, yome stoppin' 'ere with ya' fertha an' me, weem all gunna stop tergetha, that's w'at weem gunna do".

This is exactly what we did do after Mr. Neville Chamberlain made his dramatic speech to the nation on Sunday the Third of September 1939 at eleven o'clock, when he informed us that "we are now in a state of war with Germany."

The people of "Hockley Brook", along with the rest of Great Britain on that dramatic Sunday, entered a new chapter in a book that was to devastate millions of people throughout the free world, by a few MADMEN.

Epilogue

THE deep love, affection and respect I have for my parents, has unfortunately only been realised by me in later years, due to the fact I can now understand slightly, and I do mean slightly, the hardship, pain, suffering and depression they must have endured, like a good many other parents in Hockley Brook during the thirties.

How they must have fought with every ounce of strength and courage to maintain a decent type of life for us kids. How they must have cried silently and alone when through sheer desperation, to give their tortured minds and bodies a little respite, they had screamed at, or hit one of their brood.

I for one have it in me to say, thank you mom, and thank you dad. God nor anyone else needs to forgive you, because there is nothing to forgive. You did your utmost in times made more difficult by man's greatest enemy - greed. Like the verse in the song, "The rich get richer and the poor get poorer", the situation will always prevail, and a hundred reasons for, or a hundred reasons against will not alter this situation.

If we were all "gaffers" who would do the work? If we were all "workers" who would tell us what to do and provide the work for us? The only true peace in this world is the peace that exists within man's heart and mind, when he has struggled and fought hard to attain this wonderful contentment.